INTRODUCTION TO FINANCIAL ACCOUNTING

INTRODUCTION TO

FINANCIAL ACCOUNTING

Fourth edition

Christopher W. Nobes

Un

IN
I(

Lo... rk • Paris
Singapore • Tokyo • Toronto • Albany, NY • Belmont, CA • Cincinnati, OH • Detroit, MI

Introduction to Financial Accounting

Copyright © 1997 Christopher Nobes

I(T)P® A division of International Thomson Publishing Inc.
The ITP logo is a trademark under licence

British Library Cataloguing-in-Publication Data
A catalogue record for this book is available from the British Library

First published by George Allen & Unwin 1980
Revised edition 1983
Fifth impression published by the Academic Division of Unwin Hyman Ltd.
Third edition published by Routledge 1992
Reprinted 1994
This edition published by International Thomson Business Press 1997
Typeset by J&L Composition Ltd, Filey, North Yorkshire
Printed in the UK by The Alden Press, Oxford

ISBN 1–86152–165–0

International Thomson Business Press
Berkshire House
168–173 High Holborn
London WC1V 7AA
UK

International Thomson Business Press
20 Park Plaza
13th Floor
Boston MA 02116
USA

CONTENTS

Part II Accounting for business entities

FIGURES

TABLES

PREFACE TO THE FOURTH EDITION

This introductory textbook in financial accounting is intended primarily for undergraduate students in universities. However, it is hoped that parts of it may also be appropriate for use with other books for other academic or professional courses.

There are several matters relating to the structure and content of introductory textbooks on which the opinions of academic accountants differ. First, the scope of first-year courses and books varies considerably. This book deals mainly with financial accounting and those parts of business finance which fit most closely with it. There are many good introductory textbooks on management accounting that could be used with this book for courses that cover a wider area than financial accounting.

The degree to which double-entry bookkeeping is covered in introductory courses varies greatly too. This book does not base its explanation of accounting on double entry, as some do, but it does provide a fairly lengthy outline of it, after the nature of asset valuation and income measurement have been introduced at some length.

A further difference between introductory textbooks concerns the extent to which practice is discussed. This book discusses accounting standards and quotes figures from surveys of accounting practice at appropriate points. Because accounting for changing prices has been an important area of research and has had significant practical effects on published financial statements, this area is also examined.

In trying to determine the appropriate balance on the above issues I have gratefully received much assistance from a number of colleagues and students who have read various drafts of some or all of the book. These readers have also made detailed comments, and many changes have been made as a result. In particular I would like to acknowledge Margaret Crawford's assistance with Chapter 8. I cannot claim about the writing, then, that it is all my own, but I can make such a claim about any remaining unfortunate biases, mistakes or obscurities.

This edition has been up-dated to include the many major developments in accounting up to early 1997. Self-assessment and tutorial questions have now been included at the end of each chapter, with suggested answers to the former provided at the end of the book.

Christopher Nobes
University of Reading

INTRODUCTION 1

Accounting is a very ancient art. Archaeological investigation shows that wherever a sophisticated and organized society has developed, some form of accounting has been present. In many cases records of expenditure or taxation are the most important relics of a once mighty civilization. 'Keeping account' has always been part of an ordered society, 'giving account' has always been the duty of chancellors and stewards and 'auditing' (or hearing) of these accounts has been a requirement of kings and lords (and, later, of the owners of industry). This need to keep and give account was an important stimulus in the development of writing and arithmetic.

The essential purpose of accounting is therefore to communicate relevant financial information to interested persons. The original nature of accounting was concerned with explaining what *had* happened – how stewards had collected and used their lords' money. This *accountability* or *stewardship* role now applies as much to directors and shareholders as it did to stewards and lords. However, other uses for financial information have also become important. The owners of businesses may wish to compare their success with that of other businesses, and they may wish to use financial information to make decisions about the future. Other parties (e.g. lenders, employees and tax authorities) have other uses for financial information.

This chapter looks at the different functions of accounting, and outlines the structure within which they will be discussed in this book. There are also sections on the accountancy profession, the institutional context of accounting, and the nature of accounting theory.

1.1 Accounting functions

The central concerns of accounting are with the valuation of assets and the measurement of profit. There are many difficult problems of definition in these areas, some of which will be discussed in the early chapters of the book. Having already identified the main function of accounting as the communication of financial information, it is clear that a subsidiary function of capturing the relevant data is necessary. This recording or memory function of accounting developed into the 'Italian method' of *double-entry bookkeeping* by the early fourteenth century. The method is still used in a very similar manner today. However, the method of bookkeeping used is not fundamental to the definitions of value and profit. It does not determine the accounting conventions used. That is why, in contrast with the layout of some books and courses, in *this* book the fundamental measurement problems will be discussed before bookkeeping, out of the context of any

particular method, which is just the initial recording of the relevant economic events that can be quantified in money terms.

However, the information on double-entry bookkeeping in Chapters 7
and 8 should prove useful for understanding the rest of accounting, which
now covers a much larger area. Some of this larger area is the province of
Parts II and III.

Part II deals with the presentation and publication of accounting information. Chapter 9 looks at accounting for partnerships, Chapters 10 and
11 at accounting for companies. These two chapters on companies discuss
the relevant law, some taxation matters, the types of owners and capital
raising, as well as the publication and audit of financial statements. If
accounting information is to be used for decision-making rather than for
stewardship reporting, it may be better if based on current costs and
prices. Whole new underlying frameworks for accounting have been suggested to take account of inflation and relative price changes. These will
be examined in Chapter 12.

All the matters of Part II can be looked at again on a comparative international basis. This is useful in that it puts UK accounting into perspective,
opens the door for further study and provides indications of the direction of
future changes. Chapter 13 will look at the influences that have caused
international diversity, the nature of the differences in accounting and
reporting, and the progress of harmonization.

Another function of accounting is to assist in the interpretation of financial statements. This is necessary before economic decisions can be made.
Part III will look at measures of profitability (Chapter 14), liquidity (Chapter
15) and the worth of a business (Chapter 16).

An area of accounting that has developed particularly rapidly in the
twentieth century is management accounting. This concerns the use of
accounting data to aid decision-making by managers about the allocation
and management of the resources of a business. Accounting can provide
information for planning and control, for investment appraisal and so on.
Management accounting is different from financial accounting in many
important ways. It is concerned with providing information to insiders
(not outsiders), it generally looks forwards (not backwards), it must rely
on estimates (not historical facts) and it is largely a product of twentieth-
century America (not Renaissance Italy and later European development).
This large area of accounting is not covered in this book. Good introductions to management accounting are available elsewhere.

1.2 Accountants

The diversity in the work performed by accountants reflects the wide range
of functions of accounting discussed above. There are over 200,000 qualified
accountants in the United Kingdom. By international standards this is a
high proportion of the population (see Chapter 13). Accountants are

engaged in the preparation of accounts for all types of businesses and public institutions, auditing the accounts of companies and public authorities, advising about and calculating personal and corporate taxation, preparing accounting information for managers, acting as management consultants and teaching and researching in accounting.

An important divide between accountants is that some are in private professional practice as members of firms of accountants who work for clients, and others are in the direct employment of organizations that require accounting services.

There are six important professional accountancy bodies in the United Kingdom and Ireland. These are the three Institutes of Chartered Accountants – that in England and Wales (ICAEW), that of Scotland (ICAS) and that in Ireland (ICAI) – the Association of Chartered Certified Accountants, the Chartered Institute of Management Accountants and the Chartered Institute of Public Finance and Accountancy. These bodies act together on a number of matters through the Consultative Committee for the Accountancy Bodies (CCAB). This body liaises with the government, the Inland Revenue, the European Commission and so on. One very important function of the profession concerns the setting of auditing standards through the Auditing Practices Board, which issues auditing standards.

The technical rules of accounting valuation and measurement are to be found mainly in company law and in accounting standards. The latter were once set by a committee of the CCAB, the Accounting Standards Committee. However, from 1990, an independent committee, the Accounting Standards Board, has been setting standards.

1.3 Institutional context

This book is largely concerned with financial reporting in the United Kingdom, and particularly with the annual financial reporting of companies. The context within which companies operate is discussed at some length in Chapters 10 and 11. However, a short introduction is necessary here in order to understand the chapters before that.

Since 1844, British Companies Acts have regulated some aspects of corporate financial reporting, and special Acts relating to banks, railways etc. provided regulations before that. At present the Companies Act 1985, as subsequently amended, establishes rules for the preparation, contents, presentation, audit and publication of accounts. Directors of companies are responsible for arranging these matters, and for ensuring that the financial statements give 'a true and fair view' of the state of affairs and profit and loss of a company. This is discussed further later.

Many of the details of the rules for accounting are to be found outside the law. As has been said, the most important source of such rules is accounting standards. These are not binding on directors, but are highly persuasive, particularly as directors are required by law to disclose departures and auditors are required to use them by their professional bodies.

Unlike the case in most continental European countries, the rules of taxation are of small importance for British financial reporting. Accounting rules were established before tax rules, and the calculation of taxable income is a separate activity which starts from accounting figures but involves many adjustments.

1.4 Accounting theory

The word 'theory' in accounting is sometimes used to express a concept that occupies a very different place from theory in the natural sciences, or even from its place in such a social science as economics. In a natural science a theory is developed to explain how things *are* and why they behave as they do. In accounting, theory can be *positive* in this way, but it can mean something *normative* (e.g. the body of invented conventions that have evolved over centuries and are now used to determine what behaviour *should be*). To a large extent accounting practice does not follow one consistent underlying normative theory of how assets should be valued, how income should be measured and so on. However, academic accountants and others have criticized this weakness and made suggestions; the Accounting Standards Board has been drafting such a framework in the 1990s.

Theoretical research and experimentation in this area have been particularly concerned with whole new underlying frameworks for accounting, which have been suggested to take account of inflation and relative price changes. There is also a practical scientific side to accounting research. Research is carried out using analytical and empirical methods to discover and explain the behaviour of companies, investors and managers, the way in which accounting practices have developed, and the effects of different practices. For these purposes, theories and models are proposed and tested in a similar way to other scientific research.

Self-assessment questions

Suggested answers to the self-assessment questions are given at the end of the book.

1.   Management accounting is:

   (a) Any financial work done by managers instead of by accountants.
   (b) Work done by accountants to aid the decisions of managers.
   (c) Any work done by accountants inside a corporation.

2. Bookkeeping is normally seen as:

   (a) Part of financial accounting.
   (b) Part of management accounting.
   (c) Part of budgeting.
   (d) Not part of any of the above.

Tutorial questions

1. Distinguish between the role of management accounting and the role of financial accounting.
2. 'Financial accounting is concerned only with past events whereas management accounting is concerned only with potential future events.' How appropriate is this description in today's business environment?
3. 'The only user of accounting information is the accountant.' Discuss.
4. Outline the major functions which professional accounting bodies perform.

Further reading

Nobes, C.W. (1995) *Pocket Accounting*, London: Hamish Hamilton and *The Economist*.
Parker, R.H. (1992) *Dictionary of Accounting*, London: Macmillan.

PART I

THE ACCOUNTING

METHOD

This first part of the book discusses 'the accounting method', whereby financial information is selected and processed in order to present valuations of assets and measurements of income. Chapter 2 introduces the different ways of valuing and measuring. In Chapters 3 and 4 the conventions that accountants use for these purposes and the way in which value is linked with profit are discussed in greater detail. Chapters 5 and 6 examine two of the most important problems that affect both asset valuation and profit measurement: the measurement of depreciation and the valuation of stocks.

Chapters 7 and 8 look at how transactions are recorded by the double-entry system in order to supply the raw material for the calculation and presentation of financial information about value and profit.

VALUE AND PROFIT 2

As may be seen from the discussion of accounting functions in Chapter 1, two of the fundamental problems facing accountants are the measurement of value and the measurement of profit. As will be shown, there are many ways of making these measurements. Some have much to recommend them; all may be sensibly criticized. The difficulty is to find methods of measurement that are theoretically sound, produce useful and verifiable information, and are practicable, given the time and expertise that are available to a business. A further consideration is that there are several different parties interested in such accounting information who might prefer different methods of measurement. These problems are explored in an introductory way in this chapter.

2.1 Value

If practical problems are temporarily ignored, one way of measuring the value of a business is to add together all future net benefits that the owner will receive from it. For example, if a business were to yield £1,000 cash this year, £1,500 next year and £2,000 the year after that, and so on, its owner could add together these expected future flows to obtain a valuation. Before adding the amounts, account would need to be taken of the fact that money *now* is preferable to money in the future, for various reasons which will be discussed later (see Section 16.3). Adjusting the future flows for this factor is called *discounting*. The sum of the discounted amounts is called the *present value*, because the discounting adjustment leads to the value today of the future flows.

This present value may be considered by the owner and by buyers in the event of a proposed sale. It is a forward-looking value. It values the business as a whole, and if it can be performed accurately it is very useful for decision-making. However, many of the estimates involved must be regarded as vague and uncertain. Therefore it is difficult for different accountants to agree on the same figure, and for outsiders to believe such numbers when they are presented by managers: in other words there is a lack of *objectivity*. This is the main reason why this method is not used by accountants under normal circumstances for valuing a whole business.

Alternative methods of valuing a business start by identifying the individual *assets* (generally, things owned; see the more detailed definition in Section 3.2) and *liabilities* (generally money owed) of the business. A statement of the assets and liabilities of a business at a particular moment is called a *balance sheet*. As will be seen, accountants use a number of conventions to decide which assets and liabilities to include and how to value them. For example, one of the conventions is objectivity (mentioned above).

This means that since it is very difficult to reach an agreed measure for the value of the loyalty of customers, this is usually omitted. The same applies to the value of a skilled and hard-working management team.

There are two main categories into which methods of valuing assets may be put: *historical cost* and *current cost*. The historical cost system uses valuations that rest upon recordable facts about prices paid for assets in the past or amounts agreed to be owing to, or owed by, a business. There are some problems in defining when assets have been bought or sold or when they can be agreed to have risen in value, but these are usually resolved by relying on the evidence of actual external transactions. This way of adding up the assets has been used with variations over the past centuries, because it is usually simple, objective and prudent.

Current value accounting is a more recent idea and more complicated. However, it addresses many of the problems associated with historical cost accounting, particularly in times of inflation. The main asset valuation bases used within current value accounting are *replacement cost, net realizable value* (i.e. expected sale receipts *less* costs involved in a sale) and *economic value* (i.e. the net present value of the particular asset). Depending on the circumstances, a choice must be made concerning which base to use for valuing a particular asset at its current value. A useful method of doing this is to consider what the *deprival value* of the asset is. The value to the business of any asset may reasonably be said to be the maximum amount that the business would lose if it lost the asset – in other words the deprival value of the asset. The precise meaning given to deprival value and the ways in which the three bases of valuation are used will depend on which system of current value accounting is chosen. It can easily be seen that, although these values may be more relevant and current than past values, they involve much more subjectivity than historical cost valuations. In practice, as we shall see, it is possible to introduce some conventions to narrow the range of choice. The alternatives mentioned in this section are summarized diagrammatically in Figure 2.1.

The choice of valuation method may also depend on who requires the valuation. Owners and prospective buyers will want the most realistic estimate of the worth of the business as a going concern. On the other hand, lenders may want a much more conservative valuation, based on the lowest likely valuation of the individual assets in the event that the business has to be closed down. Managers, of course, will also be interested in accounting information, but this book is mainly concerned with information presented to outsiders, for example in the form of published annual reports of companies.

2.2 Profit

There are two main ways of measuring the profit of a business. First, it may be done by comparing the value of the business at two different dates using

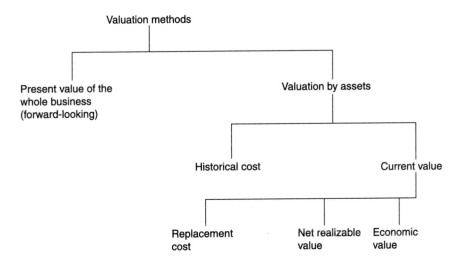

Figure 2.1   Valuation methods

the same valuation methods. After adjusting for any additions or subtractions from the business by its owners, the difference between the values at the two dates is the profit for the period. The same sort of definition can be applied to individuals. An individual's *income* for a week has been defined as 'the maximum value he can consume during the week and still expect to be as well off at the end of the week as he was at the beginning' (Hicks, 1946).

Clearly, the validity of measuring profit in this way depends upon the validity of the methods used to measure 'well-off-ness'. Hicks was certainly thinking of a present value method of valuation. Since we have already noted that this may not be a practicable method for accountants, we can immediately see one problem in trying to measure profit in this way. Particularly when prices are changing, the comparison of the valuations of a business at two different dates can lead to several plausible results. For example, does one measure any increase in value in money terms, real worth terms (taking account of general inflation) or physical terms?

Consequently, accountants have traditionally measured profit in an alternative way; that is, they have taken the difference between the *revenues* and the *expenses* that relate to the business for the period in question. Unfortunately, this method also is not as simple as it first appears. There are problems (e.g. in defining a relevant revenue). It is difficult to define revenues and expenses without using the concepts of assets and liabilities.

In order to maintain objectivity and prudence, increases in the value of stocks due to the operations of a business are not included in profit until there is a sale. On the other hand, when sales are made, unless some adjustment is performed, this means that gains due to increases in value during previous years are included in this year's profit.

Despite these problems, accountants continue to measure profit by comparing revenues with expenses. The accounting statement that deals with this is called the *profit and loss account* (or *income statement* in the United States). Several adjustments to correct the profit and loss account for the above problems have been proposed as part of current value accounting systems. These will be discussed from time to time in this book, especially in Chapter 12. The methods of profit measurement are illustrated diagrammatically in Figure 2.2.

As with valuation of the business, there are many users of profit information, who are interested for different reasons. Owners may be interested in the size of their share of the profits of a business, so that they can make decisions about consumption. Prospective investors are particularly interested in the profit of a company in order to compare the merits of different companies. Also, managerial performance can be measured by using profit as an indication of the efficiency of the business. The Inland Revenue uses adjusted profit calculations to assess tax, and employees may use profit figures for wage bargaining. Some writers (e.g. Edwards and Bell, 1961) have therefore suggested that more than one profit figure should be calculated, because these different users require different sorts of information.

2.3 Summary

In this chapter we have briefly looked at two of the major concerns of accounting: value and profit. There are many ways of measuring these. It is generally the case that the most attractive methods from a theoretical point of view turn out to be too expensive, too slow, too difficult or too subjective to be practical. Consequently, accountants represent the financial state of a business by adding up most of its assets and liabilities, and they measure its profit by comparing revenues and expenses. There are several conventions that help accountants to decide when to include an asset or a liability in the balance sheet and how to identify a relevant revenue or expense for the profit and loss account. The conventions used for traditional historical cost accounting have been severely criticized, and there has been

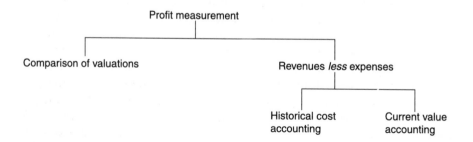

Figure 2.2 Profit measures

experimentation with current value accounting systems for the measurement of value and profit. Nevertheless, historical cost accounting is still the basic system in use at present.

Self-assessment questions

Suggested answers to the self-assessment questions are given at the end of the book.

1. The value of an asset could reasonably be thought of as:

   (a) Its replacement cost.
   (b) Its realizable value in a market.
   (c) The future benefits which will flow from it.
   (d) All of the above.

2. Having eliminated transactions with the owners, the profit of a business can be seen as:

   (a) The increase in the worth of the business over a period.
   (b) Its total sales for a period.
   (c) The expenses of a period *less* the revenues.

Tutorial questions

1. Examine the various ways in which assets can be valued. Can you think of any practical difficulties in measuring these values?
2. Is it better to measure profit by looking at changes in values in a period or by looking at the transactions of the period?

References

Edwards, E.O. and Bell, P.W. (1961) *The Theory and Measurement of Business Income*, Berkeley, CA: University of California Press.
Hicks, J.R. (1946) *Value and Capital*, London: Oxford University Press, ch. 3.

THE BALANCE SHEET   3

One of the tasks of accounting which we looked at in Chapter 2 was the preparation of a periodic balance sheet to show the financial position of a business at one moment of time. Since it is the affairs of the business that interest us, it is important that all the financial records be drawn up on the basis that the business is a totally separate financial entity from its owner or owners. In the case of a large company with many owners (i.e. its shareholders) there will be little likelihood that the assets or the incomes of the company will be confused with those of the owners. However, in the case of a sole trader (e.g. the grocer who runs a one-man business) it is all too easy for the financial records of the business and of the owner to become confused. It is particularly important, though, that the two be kept entirely separate in order to provide useful information about the business to the owner, lenders, prospective buyers of the business and the Inland Revenue.

3.1 The business entity

Separating the business from its owners will allow the drawing up of a statement as in Table 3.1. Such a statement of financial affairs is usually called a balance sheet. It represents a snapshot of the business at one moment – most typically the end of the business's accounting year. All the assets have been grouped on one side and all the liabilities on the other. The conventional order in the United Kingdom for assets and liabilities is to place the longer-term, less liquid, items nearer the top.

Because of the separation of the business from its owner, the capital figure is needed to represent the amount that the owner has contributed to the business. It is often not possible for an owner to reclaim the amount contributed. For example, a shareholder cannot normally get money back from a company in return for giving up his shares; he has to sell them to another investor through the stock exchange or otherwise. Therefore, the capital is not a liability of the business, whereas loans are. From now on, the word 'liability' will exclude the capital of the owners.

The reader will have noticed that the balance sheet in Table 3.1 balances. This is connected with the fact that the business is a separate entity from its owners. This is sometimes called the *entity convention*. The total amount owned by the business (i.e. the assets), *less* the total amount owed (i.e. the liabilities) leaves the *capital* figure. That is,

$$\Sigma A - \Sigma L = C$$

which is the same as

$$\Sigma A = C + \Sigma L$$

Table 3.1   Balance sheet of the business of P. Smith as at 31 December 1998 (£)

Fixed assets:			Capital		10,200
Property		10,000			
Machines		2,000			
Vehicles		1,500			
		13,500	Loans		3,000
Current assets:			Current liabilities:		
Stock	500		Overdraft	800	
Debtors	300		Creditors	500	1,300
Cash	200	1,000			
		14,500			14,500

which we see in the balance sheet, where *A* is assets, *L* is liabilities and *C* is capital.

If profit is earned during the year, the excess of the assets over the liabilities will become greater; therefore the capital figure will become greater. Since the profit belongs to the owners, it is not surprising that making profit increases the capital figure.

3.2 Types of asset

The assets on the balance sheet in Table 3.1 have been divided into *fixed assets* and *current assets*. Fixed assets are those intended for continuing use in the business, and they would not generally be sold in the normal course of trade. Examples of these are land, buildings, plant and machinery. Current assets are those which are generally transformed into something else in the normal course of trade. They include stocks (of raw materials, work in progress and finished goods), debtors (i.e. amounts of money owed to the business, mostly as a result of credit sales) and cash (which includes cash at the bank). One would expect the stock to be sold, the debtors to pay off their debts and the cash to be used for buying more stock, paying creditors (i.e. people to whom the business owes money; see Section 3.5), and so on.

There will be some assets that it is difficult to put into the fixed or current category, and there will be some cases of doubt about whether an item is an asset of the business at all. Assets must have expected future economic benefits, either because they can help to make profit or because they have a market value. There must also be a legally enforceable right of control, which has been acquired by the loss of another asset (e.g. cash) or the incurrence of a liability.

A number of items are excluded from being recognized as assets of a business by these criteria. For example, a warehouse on loan from another business is still an asset of the other business; a worn-out machine that a business intends never to use again and has no scrap value is not recognized as an asset, for it has no future benefits; a motorway may be of benefit to the business, but ownership has not been acquired; large sums may have been spent on unfruitful research, which cannot be called an asset because there is no expected future benefit.

Other items may be regarded as assets but are excluded from balance sheets because they fail to satisfy various accounting conventions, looked at below. For example, a business's high calibre staff or good reputation with customers cannot normally be included as an asset in the balance sheet, because there has been no specifically identifiable payment for it and it has no readily assessable value. This topic is taken further in Chapter 11.

3.3 Valuation conventions

There are several conventions relating to the inclusion and valuation of assets in the balance sheet. Some of these conventions are specifically required by law and standards, as discussed in Part II of this book. As mentioned below, these conventions need adjustment when using current value accounting.

3.3.1 Prudence convention

The convention of prudence or conservatism means that, as far as valuation is concerned, accountants will tend to use the lowest of all reasonable values for an asset. The convention is also relevant to the measurement of income, discussed in Section 4.5. This section also suggests that it may be possible to distinguish between degrees of prudence; a slightly stronger concept of conservatism is more associated with continental accounting (see Chapter 13).

The prudence and caution of accountants have traditionally been regarded as a balance for the optimism of businessmen. The accountant has seen prudence as a necessary state of mind in an uncertain world in order to fulfil his responsibilities to those to whom he or she is providing information (i.e. shareholders and creditors in particular).

It is now the view of many accountants that prudence may be too strong a convention and that often the most likely value is sacrificed in order to present the lowest value. From time to time complaint will be made in this book that, on a particular point, the receivers of information (now a much wider group than shareholders and creditors) would be better served by seeing the most realistic estimate of a figure rather than the lowest.

3.3.2 Objectivity convention

The convention of objectivity is that reliable facts relating to one way of valuing an asset are better than estimates relating to another way, even if the latter method is more realistic. If there is one way of valuing an item that would lead several accountants to arrive at similar figures, it will be preferred to another way that requires greater judgement and estimation. The attraction of objectivity to shareholders, creditors and government is that it provides a more certain figure, which is less manipulable, less likely to suffer from bad judgement or optimistic estimation, and more easily verifiable by such independent experts as auditors.

The desire for objectivity affects several of the other conventions below. Its effect is felt when measuring revenues and expenses just as much as when valuing assets or liabilities. Current value accounting leads to a weakening of this convention in favour of what its proponents would call greater 'realism' or 'relevance'.

3.3.3 Money measurement convention

The money measurement convention means that accounting information includes only those items which are capable of expression in money terms. There may be many pieces of information that have considerable effects on the value of the company and its ability to make profit but cannot easily be measured and communicated in money terms. Examples already mentioned are skilled management and customer goodwill. The great advantage of expression in money terms is that information is more readily understood and added together. Accounting as practised at present would be impossible without this important simplification.

3.3.4 Historical cost convention

The historical cost convention is closely related to money measurement. The convention is that assets are recorded at their cost when they are bought and that they continue to be recorded at cost (or some proportion of cost, if they have been partially used up or worn out) throughout their useful lives. Therefore, the 'values' of assets shown in the balance sheet are their historical costs (i.e. *input values*), not their income-generating potentials or realizable market values (i.e. *output values*). Of course, some assets have market values that are identical to their costs (e.g. cash), but many have widely different values (e.g. land bought fifty years previously).

The great advantages of recording and valuing assets at historical cost are the simplicity and the objectivity of doing so. Compared with trying to be sure about a market value or a series of future cash flows from an asset, its historical cost is a definite figure upon which different accountants can agree.

3.3.5 Stability convention

The stability convention is used in conjunction with the conventions of money measurement and historical cost. It means that an assumption is made that the currency does not change in value. This has clearly been untrue, particularly in the 1970s.

Suppose that a business bought a new factory for £100,000 in 1985. By 1995 it wished to expand by buying the identical factory next door, which was up for sale at the now reasonable price for either factory of £200,000. In the balance sheet these conventions will cause us to record the two factories together at £300,000, if pounds of 1985 are added to pounds of 1995 as though they are the same units. This is the problem arising from the stability convention. The problem from the historical cost convention is that for many purposes it is misleading to have two identical assets in a balance sheet at widely differing values.

3.3.6 Current value convention

It was in the 1970s that serious attention began to be given by the UK accountancy bodies and the government to the problems of historical cost accounting mentioned in the previous paragraph. There will be discussion of this later. It can be said here that, when current value accounting is used, the valuation of an asset in normal circumstances is related to the *replacement cost* of the asset rather than its historical cost. The principle of the current value convention is that the value to the business of an asset is its deprival value, which is the maximum that the business would lose if deprived of the asset. Usually the deprival value is related to the cost of replacement.

3.3.7 Going concern convention

The going concern convention means that there is an assumption that the business will continue for the foreseeable future. Therefore the value of most fixed assets depends not on what they could be sold for (because the business does not intend to sell them) but on what they can contribute to the profit-making of the business. This assumption therefore has an important effect on the value of the assets shown in the balance sheet, particularly if an asset is specific to the activities of the business concerned. For example, if a business owns certain machines that have been made especially for it and would not be useful to other businesses, and if the machines have low scrap value, their market value may be very small. However, their value to the business in terms of productive potential or the avoidance of the need to replace them will be much larger than their market value.

The majority of businesses may reasonably be considered to be going concerns; hence, it may seem reasonable that the market value is usually ignored in balance sheets. However, the going concern convention seems to encourage a value-in-use approach, which entails consideration of the future benefits from an asset. The fact that historical cost has so far been used instead of this economists' approach is partly an indication of the strength of the desire for objectivity. Past facts (even though manifestly irrelevant for many purposes) have a strong attraction for the accountant in an uncertain commercial world with out-of-date statutory obligations, when compared with unprovable opinions about the future. Many accountants believe that current value accounting produces a considerable movement towards what is approximately right rather than precisely wrong.

3.3.8 Consistency convention

The convention of consistency comes into play when a choice must be made between methods of valuation of assets, of allocation of expenses to different periods, and so on. This convention suggests that the same methods should be used by a business from year to year. Accounting information is of very limited use *in vacuo*; its interpretation relies upon comparison. The accounts of a company for one year need to be seen in the context of previous years' figures – hence the need for consistency. It is clear, too, that readers of financial statements need to be told if methods are changed and what the effects of any changes have been. The other main type of comparison that aids understanding is that between one company's accounts and the accounts of other companies. The promotion of *uniformity*, which should enable more sensible comparisons of this sort, is part of the work of the Accounting Standards Board (ASB), mentioned in Chapter 1.

3.3.9 Materiality convention

The convention of materiality states that there are some transactions or events that are not significant enough for accountants to record or disclose with strict correctness. For example, if new door handles were bought for an office block, the business could add their cost to the value of the building in the balance sheet (and provide depreciation on them). However, most accountants would consider that attention to this sort of detail was not worth the time. The purchase would be treated as an expense, because that would be easier. The balance sheet and profit and loss account would not look *materially* different.

Materiality applies to the disclosure of detail in accounts too. Many types of asset or expense could be separately shown in the accounts to provide readers with more detailed information. However, the greater is the detail, the more difficult it is to see the important points and the overall situation. Therefore, similar items may be recorded together during the year and presented as one total figure in the accounts. Only material items need to be disclosed separately.

There are other conventions that accountants use. These are more related to profit measurement than to asset valuation, and so they will be looked at in Chapter 4. Four conventions are mentioned as fundamental concepts in the accounting standard on disclosure of accounting policies (SSAP 2). These are the going concern, accruals (see Section 4.2), consistency and prudence conventions. They are considered to be sufficiently basic for disclosure to be necessary only if they are *not* being used. These four conventions were also laid down in the Companies Act 1981 (now the 1985 Act). This is discussed further in Chapter 11.

3.4 Asset valuation practice

Readers will have noticed that several of the conventions dealt with above seem to be inconsistent with each other, or to be alternatives. One major example of this (concerning sub-sections 3.3.3 – 3.3.6 above) should be clarified here.

In the United Kingdom most companies value most assets on the basis of historical cost, with an allowance for wearing out or depreciation (see Chapter 5). However, many large companies occasionally revalue some major assets (such as land and buildings) in order to show more up-to-date values. Very few companies revalue all assets every year to a current value basis. These issues are taken further in Section 5.4 and in Chapter 12.

3.5 Liabilities

Liabilities are obligations to outside entities (including individuals, businesses or governments) that exist at the date of valuation. They involve payments to be made in the future, and their values must be quantifiable with reasonable accuracy. We can see that the capital figure in a balance sheet does not comply with the first criterion, because the business is not obliged to pay back the capital in the normal course of events. Therefore the items on the right-hand side of the balance sheet in Table 3.1 are summarized as 'owners' capital and liabilities'.

In general the conventions of Section 3.3 apply to liabilities as well as to assets. Particularly relevant conventions are prudence, stability, money measurement and consistency. For example, a prudent approach is to tend to overstate liabilities rather than to understate them. Also, analogous to current assets are *current liabilities*. These are the liabilities which will fall due within the year. For example, a current liability called *trade creditors* represents those amounts which are due to suppliers and others within the year.

An obligation that will be incurred at a future date (e.g. a contract to buy goods on credit next year) is not recognized as a liability; nor is the remote possibility of a future obligation (e.g. a lawsuit for damages pending at the valuation date, but which will probably not be lost), which is known as a *contingent liability*. Information about these should be given in the notes to the balance sheet. However, a liability that is probable, even if of an unknown amount, should be estimated and entered into the accounting records.

Liabilities have traditionally been, and still are, recorded in balance sheets at their face money value. However, in times of inflation any liabilities that need not be paid for several years (e.g. long-term loans) are less onerous than they appear. When their payment becomes due, their value will still be the same in money terms but will be smaller in the real terms of that future period. In this sense, there is a gain involved in having these liabilities which are measured in money terms. The treatment of this gain has caused much controversy in the debate about methods of accounting for inflation (see Chapter 12).

3.6 Capital

The amount of capital is sometimes called owners' interests (or *shareholders' interests* or *owners' equity* for limited companies). The closing capital amount in a balance sheet will be:

opening capital (from the last balance sheet)
+   profit (since last balance sheet)
−   drawings of owner (e.g. dividends, for companies)
+   introductions of capital (as cash or other assets from owners)

It has been pointed out in Section 3.1 that, because of the separation of the business from its owner, the balance sheet balances:

$$\Sigma A = C + \Sigma L$$

This implies that any transaction that affects a figure in the balance sheet must affect another figure in order to maintain the balance. For example, let us start a business by getting Mr Q. Jones to introduce £10,000 cash. The balance sheet of Jones's business will look like this:

Balance sheet (£)			
Cash	10,000	Capital	10,000

Let us assume now that £600 worth of stock and £7,500 worth of machines are bought. Each transaction causes one effect on cash and one effect on another asset, leaving:

Balance sheet (£)			
Machines	7,500	Capital	10,000
Stock	600		
Cash	1,900		

Now, half of the stock is sold on credit to Smith for £500. The profit on this transaction will be £200 (i.e. sales, £500, *less* half of the stock, £300). The balance sheet will become:

Balance sheet (£)

Machines	7,500	Capital	10,000
		Profit	200
		Closing capital	10,200
Stock	300		
Debtor	500		
Cash	1,900		

Check that the balance sheet still balances. If it does, it is because the sale transaction caused the following changes on the balance sheet:

Balance sheet (£)

		Profit	+200
Stock	−300		
Debtor	+500		

Finally, the bank grants Jones's business a £1,000 overdraft for future expansion:

Balance sheet (£)

Fixed assets:		Capital	10,200
Machines	7,500		
Current assets:			
Stock	300	Current liability:	
Debtor	500	Overdraft	1,000
Cash	2,900		
	11,200		11,200

Here, the duality convention can be seen at work. That is, each transaction gives rise to two (sometimes more) effects on the accounting records of a business. This will be further discussed in the next chapter, and then in Chapter 7 it will be used as a basis for a consideration of double-entry accounting.

3.7 Summary

We have seen in this chapter that the separation of a business from its owner for the purposes of accounting enables a two-sided balance sheet to be drawn up. This shows the financial state of affairs of a business at the end of an accounting period. The difference between the assets of a business (i.e. what it controls) and its liabilities (i.e. what it owes) is the capital or owner's interest.

Assets are given a fairly precise definition and are valued with the aid of several accounting conventions. Assets can be divided into fixed and current. They are normally presented on a balance sheet in order of decreasing permanence or increasing liquidity. Hence, we find land at the top and cash at the bottom. Liabilities can also be defined with some precision and are traditionally recorded at face money values. The capital figure, which is not a liability, can be seen to change when profit is earned or when the owner withdraws or introduces capital.

Self-assessment questions

Suggested answers to the self-assessment questions are given at the end of the book.

1. A tractor held by a farm implement company for sale to farmers is a fixed asset.

   (a) True.
   (b) False.

2. Which of the following would *not* be included in the cost of land?

   (a) Commission to estate agent.
   (b) Cost of clearing an unneeded building from the land.
   (c) Property tax paid to local government for sewer usage.
   (d) Legal fees for purchase.

3. The convention of consistency refers to consistent use of accounting principles:

   (a) Among firms.
   (b) Across accounting periods.
   (c) Throughout the accounting period.
   (d) Within industries.

4. A practical decision to expense small capital expenditures rather than record them as plant assets and depreciate them is probably made on the basis of the convention of:

   (a) Consistency.
   (b) Materiality.
   (c) Conservatism.
   (d) Full disclosure.

5. A company would properly classify land held in order to build a planned factory as:

   (a) A current asset.
   (b) An investment.
   (c) A tangible fixed asset.
   (d) An intangible asset.

6. Which of the following is not properly classified as a current asset?

   (a) An investment expected to be needed for operations in the next year.
   (b) A three-year prepaid insurance policy.
   (c) A five-year-old lorry that is expected to be sold in the next year.
   (d) A tobacco inventory that must cure for eighteen more months before it is made into cigarettes.

7. Which of the following is properly classified as an intangible asset?

   (a) Debtors.
   (b) Accumulated depreciation.
   (c) Land held for future use.
   (d) Trademarks.

8. Accountants include the following as balance sheet assets:

   (a) All items on which cash is spent.
   (b) All items that the business gets benefit from.
   (c) Items that are controlled and will bring future benefit.
   (d) Only the physical items under (c).

9. A gain on the value of a building would be recorded in the profit and loss account when:

   (a) It is sold.
   (b) Cash from the sale is received.
   (c) Its increased value is recorded in a balance sheet.
   (d) Its selling price rises.

10. Creditors are:

    (a) Non-monetary assets.
    (b) Monetary liabilities.
    (c) Monetary assets.
    (d) Non-monetary liabilities.

11. The basis of fixed asset valuation (after adjusting for depreciation where appropriate) is normally:

    (a) The selling price of the asset.
    (b) The original purchase cost.
    (c) The current purchase cost.
    (d) The future net benefits.

12. A balance sheet is designed to show:

    (a) The financial position of a business under accounting conventions.
    (b) What the business could be sold for.

(c) The performance of the business for the year.

(d) What it would cost to set up a similar business.

Tutorial questions

1. Define a balance sheet.
2. Define fixed assets, current assets, capital, long-term liabilities, current liabilities, drawings and introductions.
3. Explain and discuss the various accounting conventions and principles which govern the inclusion and valuation of assets in the balance sheets.
4. What do you understand by the 'entity concept'? How do you reconcile the fact that records are kept from the viewpoint of the 'entity' with the fact that the business belongs to its proprietors?
5. To what extent does a balance sheet disclose what a business is worth?
6. State which of the following are shown under the wrong classification for John Black's business:

Assets	Liabilities
Loan from Julie Brown	Stock of goods
Cash in hand	Debtors
Machinery	Money owing to bank
Premises	
Motor Vehicles	

REVENUES AND EXPENSES

4

In Chapter 2 we saw that accountants do not usually measure profit by looking at changes in the worth of a business. A method that involves less subjectivity is to concentrate on transactions and to compare expenses with revenues, as in the simple case in the last chapter where stock used was compared with sales. This may be represented by:

$$\pi = \Sigma R - \Sigma E$$

where π is profit, R is revenues and E is expenses.

To measure the profit for a period it is necessary to match precisely the expenses of that period with its revenues. In this chapter we look at the definition of revenues and expenses as conventionally used for accounting. However, recently it has become clear that there is no strong conceptual basis for present practice. The Accounting Standards Board has suggested that revenues should be defined in terms of increases in assets and decreases in liabilities (and vice versa for expenses). This is taken further in Chapter 11.

It should be noted that accountants and the Inland Revenue may have different rules about how exactly to match expenses and revenues. Therefore they will arrive at different profit figures. This is important for determining how much profit may be paid out to the owners (see Chapter 11) and how much tax should be paid (see Chapter 10).

4.1 Accounting periods

It has been mentioned that a business is normally regarded as a going concern. It is usually impossible to divide its trading up into identifiable projects that begin and end within a short time and for which profit can be calculated. Consequently, since it is important for the owners, managers and other groups to know how the business is performing, it is necessary to divide its trading up into arbitrary lengths of time over which profit can be measured. For the purposes of comparison of one period with another it is useful if all the periods are of the same length; and since a full-scale calculation and publication of profit is expensive, it should not happen too often. So, the normal accounting period is one year. Profit for the year is calculated by matching all (but only) the expenses of the year against all (but only) the revenues of the year. Businesses do not all use the calendar year for this purpose; for example, many businesses use 31 March as their year end, because this is the corporation tax year end.

Accounting revenues are not the same as receipts. Many cash receipts during a year will not count as revenues of that year, and many revenues of a year will not have been associated with cash receipts in the year. Revenues are the receipts (past, present or future) that *relate* to the accounting year. This is called the *accruals* or *matching convention*.

It is not immediately obvious in some cases which receipts do relate to a year. Consider the following example:

12 January	Buy raw materials, store them
19 February	Begin work on processing the materials
3 April	Finished goods produced, store them
10 May	Receive order for goods, order accepted
17 May	Goods delivered, customer invoiced
5 June	Customer pays invoice for goods

It is clear that the eventual profit will be the difference between the final sales receipts and the various costs involved. However, at what point is the revenue (and hence profit) recognized? Is the profit earned gradually over the manufacturing process, when a contract of sale is agreed, when the goods are delivered or when cash is finally paid? The answer for accountants is given by the *realization convention*. In this case, the convention would require that revenues are not recognized until a sale has been agreed – that is, profits that have not been realized are not recorded. This conforms with the conventions of prudence and objectivity, because there is no certainty of revenue or profit until the sale is made.

If the sale is on credit rather than for cash, the acquisition of a debt is considered to be sufficiently objective. So, revenue recognition occurs at the time when legal rights and obligations for the sale are set up (10 May in the above example), not on cash payment. In practice, an invoice may not be issued until delivery and the latter date may be used. There are a few exceptions to this. We shall see in Chapter 6 that some profit is taken on long-term contracts before they are complete; and realization is re-examined in Chapter 11.

4.2 The accruals convention (revenues)

There are many situations where receipts of one year *are* revenues of that same year. Examples of these are rent received for periods fully within the accounting year; cash sales; and cash received from debtors for sales made earlier in the same accounting year. In other cases there is a difference between the year of receipt and the year of recognition of revenues. Some instances of this are now discussed.

4.2.1 Receipts last year, revenues this year

There are examples where receipts of last year may be revenues of this year. If a business lets some premises and asks for rent in advance, there may be some rent paid to the business last year on behalf of this year. A cricket club may have received some of this year's subscriptions during last year. In cases like this cash is received in the accounting year before the one in which it is recognized as revenue. At the time of its receipt there are these effects:

During last year	
+ Cash	+ Prepaid revenues (creditors)

At the beginning of this year the effects are:

This year	
	+ Profit
	− Prepaid revenues

4.2.2 Receipts this year, revenues next year

There may be receipts of this year that are revenues of next year. A business may receive rents in advance, part of which relate to next year, or subscriptions in advance that relate fully to next year. The effects will be similar to those in Section 4.2.1, except that the two years will be 'during this year' and 'next year'.

4.2.3 Receipts next year, revenues this year

There may be examples of reverse situations to those above. That is, at the end of the year there may be rents not yet received that relate to the year, by customers or credit sales not yet paid for. When these are paid during the following year, the cash receipts of that later year will be the revenues of this year. At the end of this year there will be cash due:

During this year	
+ Receipts due (debtors)	+ Profit

Next year	
− Receipts + Cash	

4.2.4 Receipts this year, revenues last year

There may be receipts of this year that are revenues of last year. If a business receives cash from debtors this year in payment for last year's sales, the effects will be similar to those in Section 4.2.3, except that the two years will be 'during last year' and 'this year'.

4.3 The accruals convention (expenses)

Just as some of the receipts of a year are not the revenues of that year, and vice versa, so not all the payments of a year are expenses of that year. That is, expenses are payments (past, present or future) that *relate* to the current accounting year. This is the application of the accruals convention to expenses.

Many payments of a year *are* expenses of the same year (e.g. wages, electricity expenditure and rent paid for periods fully within the accounting year). These involve a payment of cash that is equal to the size of the increase in expense (or reduction of profit):

During this year	
− Cash	− Profit

In other cases there is a difference between the year of the payment and the year of the expense.

4.3.1 Payments last year, expenses this year

Payments of last year may be expenses of this year. Examples of this are rents or insurance premiums paid last year by a business to cover part of this year. This gives rise to:

During last year	
+ Prepayments −Cash	

This year	
−Prepayments	− Profit

4.3.2 Payments this year, expenses future years

Payments of this year may be expenses of future years. This arises, for example, when a bill for next year's rates is paid in advance or a fixed asset is bought. In order to record the prepayment the same procedure as in

Section 4.3.1 is used, except that the years will be 'during this year' and 'next year'.

The purchase of a fixed asset is a little more complicated. The asset is not used up in the year of purchase, and so it would be unfair to treat the whole payment as an expense of that year. To do this would produce too low a profit figure. However, *some* of the asset is used up during the year. A charge to recognize this is called a *depreciation* expense. An expense involves the consumption of part of the assets of the business in order to make profit. On the other hand, the purchase of a fixed asset transforms one asset into another, rather than using up an asset. Therefore the actual purchase of a fixed asset does not affect profit:

This year	
+ Fixed asset	
−Cash	

4.3.3 Payments next year, expenses this year

Some payments of next year may be expenses of this year. For example, the business may hire property, the rent of which is not to be paid until next year. Also, there may be purchases bought on credit which have not yet been paid for. These cause an increase in expenses (i.e. a reduction in profit) and an increase in current liabilities to next year or to creditors. The former is called *accrued expense*:

This year	
	−Profit
	+ Creditors or accruals

During next year	
−Cash	−Creditors or accruals

4.4 Debtors and bad debts

It has been said that the realization convention assumes that a credit sale produces a sufficiently certain asset (i.e. the debt) that revenue can still be recognized at the point of sale. However, in some cases this turns out to have been an optimistic assumption. It is an unusually fortunate business whose debtors all pay their debts. It may become clear during a year that some of the credit sales included in the revenue will never give rise to receipts. These amounts are known as *bad debts* and they reduce the revenue figure (in practice this is treated as an increase in expenses), thereby reducing profit. At the same time, of course, the current asset figure for debtors is reduced:

During this year	
−Debtors	−Profit

Sometimes, it may be suspected rather than certain that some of the debtors will never pay their debts. If an accountant suspects specific debtors, a specific provision against this can be made. This will involve a charge against profit and the creation of a liability. If experience shows that some proportion of any debtors' figure will eventually become bad, a general provision for the relevant amount can be made, with a corresponding expense to reduce profit:

During this year	
	−Profit
	+ Provision for doubtful debts

In the balance sheet it is usual to show the provision as a deduction from the debtors' figure on the other side. This will be discussed in Section 7.6.

4.5 Profit measurement conventions

A number of conventions used by accountants to ascertain and value assets have been defined in Chapter 3. Some of these (e.g. consistency, materiality and prudence) apply when measuring revenues and expenses. Another important convention is the accruals convention, discussed in Sections 4.2 and 4.3. A brief explanation of the application of the convention of prudence to profit measurement may be useful here.

Prudence suggests that likely losses should be taken immediately they are suspected, whereas likely profits must wait until realization. That is, in general profit should be underestimated rather than overestimated. It may be suggested that many users of accounts will now prefer a 'best guess' approach rather than the lowest estimate. UK accounting, at least, tends towards prudence rather than stricter conservatism. For example, it would in principle be possible to recognize revenue and profit only when cash was received, whereas it has already been mentioned not only that revenue is usually recognized at the point of sale (which may be earlier), but also that on long term contracts some profit may be taken before completion. It is sometimes possible to delay charging current development expenditure until the expected revenues from it materialize (see Chapters 11 and 16). This is clearly not fully conservative, although it may not be imprudent.

4.6 The accounting equation

We have seen that profit is the difference between revenues and expenses, defined according to certain conventions. This was represented earlier by:

$$\pi \ = \ \Sigma R - \Sigma E \tag{1}$$

Also, in Chapter 3 it was shown that:

$$\Sigma A \ = \ \Sigma L + C \tag{2}$$

After a year's trading (ignoring any withdrawals or extra introductions of capital) it will also be true that:

$$\Sigma A_1 \ = \ \Sigma L_1 + C_0 + \pi_1 \tag{3}$$

where ΣA_1 is the total assets at the end of the year, ΣL_1 is the total liabilities at the end of the year, C_0 is the capital at the beginning of the year and π_1 is the profit of the year. Therefore, by combining (1) and (3) it follows that:

$$\Sigma A_1 \ = \ \Sigma L_1 + C_0 + \Sigma R_1 - \Sigma E_1$$
$$\therefore \ \Sigma A_1 + \Sigma E_1 \ = \ \Sigma L_1 + C_0 + \Sigma R_1$$

This equation explains the relationships between the five accounting totals that we have been discussing. This could be arranged as follows:

Profit calculation:	ΣE_1	ΣR_1
	$+$	$+$
		C_0
Balance sheet:	ΣA_1	ΣL_1

Postponing the calculation of profit until the end of the year and leaving the capital figure at C_0 until then, we can examine any transaction that affects the business in a more detailed way than before. For example, the payment of an electricity bill relating to the current year would have this effect:

Profit calculation:	+Expenses	
Balance sheet:	−Cash	

The receipt of rental income or subscription relating to the year would produce:

Profit calculation:		+Revenues
Balance sheet:	+Cash	

The payment of creditors in cash would have this effect:

Profit calculation:		
Balance sheet:	−Cash	−Liabilities

In all cases the two effects would leave a balance between the left-hand and the right-hand side of the equation. The profit calculation can be much more detailed, and when rearranged may appear as in the example in Table 4.1.

The top part of the table is sometimes called the *trading account,* which deals with the calculation of trading profit or *gross profit.* There are various financial, administrative and marketing expenses to be paid out of this. The remainder is *net profit.* The whole calculation is called the profit and loss account or income statement.

Let us return to the presentation of the accounting equation, using the revenues and expenses in Table 4.1. Also, let us assume that the capital at the beginning of the year was £10,000 and that the assets and liabilities are £12,000 and £1,800 respectively. The balance sheet shows an excess for assets of £200 because of the earning of profit which has not yet been recorded:

$$\text{Profit calculation (£):} \quad \Sigma E_1 = 2,800 \qquad \Sigma R_1 = 3,000$$
$$\text{Balance sheet (£):} \quad \Sigma A_1 = 12,000 \qquad C_0 = 10,000$$
$$\Sigma L_1 = 1,800$$

This will be taken further in Chapter 7.

4.7 Profit, drawings and cash

Withdrawals by the owner from the business are usually in the form of cash, but sometimes stock may be taken as well. For companies the equivalent to the drawings of the owners are *dividends.* In all these cases drawings do not affect the calculation of the profit figure, but they do reduce the capital figure. Similarly, any introductions of capital in the form of cash or other assets affect capital but not profit:

$$C_1 = C_0 + \pi_1 + \text{introductions} - \text{drawings}$$

where C_1 is capital at the end of the year.

Table 4.1   A profit calculation (£)

Revenues: Sales			3,000
less Trading expenses (cost of sales):			
Materials	500		
Labour	800		1,300
Gross profit			1,700
less Administrative expenses:			
Wages	200		
Stationery	50		
Interest	300		
Rent	150	700	
less Distribution expenses:			
Travelling	300		
Commission	500	800	1,500
Net profit			200

This is one explanation for the fact that a profitable business may have little cash. If the owners withdraw much of the profit, the business may not have enough cash to stay in operation. Other explanations are that most of the profit may be due to credit sales, which means that the business has debtors rather than cash, or that the business has been buying stock or fixed assets or paying off loans. All these items affect cash, but they do not directly affect profit. Therefore a profitable business may run out of cash if it does not set up systems to monitor and manage its liquid resources.

Although the conventions of accounting are very useful for some purposes, we may wish to calculate profit by looking at a business from a different point of view. This will involve the imputation of costs that have not actually been incurred and the abandonment of some conventions such as historical cost. For example, consider a one-man business for which the accounting profit is £30,000. The owner wishes to know if this is the amount that he has gained in the year due to running the business. Assume that he has invested £100,000 capital in addition to the premises, which he owns, and his time, which he uses up. The imputed *opportunity cost* of these may be:

	£ p.a.
Interest that could have been earned on £100,000	10,000
Rent that would have been received for premises	8,000
Salary that could have been earned elsewhere	40,000
	58,000

It appears, then, that a more reasonable answer to the owner's question would be that he was losing £28,000 p.a. (i.e. £30,000 – £58,000) as a result of running the business. On the other hand, the business may be expected to do much better in the future, the owner may put a value on being his own master, and any capital gain on the £100,000 worth of assets has not been included. This alternative concept of profit (in this case the loss of £28,000), which takes account of these opportunity costs of the owner's resources, can be called *economic profit*.

4.8 Summary

Profit is measured by deducting expenses (i.e. payments that relate to the period) from revenues (i.e. receipts that relate to the period). Profit is usually measured over the period of a year, even though the activities of the business do not normally stop and start every year. There are many reasons why revenues may not equal receipts and why expenses may not equal payments. Several conventions are used in measuring and recording revenues and expenses.

It is possible to combine movements of assets, liabilities, capital, revenues and expenses into one equation. This accounting equation shows how the balance sheet and the profit and loss account fit together. It will be used to explain the double-entry system in Chapter 7.

Changes in capital figures from the beginning to the end of a year are not explained by profit only. Withdrawals of profit by the owners or introductions of more capital affect the capital figure.

Self-assessment questions

Suggested answers to the self-assessment questions are given at the end of the book.

1. Gross profit equals the difference between:

    (a) Net profit and operating expenses.
    (b) Revenues and cost of goods sold.
    (c) Revenues and administrative and distribution expenses.
    (d) Revenues and cost of goods sold *plus* other expenses.

2. A net profit will result if gross profit exceeds:

    (a) Cost of goods sold.
    (b) Administrative and disbtribution expenses.
    (c) Purchases.
    (d) Cost of goods sold *plus* operating expenses.

3. Which of the following transactions results in an immediate increase in expenses?

    (a) Purchase of office equipment on credit.
    (b) Payment of accounts payable.
    (c) Payment of wages.
    (d) Repayment of bank loan.

4. In practice, accountants record sales revenue when:

    (a) An order is placed by a customer.
    (b) Cash is received for the sales.
    (c) A product is finished and ready for sale.
    (d) An invoice or account is sent to the customer.

5. Revenues of a period could be defined as:

    (a) Those receipts of the period that relate to the period.
    (b) All receipts of the period.
    (c) Receipts of any period that relate to the period.

    (In each case assume that the receipts are related to earning profits at least in some period).

6. A trader's net profit for the year may be computed by using which of the following formulae?

   (a) Opening capital + drawings − capital introduced − closing capital.
   (b) Closing capital + drawings − capital introduced − opening capital.
   (c) Opening capital − drawings + capital introduced − closing capital.
   (d) Closing capital − drawings + capital introduced − opening capital.

7. The profit earned by a business in 19×7 was £72,500. The proprietor injected new capital of £8,000 during the year and withdrew goods for his private use which had cost £2,200.

   If net assets at the beginning of 19×7 were £101,700, what were the closing net assets?

   (a) £35,000.
   (b) £39,400.
   (c) £168,400.
   (d) £180,000.

8. The net profit earned by a business in the year ending 31 December 19×9 was £8,500. Balance sheets of the business at 1 January and 31 December showed net assets of £84,300 and £92,500 respectively. The proprietor made regular cash drawings of £150 per month and also withdrew goods for his own use on several occasions during the year. On 30 September he had a lottery win and put the whole of his winnings into the business as new capital.

   Calculate the amount by which the cost of *goods* withdrawn by the proprietor exceeds or falls short of the amount of his lottery win:

   (a) Goods withdrawn exceed lottery winnings by £300.
   (b) Goods withdrawn exceed lottery winnings by £1,500.
   (c) Goods withdrawn fall short of lottery winnings by £300.
   (d) Goods withdrawn fall short of lottery winnings by £1,500.

9. Mr Bod has paid rent of £2,400 for the period 1 January 19×8 to 31 December 19×8. His first accounts are drawn up for the nine months ending 30 September 19×8.

   His first accounts should show:

   (a) Only a rent expense of £2,400.
   (b) A rent expense of £1,800 and a prepayment of £600.
   (c) A rent expense of £1,800 and accrued expenses of £600.
   (d) A rent expense of £2,400 with an explanatory note that this is the usual change for twelve months.

10. An electricity accrual of £375 was treated as a prepayment in preparing a trader's profit and loss account. As a result his profit was:

(a) Overstated by £375.
(b) Understated by £375.
(c) Overstated by £750.
(d) Understated by £750.

Tutorial questions

1. Define 'expenses' and 'revenues':

   (a) in the conventional way by reference to transactions; and
   (b) by reference to assets and liabilities.

2. When measuring performance, why is it useful to separate a business from its owner?

3. Explain various reasons why a business may have made a profit for the year even though its cash has fallen.

DEPRECIATION 5

If a business buys goods or services (e.g. electricity, stationery or labour) that are to be used up in the current year in the process of earning profit, they are charged to the profit and loss account. We have seen that what is charged in the accounting year in question is not the amount paid in the year but the amount that relates to the year. That is, if the business pays for some of next year's rent, it is not treated as an expense of this year. Similarly, an expense of this year may well be due to a payment during last year, this year or next year. This is a practical working out of the accruals convention met in Chapter 4.

5.1 The traditional concept

A more important result of the accruals convention relates to cases where a company buys goods of significant value that are *not* to be used up in the current year. In such cases the cost should be treated as a capital purchase (see (2) below), not as a current expense (see (1) below). We see the difference in effect on the balance sheet:

(1) e.g. Expense of £1,000:

Assets (£)		Capital and liabilities (£)	
Current assets:	−1,000 cash	Capital:	− 1,000 profit

(2) e.g. Capital purchase of £1,000:

Assets (£)		Capital and liabilities (£)
Fixed assets:	+1,000 machine	
Current assets:	−1,000 cash	

However, it would be unreasonable to charge nothing against profit for the use of the machine. If it were hired, there would be a charge. So, if the asset is owned and is wearing out there will be a charge too. If the machine will last for ten years, the cost is spread over ten years rather than charged totally to the year of purchase or not charged at all. This concept is just an extension of the treatment of something paid for currently that is an expense of future years.

The corollary of this is that, just as it is reasonable to charge for the services provided, so the fixed asset is used up because it has provided the services. The asset may be used up or become less useful for a variety of reasons, which can be divided into two categories:

(1) Physical reasons – deterioration or wearing out with use; the expiration of a lease or patent; the exhaustion of a mine;

(2) Economic reasons – the obsolescence of the asset or the product that it makes; a change in company policy leading, for example, to the hiring of machines; expansion of the business causing an asset to be inadequate in size or performance.

So, it is reasonable to allocate the cost to expense over the life of the asset and to recognize that the asset is being used up. The 'life' in question is the *useful economic life*, which takes into account the fact that a machine may be obsolete before it is worn out or vice versa. The expense is labelled 'depreciation'.

For example, suppose that a £1,000 machine is estimated to last ten years and to be worthless at the end. An obvious and simple method of depreciation would be to allocate £100 of the cost as an expense of each of the ten years. For example:

1 January 1996	Purchase:	machine	+£1,000
		cash	−£1,000
31 December 1996	Depreciation recognized:	machine	− £100
		profit	− £100

So the machine stands at £1,000 − £100 = £900 in the balance sheet. This £900 is the amount of the cost not yet treated as an expense. It is sometimes called the *net book value* (NBV) or the *written down value* (WDV). This method of depreciation is called the straight line or fixed instalment or *constant charge method*. It is illustrated in Figure 5.1.

If a scrap value (residual value) of £300 were estimated and the life were expected to be seven years, the depreciation charge would again be £100, as in Table 5.1. Notice that the written down value is not an estimate of the market value of the asset. Because the business is a going concern, it may be reasonable for outside users of the accounts to ignore market values of assets that are not going to be sold. For example, if a machine were very specific to the company, there would be no buyers for the

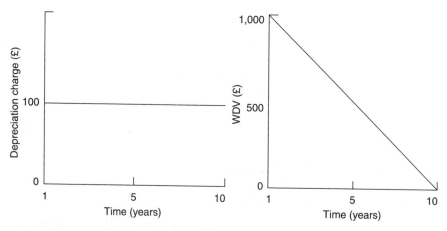

Figure 5.1   Straight line depreciation

Table 5.1 Straight line depreciation of net cost (£)

End of year	Depreciation charge recognized	WDV
0	–	1,000
1	100	900
2	100	800
3	100	700
4	100	600
5	100	500
6	100	400
7	100	300

second-hand machine, and so its market value would be zero immediately after purchase.

Companies must show the gross figure for assets as well as the WDV in the balance sheet (or in notes to it). At the end of year 6 in the example of Table 5.1 the balance sheet or the notes would show:

	£
Fixed asset: Cost	1,000
Cumulative depreciation	600
WDV	400

The depreciation charges represent the using up of the asset, not the provision of money for the replacement of the asset (see Section 5.5). Neither is the depreciation expense the amount that is allowed for tax purposes. Strictly speaking, in the United Kingdom, no depreciation is allowed as an expense for tax purposes. The system of capital allowances, however, allows most fixed assets (e.g. machinery) to be treated as expenses faster for tax purposes than for accounting purposes. This is not directly an accounting matter, however, but an investment incentive (see Chapter 10). In may other countries (e.g. Germany and Japan), accounting depreciation expenses are the ones used for tax purposes. Therefore, companies will usually charge in the accounts the maximum that is allowed for tax purposes, in order to reduce taxable profit. This often means that reducing balance depreciation is used, because this speeds up the expense.

It would be useful at this point to look at some definitions of depreciation. The Standard on depreciation (SSAP 12) states that 'depreciation is a measure of the wearing out, consumption or other reduction in the useful economic life of a fixed asset whether arising from use, effluxion of time or obsolescence through technological or market changes. Depreciation should be allocated so as to charge a fair proportion of cost or valuation of the asset to each accounting period expected to benefit from its use' (SSAP 12, para. 3).

A statement by the American Institute of Certified Public Accountants (AICPA) says that depreciation accounting is a system of accounting that aims to distribute the cost or other basic value of tangible capital assets, *less* salvage value (if any), over the estimated useful life of the unit (which may be a group of assets) in a systematic and rational manner. It is a process of allocation, not of valuation (AICPA, 1953).

The main problem with these definitions is that both use historical cost as the basis for depreciation. The allocation of the historical cost of an asset over its useful life is a relatively uncomplicated task and neatly disposes of exactly the net cost of the asset, if allowances for bad estimates are made when the asset is eventually scrapped (see Section 5.4.6). However, a realistic cost of using up one-tenth of an asset bought several years ago is very unlikely to be one-tenth of its historical cost if prices have been changing in the interim.

Let us consider again the asset bought for £1,000 that will last ten years with no scrap value. After five years the replacement cost of the asset might be £2,000. It seems more reasonable to base depreciation on the £2,000 rather than the £1,000, for it is a proportion of a machine that currently costs £2,000 that is currently being used up. This would be one possible approach to the recognition of the effects of price changes. The effect of basing depreciation on historical costs in inflationary periods is to give a misleadingly good impression of profit, particularly in companies with many old fixed assets.

These problems will be dealt with more fully later. At this point we should return to the description of how the cost of an asset may be allocated over its useful life. For simplicity the treatment here is set in the context of historical cost accounting. However, most of the problems relate in a similar way to current value accounting, except that the net cost to be allocated will not be based on the historical cost.

5.2 Methods of depreciation

Following up the AICPA definition above, let us look at various methods of depreciation in order to see whether they are 'systematic and rational'. We have already looked at the straight line method, which is clearly systematic. Is it rational? In order to answer this question it is necessary to recall why depreciation is being charged. Depreciation is a charge designed to recognize the loss of services that an asset has suffered in any year. As has been said, it is an example of the results of using the accruals or matching convention. Let us look at different types of assets with this in mind.

(1) Leases, patents and some buildings can be said to require depreciation *because of the effluxion of time*. In this case straight line depreciation seems to be satisfactory.
(2) Other assets have *increasing repairs and maintenance* in such a way that the total expense per year relating to an asset increases over its life if straight line depreciation is used. So, if a reasonably constant total

charge for an asset's services is to be put to the profit and loss account, a declining depreciation charge may be appropriate.

(3) Some assets wear out *in proportion to their use*.

5.2.1 Declining charge methods

It may, then, be rational to have a declining depreciation charge for some sorts of assets. There are several ways of producing this systematically. The *reducing balance* (or constant percentage on reducing balance) *method* is one of them. With 20 per cent depreciation this would give a situation as in Table 5.2.

Table 5.2   The reducing balance method

		£
	Cost	1,000
Year 1	*less* 20% depreciation	200
	WDV	800
Year 2	*less* 20% depreciation	160
	WDV	640
Year 3	*less* 20% depreciation	128
	WDV	512

So, the WDV at the end of the third year will be £512, and the charge in the third year will be £128. How many years will it take to write down the asset to zero? The answer, inconveniently, is that it will take an infinite number of years. However, if there is a *scrap value*, this problem is avoided. If there is no scrap value, a small figure to which the asset will be written down may be chosen. The residual at that point will be an extra depreciation charge for the final year.

To find the appropriate percentage to use for a given net cost and a given useful life, a formula may be used:

$$r = 1 - \sqrt[n]{\frac{S}{K}}$$

where r is the depreciation rate, n is the life of the asset, S is the scrap value and K is the gross cost. This formula may be simply derived as in Table 5.3.

Table 5.3   The reducing balance formula

End of year	WDV	Standardized form of WDV
0	K	$K(1 - r)^0$
1	$K - Kr$	$K(1 - r)^1$
2	$(K - Kr) - (K - Kr)r$	$K(1 - r)^2$
3	etc.	etc.

At the end of the asset's life, $S = K(1 - r)^n$
Therefore,

$$r = 1 - \sqrt[n]{\frac{S}{K}}$$

As an example, let us use the asset costing £1,000, which will have a scrap value of £300 and a life of seven years. Applying the formula,

$$r = 1 - \sqrt[n]{\frac{S}{K}}$$

$$= 1 - \sqrt[7]{\frac{300}{1,000}} = 0.158 \text{ or } 15.8\%$$

The results of this are tabulated, repeating the straight line results for comparison, in Table 5.4. It can be seen that more depreciation is charged in the earlier years using the reducing balance method. This helps to stabilize the total charge (of depreciation *plus* maintenance) for the contribution of the machine to earning profits.

Another way of producing systematically declining charges for depreciation is to use the *sum of digits method*. For this, one merely adds up the digits of the number of years of useful life. For example, for a useful life of six years the sum of digits is 21 (i.e. 6 + 5 + 4 + 3 + 2 + 1). The charge for year 1 will be 6/21, that for year 2 will be 5/21 and so on. Another method that can be used to obtain a declining charge is the *double declining-balance method*. Here, the straight line depreciation rate is worked out and then doubled and applied on a reducing balance basis.

One of these three declining charge methods may be appropriate for assets that are expected to have considerable repair and maintenance costs in later years. The total amount allocated will, of course, be the same in all these declining charge methods and, for that matter, in the straight line method.

It may be that the market value of most machines actually declines in a way that is more similar to the result of declining charge depreciation than

Table 5.4 Depreciation methods contrasted (£)

Year	Straight line		Reducing balance	
	Charge	WDV	Charge	WDV
0	–	1,000	–	1,000
1	100	900	158	842
2	100	800	133	709
3	100	700	112	597
4	100	600	94	503
5	100	500	79	424
6	100	400	67	357
7	100	300	57[a]	300

[a] Adjusted for rounding differences.

of straight line depreciation. However, this is not really an argument in favour of a declining charge method, since the main aim is to get a fair yearly allocation of cost against profit over the whole life of the asset. Nevertheless, if the business is very uncertain about the useful life of the asset or the date of sale, there is an argument for rapid depreciation and for keeping the written down value fairly close to the market value at all times rather than just at the estimated end of life. In these cases a declining charge method may be more suitable.

An alternative to using a declining charge method is to create a provision for repairs and maintenance by charging equal yearly amounts out of profit over the life of the asset. Any repairs actually carried out reduce this provision, which will fall to zero at the end of the asset's life if estimates have been accurate. The cost of the asset is depreciated on a straight line basis. So the total charge for repairs and depreciation is stabilized in this way.

5.2.2 Usage methods

Assets that come to the end of their useful lives owing mainly to wearing out through use may more rationally be depreciated on the basis of use, which is called the *usage method*. That is, if the asset concerned is expected to produce 100,000 units or to run for 20,000 hours, the depreciation charge for the year will be that proportion of the original cost that the usage of the year bears to the total expected usage. For example, in the case of a machine costing £20,000 which is expected to produce 100,000 units, the usage may turn out to be as given in Table 5.5.

5.2.3 The revaluation method

Some assets are difficult to depreciate by using any of the above three methods (i.e. straight line, declining charge and usage). These assets are such things as tools, crates and livestock, for which it may be inappropriate or unnecessary to keep item-by-item records.

Table 5.5 The usage method

Accounting year	Units produced	Depreciation charge (£)
1	15,000	3,000
2	35,000	7,000
3	20,000	4,000
4	20,000	4,000
5	10,000	2,000
	100,000	20,000

In the case of tools and crates the assets may be capable of a long life, but in practice their lives are short because of damage, breakage, theft, loss, and so on. In addition their individual values are immaterial in the context of the whole company. Therefore it would be inefficient to record the purchase, the yearly depreciation charges, the disposal and adjustments to depreciation on disposal (see Section 5.4).

So, depreciation is charged using the *revaluation method*. This method involves valuing the set of similar assets at the beginning of the year, adding assets purchased and deducting a valuation of the set at the year end. This gives a measure of the using up of the type of asset, which is charged to the profit and loss account as depreciation. The year-end valuation is recorded as a fixed asset in the balance sheet. This treatment is very similar to that for stocks, discussed in Chapter 6.

5.3 Practice

The Companies Act 1985 requires that all assets with limited useful lives be depreciated. This normally includes machinery and buildings, but not land. Further, it is necessary to disclose accounting policies with respect to depreciation, and to disclose the total depreciation charge for the year. The Accounting Standard SSAP 12 gives detailed instructions on depreciation methods and disclosure.

Of the top 300 companies in the UK in 1982-3, 259 used the straight line method for all or most assets, 23 used the reducing balance method or some combination and 19 did not disclose their methods (ICAEW 1983, latest available data). The predominance of the straight line method is probably a result of its simplicity.

Of those using the straight line method, the rates most used tend to be the following:

	%
Freehold property	2
Long-lease property	2
Plant and equipment	10
Vehicles	20–25

Because of the substantial amount of information now to be disclosed about depreciation, it is normal for this to be done by way of notes, leaving only summary net figures on the face of the balance sheet.

When a change in method occurs, it affects the profit of this year and future years, so that comparisons with last year's profit figure will be upset. SSAP 12 recommends that changes in depreciation methods be disclosed. This is clearly essential for a correct understanding of a set of accounts.

5.4 Practical problems

With all the methods of depreciation discussed so far there are several practical problems, which will often lead to estimates being made. This means that at the end of an asset's life it is usually found that too much or too little of the original cost has been allocated over its life. The problems include the following.

5.4.1 Cost

What is the 'cost' to allocate over the useful life of the asset? The answer is that cost should include not only the invoice price of the asset but also all costs involved in getting the asset into a location and condition where it can be productive. So, this will include delivery charges, sales taxes, installation charges, and so on in the case of plant and machinery. For land and buildings, cost will include legal fees, architect's fees, clearing the land, and so on, as well as the builder's bill and the cost of the land.

If the company has used its own labour or materials, these should be treated not as current expenses but as capital items, which also increase the cost of the fixed asset; that is, they are *capitalized*. It is also possible to capitalize interest cost on money borrowed to create fixed assets. Table 5.6 shows that 20 per cent of companies in a survey capitalized some interest as part of the cost of assets.

Another complication is that many companies revalue some of their assets. The revalued amounts are used as a substitute for 'cost' in the calculation of depreciation. Table 5.6 shows that a majority of UK companies in a survey did revalue some assets.

5.4.2 Subsequent expenditure

Which expenditures after purchase are of a capital nature and should be taken to increase 'cost' and thus depreciation? The answer is often unclear, but in general repairs and maintenance are treated as current expenses,

Table 5.6   Asset valuation methods, 1994

	% of companies
Cost	28
Cost + interest	7
Cost and revaluation	51
Cost + interest and revaluation	13
Unclear	1
	100

Source: ICAEW (1994)

whereas improvements are capitalized. So, a new engine for a company vehicle will usually be treated as an expense, since it keeps it in running order rather than improves it, whereas the painting of advertising signs on the company's fleet of vans may well be treated as a capital item.

Obviously, the accountant needs to consider whether the amounts are material enough to capitalize them. He or she tends to treat as much as possible as expense, since this is the prudent and administratively more convenient method. If the inspector of taxes can be convinced that items are expenses this will also speed up their tax deductibility

The depreciation treatment of the new engine mentioned above will depend on the depreciation 'units' that the accountant works on. Normally, the whole vehicle will be the unit, and so the new engine will be a current expense. If the vehicle and the engine were separate units for depreciation, the new engine would be a capital item.

5.4.3 Useful economic life

What is the 'life' of the asset over which the cost is allocated? The answer is reached by asking the engineer, the economist etc. for their estimates of the useful life of the machine (assuming reasonable repairs) and taking the shorter. Clearly, the assumptions about 'units' for depreciation and about reasonable maintenance and repairs will affect the estimation of life. The accountant and engineer should consider past experience with similar machines, impending developments of products and plans for improvements in fixed assets. A small business may have to seek external advice, perhaps from its auditors.

Traditionally, accountants have tended to err on the side of underestimating the length of life of assets. This is partly a conservative reaction in the context of uncertainty and partly a way of increasing the depreciation charges (in the early years) as a way of recognizing the effect of inflation. However, the 'best' estimate will be more suitable. SSAP 12 (para. 11) notes that the life to be used is that of the asset to its present owners.

5.4.4 Residual value

What scrap value should be used? Here the answer will again require a guess about what state the asset will be in after its useful life and how much a buyer will be willing to pay. Often, because of the great uncertainty in all the guesses that need to be made and because of a suspicion that the scrap value may be immaterial, it is assumed that there will be no value. Again, though, there is a strong argument for taking the best estimate available. SSAP 12 (para. 13) requires the estimate to be made using the price levels ruling when the asset's own value was determined (i.e. usually at purchase date).

5.4.5 Mid-year purchases

What depreciation should be charged on an asset bought during the accounting year? There are two possibilities: either the appropriate proportion (usually by month) of one year's depreciation is charged in the years of acquisition and disposal, or a whole year's depreciation is charged for only those assets that are on hand at the end of the year. As long as the second method is used consistently, it should only lead to significant distortion when the business has few assets or has just acquired or disposed of a very valuable asset. This second method is the more usual.

5.4.6 Disposal

In practice the business is likely to find that its estimates of useful life and scrap value turn out to be wrong. Consequently, an amount that is smaller or larger than the net cost (i.e. cost *less* scrap value) will have been allocated over the actual life of the asset. Traditionally, the amount allocated can never be larger than the *total* historical cost, because the accountant stops charging depreciation for an asset when its written down value reaches zero.

In the above case, where the amount allocated turns out to be wrong, the implication is that previous years' depreciation charges have been incorrect. Because of the practical difficulties of correcting previous years, the correction usually occurs in the year of disposal. It will be separately shown in the notes to the profit and loss account if it is important. For example, on disposal there will be a loss or an extra depreciation charge of £100 if the cash received for an asset is £500 but the written down value is £600.

5.4.7 Increase in value

What accounting entries are necessary if the asset increases in value? This question will be considered more fully later. It can be said here that, if the asset is sold, the realized gain is recorded as a profit. If the asset is unsold and its unrealized rise in value is to be recognized, the asset figure in the balance sheet increases, and so does the 'ownership interest' total, because a revaluation reserve is recorded. After a revaluation, the calculations of depreciation and gain or loss on disposal use the revalued amount instead of cost.

5.5 Replacement

Depreciation is not charged in order to create a reserve of money for the replacement of the asset but to charge the cost of the asset against revenue over its useful life. Unless amounts of cash that are equivalent to the depreciation charges are put into a tin box or another easily accessible store, an amount equalling the cost may not be available in liquid form at the end of the asset's life. Even if cash is available, inflation will probably have caused the price of a replacement asset to rise, and so it will be insufficient. Also, in many cases the company will not want to buy a similar asset but one that is technologically more advanced, bigger or concerned with the production of completely different goods.

However, depreciation may help to preserve the original capital (in terms of historical pounds), because depreciation reduces profit available for distribution. So, less cash may be distributed, and this will build up in the company, perhaps converted into a variety of different assets such as debtors, stock and even fixed assets.

Let us look at an example of how charging depreciation may aid replacement in the extreme cases where either (1) no depreciation is charged (company A) or (2) depreciation *is* charged, and the assets that are consequently undistributed are kept as current assets (company B). The two companies are identical in other ways, and both distribute all their profits. They start by buying a fixed asset for £10,000, which will last for ten years and have no scrap value. There are also £10,000 of current assets. Table 5.7 shows the situation after the first year. If this continues for another nine years, company A will have a worthless fixed asset and £10,000 current assets and will see that its capital is only £10,000. Company B will have a worthless fixed asset but £20,000 current assets due to distributing £10,000 less 'profits' than company A did. So, company B can purchase another fixed asset and continue business with its capital intact. Company A will have a serious financial problem.

A well-run business has an overall cash and funds plan for future months and years. Included in this is the expected need to replace assets. The assets that will be bought as replacements may be identical but more expensive or they may be entirely different. It would be unusual, and probably commercially unwise, for a business to set aside amounts of money in liquid or time-matched investments in order to be prepared for the replacement of

Table 5.7   The effect on assets of not charging depreciation (£)

Company A				Company B			
Gross profit	5,000			Gross profit	5,000		
less Expenses	3,000			less Expenses	3,000		
				less Depreciation	1,000		
Net profit	2,000	distributed					
				Net profit	1,000	distributed	
Balance sheet				*Balance sheet*			
Fixed assets	10,000	Capital	20,000	Fixed assets	10,000	Capital	20,000
		Profit	2,000	less Depreciation 1,000		Profit	1,000
Current assets	10,000	less Distribution	2,000	Current assets	11,000	less Distribution	1,000
	20,000		20,000		20,000		20,000

assets. These funds could be better used elsewhere in the business, and it is not until the time for replacement approaches that a good impression of the type and cost of replacement assets is obtainable.

5.6 Further considerations

Thus far, we have been considering the traditional concept of depreciation (which conforms with current practice), which is concerned with the allocation of cost over the useful life of the asset, taking into account the effluxion of time and physical and economic deterioration.

There are a number of alternative concepts that may be considered in an attempt to find the theoretically most justifiable method of charging depreciation. The alternatives may be particularly useful when we have to adapt the idea of depreciation to fit changing circumstances.

5.6.1 Increasing charge depreciation

The method of *increasing charge depreciation* could be supported as an alternative way of allocating historical cost on a combination of grounds. First, it could be claimed that a rationally designed system of depreciation accounting should include an allowance for the fact that a reducing amount of capital is involved. If the asset provides similar services throughout its life, the depreciation charge should increase to balance a reducing cost of providing the reducing capital. Second, there may be some assets where expenses decline over the useful life.

Although there is some reason in these suggestions, it seems justifiable to say that the total cost of capital for all years is a joint cost and should be spread over the life of the asset in a systematic and rational manner, which may be more strongly affected by factors other than the cost of capital tied up. For those grounds that still remain, we have seen that there seem to be stronger reasons for declining charge depreciation.

Clearly, the weight of the arguments for declining or increasing charge will vary with the economic reality of each situation, but at least they work in opposite directions, and the simple and popular straight line method may be that much better a compromise for this reason.

5.6.2 Opposition to depreciation

Some academic accountants have argued that depreciation relies on so many estimates and is so far removed from being a real cost of the year that it should not be charged. This, of course, would be part of a more general attack on accruals accounting. In practice, some analysts of accounts do add back depreciation charges to profits because of the arbitrary and non-cash nature of these charges.

The directors of some companies, as part of attempts to show larger profits, have used various arguments to avoid depreciation charges, particularly on large assets such as buildings. For example, it might be claimed that certain hotels or shops have to be maintained in at least as good a condition as when they were purchased. Therefore they do not wear out during their life with the present owner; therefore there should be no depreciation charges.

An alternative argument, for investment properties, is that they are being held for value, and so they ought to be shown at current valuation, thereby absorbing any depreciation. Indeed, an Accounting Standard (SSAP 19) does make investment properties an exception: they must be annually revalued and not depreciated.

5.6.3 The economist's approach

The economist's approach might be to charge depreciation equivalent to the amount by which the value of the asset to the firm had declined during the period of use under consideration. The value of the asset to the firm is not the market value but the discounted expected net revenue contributions from the asset. One needs to identify the net revenues of the company with and without the asset in order to measure the net contributions of the asset.

The net contributions of the asset will be called R_1 in year 1, R_n in year n, and so on. It has been briefly mentioned in Chapter 2 that future revenues need to be discounted in order to assess their present values. The value of an asset (PV_0) can therefore be said to be:

$$PV_0 = \frac{R_1}{1 + r} + \frac{R_2}{(1 + r)^2} + \ldots + \frac{R_n}{(1 + r)^n}$$

where n is the life of the asset and r is the appropriate discount rate. This rate may be the cost of capital or the rate of return on funds (see Chapter 16). The above equation can be restated as:

$$PV_0 = \sum_{t = 1}^{t = n} \frac{R_t}{(1 + r)^t}$$

where t is the year. One year later the asset's value (PV_1) will be given by:

$$PV_1 = \sum_{t = 2}^{t = n} \frac{R_t}{(1 + r)^{t - 1}}$$

and the depreciation for the year will be $PV_0 - PV_1$.

There are, of course, great practical difficulties in isolating the net revenues or cost savings of an asset after purchase. However, if it could be done it would lead to a justifiable current measure of the using up of the asset's value during the year, taking into account repairs and maintenance or deterioration in performance caused by lack of them.

5.7 Summary

The traditional concept of depreciation is concerned with the allocation of the historical cost of a fixed asset over its useful life in a systematic and rational manner. The amounts allocated are charged against profit in the appropriate year, with the intention that the fairest estimate of profit will be made.

There are many causes that contribute towards the limited life of the asset (e.g. the passing of time, the use of the asset, escalating repair expenses, and technical obsolescence of the machine or its product). If these causes can be identified and quantified, it should be possible to decide which method of depreciation would allocate the cost most fairly over the asset's life.

The methods in use include the straight line, declining charge, usage and revaluation methods. The first is the simplest and most popular. Whichever method is used, depreciation does not provide cash for replacement (although it may mean that less cash is distributed), and it does not lead to the written down value being an estimate of market value (except at the end of the asset's life, by which time it will usually be found that estimates of life and scrap value are inaccurate).

There are several practical problems (e.g. estimating the life and the scrap value of the assets). However, by far the most serious difficulty is the effect of inflation, which makes depreciation charges based on historical costs out of date.

Self-assessment questions

Suggested answers to the self-assessment questions are given at the end of the book.

1. Depreciation refers to the periodic allocation of the net cost of a fixed asset over its useful life.

   (a) True.
   (b) False.

2. The net book value of a plant asset usually equals its market value.

   (a) True.
   (b) False.

3. Accelerated methods of depreciation result in lower net income in the last years of an asset's life than does the straight line method.

   (a) True.
   (b) False.

4. Which of the following would *not* be a basis for estimating the useful life of a piece of equipment?

   (a) Years of service.
   (b) Weight.
   (c) Potential production in units.
   (d) Hours of service.

5. Which of the following most appropriately describes the basis of calculation of depreciation?

   (a) Physical deterioration of plant asset.
   (b) Gradual obsolescence of plant asset.
   (c) Decline in value of plant asset.
   (d) Allocation of cost of plant asset.

6. All of the following are needed for the computation of depreciation except:

   (a) Disposal date.
   (b) Cost.
   (c) Residual value.
   (d) Estimated useful life to the present owner.

7. If an asset cost £24,000 and has a residual value of £3,000 and a useful life of six years, the depreciation in the second year, using the sum-of-the-years-digits method, would be:

   (a) £6,857.
   (b) £6,000.
   (c) £5,714.
   (d) £5,000.

8. Using the figures of Question 7, which of the following methods would result in the most depreciation in the first year?

   (a) Straight line.
   (b) Sum of the years digits.
   (c) Declining balance.
   (d) Cannot tell from data given.

9. The sale of equipment costing £8,000, with accumulated depreciation of £6,700 and sale price of £2,000, would result in a:

   (a) Gain of £2,000.
   (b) Gain of £700.
   (c) Loss of £700.
   (d) Loss of £600.

10. Palmer Corporation purchased a piece of equipment on 1 June, 19xx, for £15,000. The equipment has an estimated life of ten years or 25,000 units of production and an estimated residual value of £2,500. The amount of depreciation to be recorded for the year, using the straight line method of calculating depreciation and assuming a 31 December year end, is:

   (a) £1,500.
   (b) £875.
   (c) £729.
   (d) None of the above.

11. According to the information given in Question 10, the amount of depreciation to be recorded for the year, using the sum-of-the-years-digits method, is:

   (a) £1,326.
   (b) £1,591.
   (c) £664.
   (d) None of the above.

12. According to the information given in Question 10, the amount of depreciation to be recorded for the year, using the units-of-production method and assuming that 3,500 units were produced, is:

   (a) £3,660.
   (b) £4,380.
   (c) £2,129.
   (d) None of the above.

Tutorial questions

1. The distinction between current (or revenue) expenditure and capital expenditure is fundamental to the preparation of financial statements that show a true and fair view of the organisation's activites. Define and describe (with examples) captial expenditure and revenue expenditure and explain the effect on net profits if the correct classification of expenditure is not maintained.

2. Depreciation might be defined as 'the allocation of the depreciable amount of an asset over its estimated useful life'. With respect to the above:

   (a) examine *four* reasons that would result in loss of value of a fixed asset, and suggest *three* ways of calculating depreciation; and
   (b) explain what factors should be taken into account when calculating depreciation, and evaluate the difficulties inherent in this process.

3. 'In countries where finanacial reporting is closely influenced by taxation, depreciation charges have little in common with economic reality,

whilst in countries where financial reporting is not closely influenced by taxation, depreciation charges involve many estimations and are subject to large variation and manipulation. These estimations also have little in common with economic reality. Depreciation is therefore, in both situations, an accounting mechanism for profit manipulation and creative accounting'. Discuss.

4.   M Co. purchased plant and machinery at cost of £6,000 in April 19x5. The provision for depreciation was to be calculated on a straight line basis at 20 per cent per annum on cost. In August 19x8 M Co. decided to replace the machine, and sold it for £2,000.

(*Note*: A full year's depreciation is charged in the year of acquisition and in the year of disposal.)

Calculate the following:

(a) depreciation charge each year,
(b) residual value at the time of disposal,
(c) profit or loss on disposal.

Also prepare extracts of the company's balance sheet at the ends of the years 19x5, 19x6 and 19x7.

References

American Institute of Certified Public Accountants (AICPA) (1953) *Accounting Terminology, Bulletin No. 1*, New York: AICPA.
Institute of Chartered Accountants in England and Wales (ICAEW) (1983) *Survey of Published Accounts, 1983–4*, London: ICAEW.
Institute of Chartered Accountants in England and Wales (ICAEW) (1994) *Financial Reporting, 1994/95*, London: ICAEW.

Further reading

Accounting Standards Committee (1987) *Accounting for Depreciation*, SSAP 12.
Accounting Standards Committee (1991) *Accounting for Investment Properties*, SSAP 19.

STOCK

Our main concern when discussing depreciation was with obtaining a 'fair' profit figure. There was less concern with the resulting asset 'valuation' as recorded in the balance sheet. When considering stock (inventory in the United States), there will again be these two factors to bear in mind. However, as stock is a current asset, more attention is paid to valuation because of its impact on the measurement of liquidity (see Chapter 15). Nevertheless, many accountants, investors, tax inspectors and directors regard the accuracy of the profit figure as the more important. As stock is often as much as one-third of total assets, the effect of inaccurate valuation could be very important for both profit and balance sheet figures.

6.1 Profit measurement

It should be clear that the valuation of stock on hand at the end of an accounting period is directly related to the profit figure. For example, for a retail company with no opening stock,

> sales for the period
> − purchases for the period
> + closing stock at end of period
> = gross profit

Purchases of materials in the period are all treated initially as expenses.

However, the materials are not all used up in the accounting period, so that it is necessary to make an adjustment that reduces the expense for stock on hand at the year end. Although the total profit of all accounting periods is not affected by the valuation of stock (because one year's closing stock is the next year's opening stock), the profit of any individual year *is* affected.

Since the concern is with finding the fair figure for profit for the year, there must be an attempt to match the charge for the stock used against the sales that relate to it. There are many ways of valuing the remaining stock, some of which cause fairer charges for the stock used than others. The example in Table 6.1 should make it clear that any overvaluation of closing stock by £1 leads to an overstatement of profit by £1.

6.2 The count

Before *valuing* the stock left it is necessary to know how much there is. It is also useful to know what types of stock there are. Stocks are often divided into raw materials, work in progress and finished goods. The Companies

Table 6.1   The relation between stock valuation and profit (£)

Sales (revenue)		2,000
Opening stock	800	
Purchases	1,600	
	2,400	
less Closing stock	950	
Cost of sales (expense)		1,450
Gross profit		550

Act 1985 requires companies to disclose the division of their stocks into such categories.

Looking at the process of counting, let us consider first a simple case where a business owns finished goods only, because it runs a wholesale warehouse. Even here, there are several ways of estimating the quantity of stock on hand at a year end.

6.2.1 Stocktakes (or periodic counts)

The warehouse staff, perhaps assisted by administrative staff, physically count and record all items of stock on the premises. The auditors will probably wish to advise on procedures, attend the count and check the results for a few types of stock. Adjustments have to be made for goods on the premises that do not belong to the firm and for goods off the premises that do. Also, there will be adjustments for stock movements if the actual count is done on a day that is not the accounting year end, perhaps because a weekend is more convenient.

6.2.2 Continuous stocktaking (or perpetual inventory)

Using this method a record is kept by item of all stock movements as they occur. Therefore a figure for the amount of stock of each type on hand at any moment should be easy to calculate. This is supplemented by occasional counts of selected items to see whether the stock records are accurate. The method avoids a massive and disruptive effort at the year end.

In practice many stock control systems are run by computers, which record sales and purchases and produce invoices and lists of debtors. They can also report current stock figures, slow-moving lines, re-order possibilities and so on. The running of a perpetual inventory is much easier in these circumstances.

Comparing these two methods, it is clear that the latter will discover pilferage more quickly and help in signalling that a re-order of stock is necessary. Note that the periodic count gives a figure for usage during the year by residual, which obscures any pilferage and breakages. On the other hand, the perpetual inventory method counts up usage during the year but leaves closing stock as a residual figure. The figures used for profit measurement must always be the physical figures, if available. The accounting records must be adjusted to the actual stock in cases of discrepancy.

6.3 Valuation

Now we can consider potential alternative bases of valuation: *output values* and *input values*.

6.3.1 Output values

The use of output values would rely on the proposition that the value of the stock to the firm is the future receipts that will arise from it. There are several ways that could be used to measure this output value.

(1) *Discounted money receipts* can be used when there is a definite amount and time of receipt. This will seldom be the case except for contracts of supply.
(2) *Current selling prices* may be used when there is a definite price and no significant selling costs or delays. For example, stocks of gold may be valued in this way.
(3) *Net realizable value* is the estimated selling price in the ordinary course of business, *less* costs of completion and *less* costs to be incurred in marketing, distributing and selling but without deduction for general administration or profit.

There seem to be grounds for using net realizable value when sales prices and other costs are known, particularly for stocks in an advanced state of completion. However, conventional accounting is not disposed towards a consistent use of this valuation method, because profit would then be taken before the stock was sold. It can be argued that, if 90 per cent of the work has been done, then to take all the profit before sale is better than taking none. Nevertheless, the American Institute of Certified Public Accountants (AICPA) has advised its members that net realizable value should only be used when it is below cost or when cost cannot be found and the stock is immediately marketable (AICPA, 1968). The UK law and standard (SSAP 9) are even more restrictive and require that net realizable value should only be used if it is lower than cost.

6.3.2 Input values

The alternatives to output values are input values, of which we shall consider two. In each case the value will include those costs which contribute towards bringing the stock to its present location and condition. These costs should usually include the appropriate proportion of production overheads (as illustrated below). However, other overheads (e.g. administration and selling) should not be included, partly because they are difficult to assign to specific stocks and partly because they do not contribute to bringing the stocks to their present condition and location.

In a survey, 300 UK companies reported that they included overheads in ways shown in Table 6.2.

Let us look at a simple example of overhead absorption:

		£
Direct cost:	Labour	3 per unit
	Materials	2 per unit
Direct overheads (specific supervisors and machines)		40,000
Indirect overheads (rates, factory manager etc.)		60,000
Administrative overheads of the rest of the company		80,000
Selling overheads		20,000

If the year's production were 20,000 units and this type of production used one-third of the factory, the cost per unit for goods that had fully passed through production would be £8; that is,

	£/unit	
Direct costs	5	
Direct production overheads	2	(i.e. £40,000 ÷ 20,000)
Indirect production overheads	1	(i.e. £60,000 × $\frac{1}{3}$ ÷ 20,000)
Other overheads	–	
	–	
	8	

6.4 Historical cost as an input value

The two input values considered here are historical cost and current replacement cost. The former has been the usual method of valuation

Table 6.2   Assignment of overheads in 300 UK companies (%)

Overheads included	1977–8	1971–2
Production, works and manufacturing	52	24
'Appropriate'	22	17
Production etc. and administrative	4	3
None	–	1
Not stated	22	55
	100	100

Source: ICAEW (1979, latest available data)

for centuries. The latter would be the normal method of valuation under some systems of current value accounting.

The historical cost of stock can be measured by aggregating the net payments made in the past to bring the stock to its present condition and location. This will include the original cost of materials and delivery and normal costs of production. Abnormal costs (e.g. unusually great wastage or idle time) or unintended costs (e.g. inefficient buying or pilferage) are not costs of production but losses.

The advantages of a historical cost basis are that it is objective and that it is usable where selling prices and extra costs to completion are volatile or uncertain. However, when prices are changing, the valuation may soon become out of date, and there will be the problem that stocks bought at different times that are still on hand will be added together at original cost, although they are not really comparable. Also, it will usually be necessary to allocate to the stock in question the costs incurred jointly for it and other stocks.

There is a variety of different assumptions about the flow of stocks that can be used for the historical cost basis. These are necessary because, having counted a particular item of stock, it is not always clear what the historical cost is. This is because of lack of knowledge of which particular identical units of stock, bought at varying prices throughout the year, are those on hand. Very often it is physically impossible to tell which units are still held (e.g. in the case of a tank full of oil), or it may be economically unjustifiable to find out (e.g. in the case of large stocks of small items). Even if the exact initial costs and production costs of each unit can be determined, there are reasons for ignoring this and assuming another sort of stock flow for accounting purposes. This will be discussed further below.

A simple example of the problem will help to illustrate this. Suppose that the transactions listed in Table 6.3 occur. Which, for accounting purposes, are the five that were sold, and which are the five that remain? The answers will determine the size of profit and the balance sheet valuation of stock. Let us look at various possible assumptions.

6.4.1 Specific or unit cost

The specific or unit cost method can be used when the items of stock are large enough to be readily identifiable. Then it is assumed that each unit is a

Table 6.3 Example of stock purchases

Transaction date	Purchases	Cost of sales charged to profit	Remaining stock at cost
1 January	10 at £3		10 at £3 = £30
11 January		6 at £3	4 at £3 = £12
21 January	6 at £4		4 at £3 + 6 at £4 = £36
31 January		5 at ?	5 at ? = ?

specific venture, that specific costs and revenues should be matched, and that specific costs should be carried in stock until the unit's sale. In the example in Table 6.3, if specific cost were used it would be necessary to see which five units were actually on hand. There are two problems with valuing using this assumption. First, many costs are joint costs – that is, the costs are incurred for the processing of all these units and perhaps other types of units as well, and they are therefore difficult to allocate to individual types of stock, let alone to individual units. Second, profit can be manipulated by choosing which out of several similar units will be sold; if it were wished to defer some profit until next year, the most expensive units (perhaps the most recent ones) would be sold.

6.4.2 Average cost

The average cost would be used if the company's business were regarded as a series of transactions that could not reasonably be separated. The physical flow is ignored, and the problems of allocating actual processing costs to individual units are avoided.

In the example in Table 6.3 the costs of the stock used and the stock remaining would both be £18 (£3.60 per unit, i.e. £36 ÷ 10 units). This weighted average cost method is used by many companies and can be claimed to provide the fairest practicable approximation to actual cost, as required by the accounting standard on stock valuation (SSAP 9).

6.4.3 First-in, first-out

First-in, first-out (FIFO) is another method that could fulfil the SSAP 9 requirement. Here the assumption (which may have the merit of being somewhere near the truth) is that the goods that leave the firm are those which have been in stock the longest. Consequently the stock on hand is assumed to be the latest. This will lead, in times of rising prices, to higher profit figures and more realistic balance sheet values than average cost or LIFO (see below).

In the example in Table 6.3 the stock used on 31 January would be valued at £16 (four units at £3 and one unit at £4), and the stock remaining would be valued at £20 (five units at £4). This method is perhaps the most popular and is one of those suggested by SSAP 9. The problem with the method is that, although there is an approximate matching of specific costs against specific revenues, there is not a matching of *current* costs against *current* revenues. This will be considered further when we consider adjustments necessary to allow for inflation (Section 6.7).

6.4.4 Normal stock

The normal stock methods are sometimes used by particular types of company that use processing methods that rely on having a fixed 'pipe-line' of raw materials or work in progress. For example, an oil refinery might always have a number of tonnes of crude which could only be sold or used up if the refinery were to cease production. If the refinery is to be treated as a going concern, the 'pipeline' could be regarded as a fixed asset rather than a current asset. In this case the stock charged against profit is that bought in the year. This creates an approximate matching of current costs and current revenues. Also, again assuming that the 'pipe-line' does not change in size, gains and losses due just to holding the stocks are excluded from operating income.

The two versions of 'normal' stock are (i) the *base stock method*, where the normal stock is treated as a fixed asset and the rest of the stock is valued using average cost or FIFO, and (ii) *last-in, first-out* (LIFO). Using the LIFO flow assumption the example in Table 6.3 would lead to a charge against profit on 31 January of £20 (five units at £4) and a closing stock of £16 (one unit at £4 and four units at £3). So, the charge to profit is a better estimate of current costs, but the balance sheet holds an unrealistically low stock figure. However, if the normal stock is to be regarded as a fixed asset, an unrealistic valuation will be a factor that it shares with other fixed assets. A balance sheet note of the current value would be a partial solution and would provide an estimate of holding gains or losses.

Other problems, which apply particularly to LIFO, are that:

(1) When the normal stock is reduced, absurd profit figures result from the use of very old material costs.
(2) If stock values fall because of inefficient buying or deterioration, recognition will not be given to this because LIFO cost will probably still be below net realizable value.
(3) Real gains from specific price rises in excess of general price rises are not reported.
(4) Profit is artificially smoothed.

The LIFO method is allowed by law but not normally by SSAP 9, because it will not normally give a true and fair view, which is the overriding legal requirement (see Chapter 11). LIFO is also not accepted by the Inland Revenue in the United Kingdom. In the United States, however, the use of LIFO has become very widespread because the Internal Revenue Service allows it to be used as a way of postponing the recognition of a stockholding profit, and therefore postponing tax, until the stock is realized and cash is available. LIFO is also to be found in Germany, Italy and Japan.

6.4.5 Standard cost

For the purposes of cost accounting a business may have established a series of standard costs for its stocks at various levels of completion. These costs may be used for stock valuation. Further reference to standard costs is left to books on cost accounting.

6.4.6 Retail inventory and gross profit margin

The retail inventory and gross profit margin methods are used to overcome the practical problems in large shops of counting and valuing great numbers of different items. Using these methods the stock is counted on a periodic rather than a perpetual basis, and its value at selling prices is worked out. To find a value using any of the other methods discussed so far would be extremely difficult. Clearly, though, to value stock at selling prices would be to take profit before sale. Therefore ratios of cost to price are worked out item by item or class by class. Then, the values of sets of stock are reduced to cost price by the application of these ratios. Since current prices and costs will be used, there will be a result similar to FIFO. This is called the *retail inventory method*.

An alternative method uses a gross profit margin, which is worked out using a number of prior years. Here, the valuation is even quicker, because the inventory cost is worked out by taking the goods bought *plus* opening stock at cost, *less* the goods sold at selling price reduced to cost by application of the gross profit margin. So, no count is made. Consequently, this method should only be used as a check on other methods or when no other method is possible (e.g. as a result of a fire).

In summary, FIFO and average cost are the flow assumptions often used for historical cost accounting and those approved by the accounting bodies and the Inland Revenue. The main problems with them are that, in times of inflation and particularly for FIFO, the current charge for use of stock is unrealistically small and that non-comparable units of stock are added together. However, the balance sheet valuation approximately reflects current values, again particularly for FIFO.

It should be mentioned that it is important, for the comparability of profit figures from year to year, to be consistent in the method used. Standard practice is that any changes should be disclosed and quantified. This is clearly important for a proper reading of profit figures and balance sheets.

6.5 Current replacement cost as an input value

Even under historical cost accounting, current replacement cost has occasionally been used for stock valuation. It will be briefly considered here in that context. Section 6.7 will consider replacement cost as the normal basis for valuing stock under current value accounting.

It might be thought that under historical cost accounting the current replacement cost of stock in its current condition and location could be a usefully prudent basis for stock when this value is below historical cost. It could be applied in particular to the valuation of raw materials for which the net realizable value is difficult to measure.

However, the use of replacement cost is criticized in that it is not objective, particularly for stocks that cannot be replaced because they are obsolete or seasonal. Also, if a replacement cost goes up, it does not necessarily mean that sales prices go up, and so perhaps stock will not be replaced in these circumstances. Further, a fall in replacement cost will not affect the value of stock to a going concern unless net realizable value falls, and so there are good grounds for ignoring it for historical cost accounting.

6.6 Practice under historical cost accounting

Traditionally, the valuation rule of 'the lower of cost or market value' has been used. That is, 'historical cost' is the usual basis of valuation unless there has been a loss in value since purchase. Such a loss in value can occur through obsolescence, physical deterioration, inefficient purchasing or a fall in the selling price of the goods to be manufactured. It is accounting practice to recognize a loss in value of current assets as soon as it is discovered. So, profit is reduced immediately rather than at the point of sale. The market value used in the United Kingdom is the *net realizable value* (NRV). To write down stocks further than this to replacement cost (RC) will usually mean allowing for a loss that will not actually be incurred, as mentioned above.

The AICPA has recommended a slightly more complicated definition of market value, however, namely replacement cost with an upper limit of net realizable value and a lower limit of net realizable value *less* normal profit margin (AICPA, 1968). Whatever definition is used, a decision will need to be made about whether items are to be looked at individually (to see whether cost or market value is lower) or in total. The UK Accounting Standard requires that the comparison be carried out individually to avoid the setting off of foreseeable losses against unrealized profits. Consider the example in Table 6.4; the individual comparison leads to a total stock value of £720, whereas a total comparison would lead to £750 (thus hiding the loss in value suffered by stock B).

In inflationary times cost will nearly always be below net realizable value or replacement cost, and so we can see that in practice a very large majority of stocks will be valued at historical cost.

A problem with the 'lower of cost or net realizable value' rule is that it gives rise to inconsistency if, for example, opening stocks are valued at cost but closing stocks are valued at net realizable value. The profit figures will

Table 6.4   Example of stock valuation (£)

	Cost	NRV	Lower by individual comparison
Stock A	100	130	100
Stock B	400	370	370
Stock C	250	380	250
Total	750	880	720

Table 6.5   Flow assumptions for the determination of cost

	% of companies
FIFO	19
LIFO	1
Weighted average	6
Base stock	1
	27
No disclosure	73
	100

Source: ICAEW (1984).

be distorted in consequence. Nevertheless, for historical cost accounting the 'lower of cost or net realizable value' basis will remain that in general use, and SSAP 9 and the Companies Act 1985 require it.

As noted earlier, SSAP 9 is very discouraging about the use of LIFO. The most recent survey of UK practice shows a predominance of FIFO, as in Table 6.5.

6.7 Current value accounting

Under systems of current value accounting the valuation of stock is usually based on replacement cost, because this will normally be the 'value to the business' or the 'deprival value' of the stock. As an illustration of this, suppose that a business owns ten units of a common raw material. The business intends to maintain stocks at ten units. The units in stock were bought earlier in the year for £10 each. Their purchase was recorded on this basis, and they still have labels with '£10 cost' on them. At the year end, the cost of identical units has risen to £12. What is the value of the units?

Under historical cost, specific costing can be used in this case. Assuming that net realizable value is higher and that no work has been done on the units, the valuation will clearly be £100. However, under current value accounting, recognition is made of the fact that, if the business were deprived of the stock, it would buy another ten units at the current cost. Therefore the value to the business of the stock is £120.

There will still be cases where stock has lost value due to obsolescence or damage. Consequently the net realizable value of stock is to be used where it is lower than the replacement cost. So, the rule for the valuation of stock under current value accounting becomes 'the lower of current replacement cost and net realizable value'. This is a much more realistic estimate of the value of the stock to the business as a going concern.

The problems associated with deciding upon the current cost of *using up* stock to earn profit are more complicated. They will be looked at in Chapter 12.

6.8 Long-term contracts

There are particular problems relating to the valuation of the work in progress of long-term contracts that have been ordered by customers. Such work may be absorbing materials and labour, both specific and overhead, for a number of years before eventual sale. In order to avoid large fluctuations in profit and to record as fair a profit as possible in any year, it seems an appropriate use of the accruals convention to take credit for ascertainable profit while contracts are in progress. SSAP 9 requires a portion of profit reflecting the degree of completion of the contract at the accounting date to be taken, but only when the eventual outcome of the contract is reasonably certain. The profit is treated as realized. On the other hand, it is not surprising to find in SSAP 9 that any expected loss on the contract as a whole should be provided for as soon as it is recognized. It can be argued that this is unfair to the current year's profit.

The double entry for this profit might be thought to be an increase in the work in progress. However, this would mean valuing stock at above cost (i.e. at cost *plus* some profit). Therefore SSAP 9 requires the use of an account called 'amounts recoverable on contracts', which is a sort of debtor.

6.9 Summary

The valuation of stock is important for profit measurement and for balance sheet valuations. There are some practical problems attached to counting the stock, but the important theoretical problems relate to the choice of a basis for valuation. There are several possible output and input values. Traditionally, stock has been valued at the lower of historical cost and net realizable value. The historical cost is usually the lower, especially during inflation; it has therefore been the normal basis. The alternative is useful for recognizing a loss in value.

There are a number of difficulties with the use of historical cost. Which are the units left in stock? Which overheads should be included in cost? Should the comparison with the market value be universal or by item? Nevertheless, the advantages of conservatism and objectivity have for many years outweighed these practical difficulties and the lack of realism of the results.

Current value accounting systems are more interested in a realistic value to the business of the stock. Consequently, the normal basis of valuation is the current replacement cost, which usually represents the deprival value of the stock. In order to allow for losses in value, the full valuation basis is the lower of current replacement cost and net realizable value. Figure 6.1 illustrates these various valuation bases.

Whether or not current value accounting is being used, it can be seen that profit is not taken until the stock is sold. There have been arguments about the fairness of this prudent treatment. However, it clearly has strong advantages on grounds of objectivity. Nevertheless, when long-term contracts are being considered, the unfairness becomes particularly obvious and acute. This has led to acceptance of the idea of taking a proportion of expected profit at each year end.

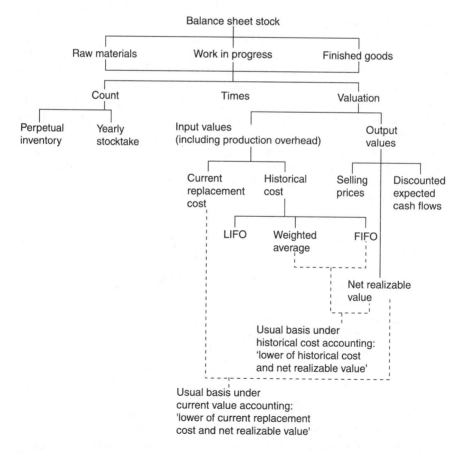

Figure 6.1   Stock valuation

Self-assessment questions

Suggested answers to the self-assessment questions are given at the end of the book.

1. Inventory costing methods such as LIFO and FIFO are different methods of determining the actual cost of specific inventory items.

    (a) True.
    (b) False.

2. An overstatement of opening stock results in:

    (a) No effect on the period's net income.
    (b) An overstatement of net income.
    (c) An understatement of net income.
    (d) A need to adjust purchases.

3. An overstatement of closing stock in one period results in:

    (a) No effect on net income of the next period.
    (b) An overstatement of net income of the next period.
    (c) An understatement of net income of the next period.
    (d) An overstatement of the closing stock of the next period.

4. In a period of *declining* prices, which of the following methods generally results in the lowest balance sheet figure for stock?

    (a) Average cost method.
    (b) LIFO method.
    (c) FIFO method.
    (d) Cannot tell without more information.

5. In a period of *rising* prices, which of the following methods generally results in the lowest net income figure?

    (a) Average cost method.
    (b) LIFO method.
    (c) FIFO method.
    (d) Cannot tell without more information.

6. A retail company has goods available for sale for the year of £500,000 at retail (= £300,000 at cost) and closing stock of £50,000 at retail. What is the estimated cost of goods sold?

    (a) £30,000.
    (b) £50,000.
    (c) £450,000.
    (d) £270,000.

					£
7. June	1	Stock	100	@	1.00
	6	Purchased	150	@	1.10
	13	Purchased	50	@	1.20
	20	Purchased	100	@	1.30
	25	Purchased	25	@	1.40
	27	Sold	125	@	——

Using the average cost method, and rounding to the nearest pound, the cost assigned to the closing stock from the foregoing information is:

(a) £216.
(b) £144.
(c) £346.
(d) None of the above.

8. Using the information from Question 7 and using the specific identification method, and assuming that 100 of the items sold came from the 20 June purchase and that the rest came from the 13 June purchase, the cost assigned to the closing stock is:

(a) £160.
(b) £330.
(c) £400.
(d) None of the above.

9. Using the information from Question 7 and the last-in, first-out (LIFO) method, the cost assigned to the closing stock is:

(a) £325.
(b) £165.
(c) £590.
(d) None of the above.

10 Using the information from Question 7 and the first-in, first-out (FIFO) method, the cost assigned to the closing stock is:

(a) £590.00.
(b) £362.50.
(c) £227.50.
(d) None of the above.

11. Using the information from Question 7 and the last-in, first-out (LIFO) method, the cost of goods sold is:

(a) £165.
(b) £325.

(c) £590.
(d) None of the above.

12. *Stock*   *Quantity*   *Cost (£)*   *Market*

Stock	Quantity	Cost (£)	Market
Item A	200	1.00	0.50
Item B	100	2.00	2.10
Item C	100	3.00	2.50
Item D	300	2.50	2.00
Item E	200	3.00	3.10

Using the item-by-item method of applying the lower-of-cost-or-market rule to valuing the stock, the value assigned to stock item C for inclusion in total stock on the balance sheet is:

(a) £300.
(b) £250.
(c) £50.
(d) None of the above.

13. Using the information from Question 12 and the item-by-item method of applying the lower-of-cost-or-market rule to valuing the stock, the total value of stock appearing on the balance sheet is:

(a) £1,750.
(b) £2,090.
(c) £1,760.
(d) £1,780.

14. Assuming that net purchases cost £250,000 during the year and that closing stock was £4,000 less than the opening stock of £30,000, how much was cost of goods sold?

(a) £280,000.
(b) £246,000.
(c) £254,000.
(d) £276,000.

15. Assume a company has a periodic inventory system with an opening balance of £20,000, purchases of £150,000, and sales of £250,000. The company closes its records once a year on 31 December. In the accounting records, the stock account would be expected to have a balance on 31 December prior to adjusting the closing entries that was:

(a) Equal to £20,000.
(b) More than £20,000.
(c) Less than £20,000.
(d) Indeterminate.

16. Selected account balances relevant to the income statement for County Sporting Goods appear as follows:

Account name	Debit	Credit
Sales		500,000
Sales returns and allowances	10,000	
Sales discounts	10,000	
Purchases	130,000	
Purchases returns and allowances		10,000
Purchases discounts		20,000
Freight in	20,000	
Selling expenses	50,000	
General and administrative expenses	170,000	

In addition, opening merchandise stock was £27,000 and closing merchandise stock was £20,000. Net sales for the period are:

(a) £500,000.
(b) £480,000.
(c) £490,000.
(d) None of the above.

17. According to the information given in Question 16, net purchases for the period are:

(a) £100,000.
(b) £120,000.
(c) £110,000.
(d) £150,000.

18. According to the information given in Question 16, cost of goods sold for the period is:

(a) £147,000.
(b) £107,000.
(c) £127,000.
(d) None of the above.

19. According to the information given in Question 16, gross profit for the period is:

(a) £353,000.
(b) £333,000.
(c) £303,000.
(d) None of the above.

Tutorial Questions

1. A firm buys and sells a single commodity. During a particular accounting period it made a number of purchases of the commodity at different prices. Explain how assumptions made regarding which units were sold will affect the firm's reported profit for the period.

2. What is meant by 'lower of cost and net realizable value'? What difficulties exist in the application of this rule?

3. Marks Co. has been in operation for three years. The purchases and sales information below represents the company's activities for its first three years:

	19×5	19×6	19×7
Sales (unit)	12,000 @ £50	20,000 @ £60	18,000 @ £65
Purchases (units)	4,000 @ £20	8,000 @ £35	7,000 @ £40
	7,000 @ £20	4,000 @ £30	5,000 @ £35
	8,000 @ £30	1,000 @ £40	8,000 @ £25

Prepare a schedule illustrating the number of units held at the end of each year.

4. Using the information contained in Question 3 calculate the value of the year-end inventories using FIFO and LIFO. Also prepare profit and loss accounts showing the gross profit under each of the valuation methods for all three years.

5. Reginald and Arthur are brothers. Recently their maiden aunt died bequeathing them £1000 each. Initially they intended to set up in partnership selling 'milds' and 'bitters'. However Reginald felt that there was no future in the 'bitter' market, whereas Arthur expected that 'bitter' sales would boom. After an argument the brothers decided to set up their own businesses, Reginald trading in 'milds' and Arthur in 'bitters'.

The following shows the transactions undertaken in their first trading period.

Purchases	260 milds at £1.25 each
Purchases	100 milds at £1.50 each
Purchases	200 milds at £3.75 each
Then, sales	300 milds at £4 each

Whilst Reginald was finding that prices were rising swiftly in the market for 'milds', Arthur by shrewd buying was able to obtain a lower price per unit for each successive purchase he made. The transactions which Arthur undertook were:

Purchases	200 bitters at £1.75 each
Purchases	200 bitters at £1.70 each
Purchases	200 bitters at £1.55 each
Then, sales	500 bitters at £2 each

(a) At the end of the period both brothers wish to withdraw all their profits (all transactions were made in cash). How much will each brother be able to withdraw:

(i) calculating profit on a FIFO basis?

(ii) calculating profit on a LIFO basis?

(b) After withdrawing all profits in cash, what ability has each brother to replenish the stock of the goods he trades in? What assumptions do you need to make in answering this question?

References

Accounting Standards Committee (1988) *Stocks and Long-term Contracts*, SSAP 9.

American Institute of Certified Public Accountants (AICPA) (1968) *Accounting Principles, Bulletin No. 43*, New York: AICPA.

Institute of Chartered Accountants in England and Wales (ICAEW) (1979) *Survey of Published Accounts, 1978*, London: ICAEW, s. 15.

Institute of Chartered Accountants in England and Wales (ICAEW) (1984) *Financial Reporting, 1984/85*, London: ICAEW.

THE 'ITALIAN METHOD'

7

This chapter begins to look at the mechanics of accounting. Historical cost accounting will continue to be used for this purpose, because it is simple and is still the basic system of accounting.

7.1 History

The earliest records of financial information date from the fourth millennium BC in Assyria and then later in Egypt. These were lists of expenditures or incomes of major projects. The 'accounting' was performed in the absence of a common monetary unit, and so no totalling or complex analysis was possible. Records are more abundant from Greek and Roman times. There were units of currency by then, but there was no systematic bookkeeping. The receipts and payments records were mixed.

The leaders in organized production, banking and trade in the early Renaissance were the Italian city states such as Florence, Venice and Genoa. Development of commerce had been facilitated by the laws protecting private property, the accumulation of capital and considerable trading on credit. These city states had most need of sophisticated accounting. The need was particularly great because of the increasing use of partnerships and overseas agencies. The first certain records of double-entry accounting are those of an Italian firm in Provence around the year 1300 (Lee, 1977); some survive from another Italian firm in London from 1305 to 1308 (Nobes, 1982). The first book to include a substantial description of accounting was published in Venice in 1494 by Luca Pacioli, a Franciscan friar and mathematics professor. Pacioli's book was called *Summa de Arithmetica, Geometria, Proportioni e Proportionalità*. It was written in Italian rather than Latin, and consequently was available to a wide readership.

Accounting based on double entry spread throughout Europe in the following centuries and became known as the Italian method. Many characteristics of modern accounting date from this period. However, at that time accounts were for private use only, and so there was no pressure for uniformity or accounting standards. The proprietor and his business were not always separated for accounting purposes, and the concept of a business as a 'going concern' producing a balance sheet and a profit figure every year had not developed. Business tended to operate on a venture basis. Later, accounting did develop periodic balancing of accounts and profit calculation. For example, in 1673 it became compulsory in France to pro-duce a 'balance sheet' at least once every two years.

In the nineteenth century, Britain and the United States experienced an enormous growth in industry and trade, which encouraged the develop-ment of accounting. By then there were many parties interested in accounts: shareholders, potential investors, creditors, the Revenue and the govern-ment. They needed accounting information, and they needed it to be rea-sonably reliable and uniform. Accounting and the accountancy profession as we see them today were founded in these places and in this period. Twentieth-century developments are looked at throughout this book.

7.2 Double entry: explanation and justification

It has been pointed out (in Section 4.6 and elsewhere) that any transaction has at least two effects. For example, when a £5,000 building is bought for cash, the asset records show an increase of £5,000 and the cash records show a decrease of £5,000. It has been shown, too, that a credit sale of £500 for stock that had cost £300 will give rise to three effects:

Balance sheet			
Stock	−300	Profit	+200
Debtor	+500		

In practice it will usually be very difficult to tell how much stock (at cost) has been disposed of in a sale, particularly if several types of material and labour have been combined to make a product. Therefore, it will also be difficult to calculate the profit on every small sale. So, accountants wait until the end of an accounting period to calculate profit. At that point the stock used is taken to be the purchases during the period adjusted for the facts that (i) there was some stock handed on at the beginning of the period, and (ii) there remains some stock at the end.

Meanwhile, sales and purchases of stock are recorded without adjusting profit figures. That is, sales transactions do not give rise to the effects in the above balance sheet on a daily basis. When a business makes a £500 credit sale, the sales records show a £500 increase and debtors also show a £500 increase:

Profit calculation (£):		Sales + 500 (i.e. stock + profit)
Balance sheet (£):	Debtor + 500	

When there are £200 of purchases by the business for cash, the purchases records show a £200 increase and the cash records show a £200 decrease.

Table 7.1 contains some more examples of these and other types of trans-action. Each transaction can be said to have two opposite effects on what the business owns (controls) or owes. All the items in the 'Effect A' column can

Table 7.1 Examples of transactions (£)

Transaction	Value	Effect A	Effect B
(1) Cash sale	50	+ Cash	+ Sales
(2) Credit sale to L.D. Vinci	80	+ Debtors	+ Sales
(3) Loan raised from C.D. Medici	2,000	+ Cash	+ Lenders
(4) Asset bought	1,000	+ Assets	− Cash
(5) Asset depreciated	200	+ Depreciation charge	+ Depreciation provision
(6) Electricity bill received	100	+ Expenses	+ Creditors
(7) Electricity bill paid	100	− Creditors	− Cash

be said to represent increases in what the business owns or decreases in what it owes. That is,

(1) and (3) it owns more cash
(2)   it owns more debt
(4)   it owns more assets
(5) and (6) it 'owes' less to its owners in profit
(7)   it owes less to outside creditors

All items in the 'Effect B' column can be understood as the reverse of 'Effect A' – that is, decreases in things owned or increases in what is owed by the business:

(1) and (2) it 'owes' more to the owners as profit
(3)   it owes more to lenders
(4) and (7) it owns less cash
(5)   the assets are considered to have less value
(6)   it owes more to outside creditors

For reasons discussed below, each of the effects in column A is called a debit and each in column B is called a credit. So, at the end of a period during which the accounts are run, the total of all debits equals the total of all credits. The system is self-balancing.

There is no stigma attached to 'debit' nor congratulatory connotation attached to 'credit'; they are merely labels to describe two groupings of transactions. It can be seen that 'debit' is by no means synonymous with plus or with minus; it implies an increase in owning or a decrease in owing, as summarized in Table 7.2. This is a further consequence of the accounting equation in Chapter 4:

$$\Sigma A + \Sigma E = \Sigma L + C + \Sigma R$$

where A is assets, E is expenses, L is liabilities, C is capital and R is revenues.

The words 'debit' and 'credit' have their origins in early Italian accounting, which particularly concerned itself with debts to and from persons. The derivations of the words will be clear to those who are familiar with any Latin-based language. 'Debit' means he ought (to pay us); a debit on a person's account means that he must pay the business at some future

Table 7.2 The meaning of 'debit' and 'credit'

Debits	Credits
Increases in owning	Decreases in owning
Decreases in owing	Increases in owing
+ Assets	− Assets
+ Expenses	− Expenses
− Liabilities	+ Liabilities
− Capital	+ Capital
− Revenues	+ Revenues

date. Similarly, 'credit' means he trusts (us to pay him). From these basic entries all the others fall into place, as in Table 7.2.

In practice most accountants would not work out whether, for example, any particular transaction involved a debit to cash or a credit to cash, but would know by reflex. Many might not be able easily to work out from first principles which entry should be made. The system is merely a convention that is fairly easily learned and works well.

Let us follow the seven transactions in Table 7.1 into some accounts, performing double entry. An 'account' is just a piece of paper (or perhaps an area on a computer disk) that stores all the information relating to one type of asset, one type of expense, and so on. The convention is that the debits are stored on the left of an account and the credits on the right. So, transaction (1) (a cash sale) will be recorded on two accounts like this:

Cash account (£)		Sales account (£)	
Debits	**Credits**	**Debits**	**Credits**
Sales 50			Cash 50

The cash account records a debit to show that the business now owns £50 more cash (due to sales). The sales account records a credit to show that there have been revenues of £50 (due to cash receipts). Transaction (2) (an £80 sale on credit to L.D. Vinci) will give rise to an entry on the personal account of Vinci and an extra entry on the sales account. No cash changes hands, so that there will be no effect on the cash account.

L.D. Vinci (debtor) account (£)		Sales account (£)	
Sales 80		Cash 50	
		L.D. Vinci 80	

Notice that by looking at one entry we can find out where the other related entry is. The third transaction will give rise to two entries:

Cash account (£)		C.D. Medici (lender) account (£)	
Sales	50		Cash 2,000
C.D. Medici 2,000			

Transaction (4) will cause two extra entries (shown with asterisks):

Fixed assets account (£)		Cash account (£)	
Cash 1,000*		Sales 50	Fixed assets 1,000*
		C.D. Medici 2,000	

The double-entry accounting for depreciation will be discussed further in Section 7.7, but transaction (5) is fairly simple:

Depreciation charge account (£)	
Provision for depreciation 200	

Provision for depreciation account (£)	
	Depreciation charge 200

Transaction (6) (receiving a bill but not paying it) will be entered as

Electricity expense account (£)		Creditors account (£)	
Creditors 100			Electricity expense 100

Transaction (7) (paying the bill later) will give the two new entries shown with asterisks:

Creditors account (£)	
Cash 100*	Electricity expense 100

Cash account (£)			
Sales	50	Fixed assets	1,000
C.D. Medici	2,000	Creditors	100*

As the business year continues, more transactions will occur and give rise to double entries each time. Every sale (whether for cash or on credit terms) will be recorded on the right-hand side of the sales account as a credit.

Every receipt of cash for whatever reason will be recorded on the left-hand side of the cash account as a debit. There is no theoretical limit to the number of accounts that can be used. The accountant must strike a balance between the need for detail and the desire to avoid unnecessary work.

We have seen (in Section 3.6) that it is possible to redraw a balance sheet each time that any transaction occurs. In a normal business involving thousands of transactions in a week this would be ridiculously time con-suming. Therefore accounts (such as those above) are kept throughout the year using double entry, in order that the balance sheet need only be redrawn periodically. It is assumed here that the balance sheet is drawn up annually. In practice businesses may do this more frequently.

The accounts for assets or liabilities or capital, which are accumulating entries throughout the year, are totalled at the end of the year to provide the asset, liability and capital figures for the balance sheet. Those accounts which record expenses and revenues are combined together to form a profit and loss account for the year. The profit or loss is transferred to the capital account, which is recorded on the balance sheet. Examples of this are given later in this chapter.

7.3 The advantages of double entry

There are several important advantages to be gained from using a double-entry system. First, since there are clearly two effects from each transaction, it is useful to record them both. Before double entry, a cash sale would have been recorded only in the cash book, which contained all other transactions affecting cash. This meant that in order to find a total of recorded sales it was necessary to look through all cash transactions, picking out those relating to sales. For a large trader this would have been very laborious for even one day's sales, let alone one year's. So double entry allows an easy totalling of sales, cash, electricity bills, wages, fixed assets, and so on. Without these totals, balance sheets and profit and loss accounts would be impossible to produce.

Totalling is made particularly easy because the accounts are two-sided, allowing positive and negative effects to be stored separately on the same account. This enables quick balancing of any accounts. For example, in the accounts on the last few pages (which, of course, will normally have many more entries on them) the eventual total of cash in hand can be worked out to be £950 (i.e. £2,050 − £1,100). Table 7.3 gives the balanced account.

Table 7.3 Cash account from Table 7.1 (£)

Sales	50	Fixed assets	1,000
C.D. Medici	2,000	Creditors	100
		Balance carried down	950
	2,050		2,050
Balance brought forward	950		

Double entry has been maintained by creating a brought-forward debit of equal size to the balancing credit of £950. At the start of the next accounting period the cash account will already show £950, which is correct. Clearly, it will be a good idea to check the cash and the bank account to see if there is £950. If there is not, an investigation into shortages of cash or errors in the records should be carried out. The facts that all cash entries are on one account, that only cash entries are on it and that the entries are separated into cash in (debit, left-hand side) and cash out (credit, right-hand side) aid quick totalling. The same applies to all accounts of whatever sort.

Another significant advantage is that it is known that the whole system should be self-balancing. When the end-of-year balancing act is performed, it is unusual for the accounts of businesses of any size to balance straight away. That is, when all the debits are added together, they may not appear to equal all the credits as they should. This is due to inevitable errors of recording and analysing the entries in the accounts. Any lack of balance warns the accountant that errors should be searched for. Also, since each entry is cross-referenced to its equal and opposite entry, it is fairly easy to understand the origin of an entry.

At this point it should be said that accounting entries always carry a date in order to make it easier to understand them if they need to be checked in the future. For example, if transaction (1) (the cash sale) occurred on 3 November 1997, it might be recorded like this:

Cash account (£)		Sales account (£)	
3 Nov. 97 Sales 50			3 Nov. 97 Cash 50

Dates will only be used in accounts in this book when they are necessary for clarity.

Several of these factors make it more difficult fraudulently to manipulate items in the accounts. It has been mentioned that checking is fairly easy. Also, balancing is impossible if the totals of only one account are manipulated, and adjustments of more than one account may entail the alteration of a figure that is regularly checked (e.g. the cash balance).

It has been said that at the end of the period (we have been considering it to be a year) the revenue and expense accounts are combined to calculate profit. This is performed using double entry too. The revenue and expense accounts already met are shown below after year-end balancing and closing off procedures have occurred (new entries have asterisks).

Sales account (£)			
Profit and loss a/c 130*	Cash		50
	L.D. Vinci		80
130			130

Depreciation charge account (£)

Provision	200	Profit and loss a/c	200*
	200		200

Electricity expense account (£)

Creditors	100	Profit and loss a/c	100*
	100		100

Trading and profit and loss account (£)

		Sales	130*
Electricity	100*		
Depreciation	200*		

The reasons for the positioning of these entries in the incomplete profit and loss account should become clear in the next section. Notice that the expense and revenue accounts have now been closed down by transferring their balances to the profit and loss account. They start the next year with no balances, apart from the exceptions noted in Section 7.6.

7.4 The trading account: gross profit

Conventionally, there are two important subtotals in the calculation of profit: gross profit and net profit. As seen in Chapter 4, the trading account collects together the revenue and expense entries relating to the main trading activities of the business and leads to the calculation of gross profit. The trading and profit and loss accounts are part of the system of double entry. Less detail is shown in the published accounts of companies, as discussed in Chapter 11.

Let us look at some more transactions specifically related to trading. For simplicity consider the transactions of a new business called Artists Materials (Table 7.4). Each of these entries will be recorded on the appropriate side of the appropriate account. The accounts specifically connected with trading will look like this (the other halves of the double entries being in other accounts, as noted in the table):

Purchases account (£)

(1) Carrara Ltd 3,000	
(3) Cash 2,000	

Table 7.4 Transactions of artists materials (£)

Transaction	Debit		Credit	
(1) Purchase £3,000 worth of marble on credit from Carrara Quarries Ltd	Purchases a/c	3,000	Carrara Ltd (creditor) a/c	3,000
(2) Sell £1,000 worth of marble for cash to Michelangelo Buonarrotti	Cash a/c	1,000	Sales a/c	1,000
(3) Purchase £2,000 worth of paint for cash from Florentia Wholesale Paint Company	Purchases a/c	2,000	Cash a/c	2,000
(4) Sell £500 worth of paint on credit to Mr S. Botticelli	S. Botticelli (debtor) a/c	500	Sales a/c	500
(5) Sell £800 worth of marble for cash to Mr D. Donatello	Cash a/c	800	Sales a/c	800
(6) Return of £100 worth of paint by Mr S. Botticelli	Sales a/c	100	S. Botticelli (debtor) a/c	100

Sales account (£)

(6) S. Botticelli	100	(2) Cash	1,000
		(4) S. Botticelli	500
		(5) Cash	800

If these were the only trading entries in the accounting period, the trading account would be made up by closing down the above accounts and transferring the balances thus:

Purchases account (£)

Carrara Ltd	3,000	Trading a/c	5,000
Cash	2,000		
	5,000		5,000

Sales account (£)

S. Botticelli	100	Cash	1,000
Trading a/c	2,200	S. Botticelli	500
		Cash	800
	2,300		2,300

	Trading account (£)		
Purchases	5,000	Sales	2,200

This does not seem to be a very healthy trading position, but it must be remembered that not all the purchases will have been turned into sales. That is, there is usually some closing stock remaining at the end of an accounting period. This should be familiar from the last chapter. If stocktaking shows that there is £3,500 worth of stock of marble and paint left, the trading account will look like Table 7.5. Notice that double entry is being maintained. The gross profit entries balance each other. The closing stock (and opening stock) entries will be discussed in Section 7.6.

7.5 The rest of the profit and loss account

The remains of the profit and loss account contain all other revenues and expenses that are not raw trading transactions. Suppose that the only extra transactions in the accounting period of Artists Materials are those shown in Table 7.6. The revenue and expense account halves of these transactions will

Table 7.5 Trading account of Artists Materials for the period ending 31 December (£)

Purchases	5,000	Sales	2,200
less Closing stock	3,500		
	1,500		
Gross profit c/d	700		
	2,200		2,200
		Gross profit b/f	700

Table 7.6 Further transactions of Artists Materials (£)

Transaction		Debit		Credit	
(7)	Wages of £100 paid	Wages a/c	100	Cash a/c	100
(8)	Rent for the period of £150 (not yet paid to the landlord)	Rent a/c	150	Strozzi a/c (landlord)	150
(9)	Advertising bill for the period, paid, £30	Advertising a/c	30	Cash a/c	30
(10)	Stationery bought for £20	Stationery a/c	20	Cash a/c	20
(11)	More wages paid, £80	Wages a/c	80	Cash a/c	80
(12)	Rent received from subletting part of the premises, £40	Cash a/c	40	Rent received a/c	40

appear as below (the other halves are in the cash account and A. Strozzi account, as noted in the table).

Wages account (£)

(7) Cash	100	Profit and loss a/c 180*	
(11) Cash	80		
	—		—
	180		180

Rent (expenses) account (£)

(8) A. Strozzi	150	Profit and loss a/c 150*	
	—		—
	150		150

Advertising account (£)

(9) Cash	30	Profit and loss a/c 30*	
	—		—
	30		30

Stationery account (£)

(10) Cash	20	Profit and loss a/c 20*	
	—		—
	20		20

Rent received account (£)

Profit and loss a/c	40*	(12) Cash	40
	40		40

These accounts have been shown already closed off. The other halves of the double entry for each of the asterisked items are in the profit and loss account in Table 7.7.

As before, the double entry system is strictly maintained. What happens to the net profit brought forward depends on the type of business. This will be demonstrated in Chapters 9 and 11. The rent received is not in the trading account because it does not result from the main trading activities. It is, of course, on the credit side, just like other revenues.

The order of the expense items is not very critical, although it seems sensible to start with the most important. For companies, expenses are organized into groups ('administrative', 'distribution'). Consistency from year to year will make comparisons easier. Note that the heading of the account includes the words 'for the period ending'. This emphasizes the fact

Table 7.7 Trading and profit and loss account of Artists Materials for the period ending 31 December (£)

Purchases	5,000	Sales	2,200
less Closing stock	3,500		
	1,500		
Gross profit c/d	700		
	2,200		2,200
Wages	180*	Gross profit b/f	700
Rent	150*	Rent received	40*
Advertising	30*		
Stationery	20*		
Total expenses	380		
Net profit c/d	360		
	740		740
		Net profit b/f	360

that the profit and loss account deals with flows over time. The wording is often 'for the year ending', 'for the quarter ending' and so on.

7.6 Stock, accruals and prepayments

During the year it is usual for no entries to be made in the stock account. The business would be well advised to keep records of stock movements and levels, but these will not be part of the double-entry system. The stock account is only needed at the end of the accounting period, which is naturally the beginning of the next. Let us assume that a business has been left £2,000 of stock from the previous year. Therefore, at the start of the year the stock account appears thus:

Stock account (£)		
Opening stock	2,000	

At the end of the year, stock may be valued at £3,500. The accounting entries to record (1) the removal of the old stock, and (2) the arrival of the new stock will be:

(1) trading a/c *debit* £2,000; stock a/c *credit* £2,000
(2) stock a/c *debit* £3,500; trading a/c *credit* £3,500

This will give the asterisked entries below:

Stock account (£)			
Opening stock	2,000	Trading a/c	2,000*
	2,000		2,000
Closing stock	3,500*		

Trading account (£)			
Opening stock	2,000*	Closing stock	3,500*

The normal presentation, as in the previous trading account, is different from this, because it is clearer to show the closing stock as a negative figure on the left rather than as a positive figure on the right. It should be obvious by now that in all these manipulations accountants adhere not to naturally occurring laws that have been discovered but to conventions that have been invented and adopted because they work well.

There are other items apart from stock that can be passed from one year to another, as seen in Chapter 4, where definitions of revenues and expenses are discussed. For example, below there are two accruals and two prepayments for a business whose accounting period ends on 31 December.

(1) Rent is paid half-yearly in arrears (£500 per half year). Last payment was 30 September; next payment is due 31 March.
(2) Telephone bill is paid quarterly. Next bill is expected 31 January (always about £120 per quarter).
(3) Rates are paid half-yearly in advance (£200 per half year). Last payment was 1 October; next payment is due 1 April.
(4) Yearly insurance premium of £180 is paid on 1 November each year.

It has been explained that, in order to arrive at the profit figure, the payments *relating* to a period (i.e. the expenses), not the payments made in a period, are those included. This is the accruals convention (see Chapter 4). Let us imagine that the business started on 1 January with several premises to pay expenses for. Without taking the above points into account, the total of bills paid in the year may have been as follows:

	£
Rent	1,500
Telephone	800
Rates	1,000
Insurance	500

The previous four points imply that at 31 December,

(1) rent is in arrears by £250
(2) the telephone bill is in arrears by £80
(3) rates are paid in advance by £100
(4) insurance is paid in advance by £150

The expense accounts for the year ending 31 December, taking all this into account, will look like this:

Rent account (£)

Cash	1,500	Profit and loss a/c	1,750
Accruals c/d	250		
	1,750		1,750
		Accruals b/f	250

Telephone account (£)

Cash	800	Profit and loss a/c	880
Accruals c/d	80		
	880		880
		Accruals b/f	80

Rates account (£)

Cash	1,000	Prepayment c/d	100
		Profit and loss a/c	900
	1,000		1,000
Prepayment b/f	100		

Insurance account (£)

Cash	500	Prepayment c/d	150
		Profit and loss a/c	350
	500		500
Prepayment b/f	100		

Profit and loss account (£)

Rent	1,750	Gross profit	xxxx
Rates	900		
Telephone	880		
Insurance	350		

Thus, the actual charges in the profit and loss account are increased by amounts owing that relate to the present accounting year and are decreased by amounts paid on behalf of next year. Notice that next year's accounts have already been credited or debited with the appropriate amounts because of double entry. For example, when the £500 rent bill arrives and is paid at the end of March next year and is debited to the rent account (the cash account being credited with £500 at the same time), the account will show a net charge of £250 (i.e. £500 − £250) so far. This is correct for one quarter:

Rent account (£)

Cash	500	Accruals b/f	250

7.7 Provisions

There was a discussion in Chapter 5 about depreciation, i.e. charging amounts out of current profit in order to recognize that fixed assets are used up in making the profit. The mechanics of the associated depreciation provision are that an account is set up in which to add up the periodic amounts provided. For example, let us take the case of an asset bought on 1 January 1993 for £2,100, which has an expected scrap value of £500 and an expected life of four years. The asset's wearing out depends mainly on the effluxion of time, so it is decided to use the convenient straight line method of depreciation. This means a yearly charge of £400 (i.e. £(2,100 − 500)/4). The transactions for the first year, including the purchase, are represented below:

Asset account (£)

1 Jan. 93	Cash	2,100

Depreciation expense account (£)

31 Dec. 93 Depreciation provision	400	31 Dec. 93 Profit and loss a/c	400
	400		400

Provision for depreciation account (£)

31 Dec. 93 Depreciation expense	400

The cash account and profit and loss account are not shown. After another three years the asset and provision accounts look like this:

Asset account (£)

1 Jan. 93	Cash	2,100

Provision for depreciation account (£)

31 Dec. 93 Balance c/d	400	31 Dec. 93 Depreciation expense	400
	400		400
31 Dec. 94 Balance c/d	800	31 Dec. 93 Balance b/f	400
		31 Dec. 94 Depreciation expense	400
	800		800
31 Dec. 95 Balance c/d	1,200	31 Dec. 94 Balance b/f	800
		31 Dec. 95 Depreciation expense	400
	1,200		1,200
31 Dec. 96 Balance c/d	1,600	31 Dec. 95 Balance b/f	1,200
		31 Dec. 96 Depreciation expense	400
	1,600		1,600
		31 Dec. 96 Balance b/f	1,600

The yearly balancing of the provision account is useful in order to find the cumulative provision at the end of any year, particularly if several assets of a similar sort are being provided for on the same account. The provision account is sometimes called the cumulative depreciation account. Each year the double entry for the provision appears as a debit on the depreciation expense account and is transferred to the profit and loss account.

In the balance sheet notes the asset will be recorded at the end of year 3, for example, as:

	£
Fixed assets at cost	2,100
less Cumulative depreciation	1,200
WDV	900

This is clearly more informative than just showing the WDV of £900, which could be the result of assets costing £1,000 and cumulative depreciation of £100. The published accounts of companies must show all three figures, although the detail is usually in the notes. However, some small businesses may not be recording depreciation in this way and may use the credit side of the asset account to accumulate depreciation provisions.

Other provisions will be treated in the same way as depreciation. For example, let us look at bad debts (first discussed in Chapter 4). A business may have £5,000 worth of debtors in the debtors account at the end of the year. It may decide that identified amounts (adding up to £500) of this debt are definitely irrecoverable and that it will be safer to make a provision for possible bad debts for another unidentified 5 per cent of the remaining debtors. The accounting entries for this are as follows:

(1) recognition of bad debts: bad debts a/c *debit* £500; debtors a/c *credit* £500
(2) provision for future bad debts (5 per cent of the remaining £4,500): bad debts a/c *debit* £225; provision a/c *credit* £225

The accounts will be affected thus:

(Good) Debtors account (£)			
Balance b/f	5,000	(1) Bad debts	500
		Balance c/d	4,500
	5,000		5,000
Balance b/f	4,500		

Bad debts account (£)			
(1) Debtors	500	Profit and loss a/c	725
(2) Provision	225		
	725		725

General provision for doubtful debts (£)		
	(2) Bad debts a/c	225

Profit and loss account (£)		
Bad debts	725	

In the balance sheet the debtors' figure will appear as:

	£
Current assets:	
Debtors	4,500
less Provision	225
	4,275

Other provisions will be dealt with in a similar way. Again, in practice, only the balance will usually be shown on the balance sheet.

7.8 The balance sheet

The observant reader may have noticed that the process of transferring various items of revenue and expense from their accounts to the profit and loss account has left a number of accounts with balances remaining on them. These accounts are asset, liability or capital accounts (including the profit and loss account, which now also has a balance remaining). The total of all the credit balances should still equal the total of all the debit balances, because double entry has been maintained throughout, even in the profit and loss account. When all the balances are collected together on a balance sheet (or sheet of balances), we have a picture of what is owned by and owed to the business at that moment in time.

The balance sheet is not part of the double-entry system. The debit or credit balances on the asset, liability or capital accounts are not being transferred to the balance sheet; they are carried forward to the next period, as indeed are the real assets and liabilities that they represent. The balances are merely recorded on a balance sheet in order to show the financial position of the business at the end of the accounting period. That is, the balance sheet represents stocks, not flows. Therefore it will have 'as at 31 December 1998', for example, in its title.

Looking back through this chapter some accounts can be identified that still hold balances after the profit and loss account has been compiled. We shall expect to find these on the balance sheet. Examples of these are the cash account, debtors accounts, creditors accounts, fixed asset accounts and provision accounts. A worked example of how to prepare a profit and loss account and a balance sheet can be found at the end of Chapter 8. Published accounts will be discussed in Chapter 11.

7.9 Summary

Accounting, in the sense of the recording of financial information, is a very old art. Double-entry accounting (the Italian method) dates from the fourteenth century. It has enormous practical advantages. An account is set up in order to record all the information relating to one type of expense, revenue, asset or liability. Every transaction will have two effects: a credit and a debit. Each account has two sides in order to record separately the credits and the debits.

At the end of the accounting period the total of credit balances should equal the total of debit balances. The balances on revenue or expenses accounts are transferred to a profit and loss account, where they are combined to calculate profit. The remaining balances are carried forward to the next accounting period. In order to show the financial position of the business at the end of the accounting period, they are recorded on a balance sheet.

Self-assessment questions

Suggested answers to the self-assessment questions are given at the end of the book.

1. A capital expenditure results in a debit to:

    (a) An asset account.
    (b) An expense account.
    (c) A capital account.
    (d) A liability account.

2. Which of the following is *not* a satisfactory statement of the balance sheet equation?

    (a) Assets = liabilities − owner's equity.
    (b) Assets − liabilities = owner's equity.
    (c) Assets = liabilities + owner's equity.
    (d) Assets − owner's equity = liabilities.

3. The purchase of an asset on credit:

    (a) Increases assets and owner's equity.
    (b) Increases assets and increases liabilities.
    (c) Decreases assets and increases liabilities.
    (d) Leaves total assets unchanged.

4. The effect of a credit entry on the creditors account is to:

    (a) Decrease the account balance.
    (b) Increase the account balance.

(c) Decrease or increase the account balance.
(d) Decrease and increase the account balance.

5. Double entry was invented by:

(a) The Romans.
(b) Fourteenth-century Italians.
(c) Nineteenth-century Britons.
(d) Twentieth-century Americans.

Tutorial questions

1. Please arrange the following five symbols into an equation with no minus signs in it.

A_1 = assets at end of period
L_1 = liabilities at end of period
OE_0 = owner's equity at beginning of period
R_1 = revenues for the period
E_1 = expenses for the period

2. Rialto Co. has just completed the first eight months of its current financial year. Although it has increased sales by 25% over the previous year, it is anticipating considerably reduced profits for the year. The Sales Director is concerned about the situation. After discussions with other directors the Sales Director has discovered the following:

(i)   A customer has agreed to pay £30,000 for some stock costing £80,000. The stock was purchased four years ago and has a scrap value of £10,000.

(ii) A new delivery van is to be purchased for cash before the year end, costing £25,000.

(iii) A new item is to be introduced into the company's product range. It will involve the purchase of £40,000 of stock on credit immediately. The item will not be on sale until the next financial year.

(iv) A customer has recently ceased trading, owing the company £40,000 for sales made in the previous year. It is now unlikely that any payment will be received.

Explain the effect of items (i)–(iv) on the company's cash flow and profit during the year.

3. On 1 January 19x1, David Hume started business as an electrical contractor. He borrowed £1,000 on overdraft from the bank and used his car (value £1,500) and garage (value £5,000) for business purposes. He did most of his work for cash and purchased most of his materials on credit. Initially he drew £50 a week from his cash receipts but, as business improved, he increased this to £70 after 26

weeks. At the end of the year he prepared a list of assets and liabilities as at 31 December 19x1 as follows:

	£
Stock	5,200
Debtors	500
Bank overdraft	1,520
Creditors	2,295
Cash in hand	105

Hume had used £500 worth of the materials purchased for work done on his own home. You may assume that the value of the car and the garage was the same on 31 December as on 1 January.

You are required to:

(a) Calculate the net assets of David Hume as at 31 December 19x1.
(b) Using your answer to (a), state the profit made by the business for the year ending 31 December 19x1.
(c) Discuss what the impact on your answers to (a) and (b) would be if you were told the value of the car on 31 December 19x1 was only £1,000.

References

Lee, G.A. (1977) 'The coming of age of double entry', *The Accounting Historians' Journal*, Fall.
Nobes, C.W. (1982) 'The Gallerani account book of 1305–1308', *Accounting Review*, April.

Further reading

Edwards, J.R. (1989) *A History of Financial Accounting*, London: Routledge.
Wood, F. *Business Accounting 1*, London: Pitman, latest edition.

ACCOUNTING TECHNIQUES

8

In this chapter there will be an outline of the practical ways in which the day-to-day activities of bookkeeping and accounting are performed, and the processes which are required at the year end. Almost all organizations nowadays use a computer system, either custom made or an accounting package. Some computer systems merely duplicate manual systems and generate large amounts of paper. Some organizations operate with data stored almost entirely electronically – current information is viewed on screen and older data is stored on magnetic disk or tape. It is, however, still essential to keep a record of all transactions which have taken place.

Computer systems automate routine procedures and assist with the mechanics of the double-entry system, but it is unwise to rely on any system without an understanding of the underlying accounting concepts.

8.1 'Books' and 'ledgers'

In a manual system, *books of prime entry* such as the cash book, sales day book, and purchases day book, are used to record the details of the high volume transactions. At the end of the day, week or month, depending on the volumes, totals from these books are used to generate double entries for the accounting system. For example, the figure for sales on credit will be the total of the sales day book (accounting entries: *debit* individual debtor accounts severally, *credit* sales account in total). In the case of cash sales the initial record will appear in the cash book (accounting system: *debit* cash account, *credit* sales account).

In a computer system each transaction is entered once only and double-entry posting to the accounting system is automatic. Often a batch system is used whereby only batch totals are posted to accounts when details are unnecessary, as in the manual system. At this point an electronic record of the transaction exists and a printout of transactions can be made if required (see Appendix 8.1).

Traditionally, there have been several groupings of accounts into different ledgers. The sales ledger contains the accounts of debtors, the purchases ledger contains the accounts of creditors. These two ledgers are *personal ledgers*, as they deal with debts to and from persons (human or corporate). The ledger holding other accounts is known as the *nominal ledger*. If there are large numbers of accounts of one type, perhaps fixed asset accounts, these may also be kept in a separate ledger for convenience.

At one time each ledger would have been a separate book. Computer systems will present each 'ledger' as if it is separate and may well have passwords allowing users to access only those ledgers which they require for their work.

8.2 Control accounts

In order to maintain the double-entry system within the nominal ledger, *control accounts* keep running totals of the entries in each of the other ledgers. In a manual system a control account also acts as a check on the accuracy of entries in a personal ledger. The accounting entries from the sales day book now become: *debit* debtors ledger control account, *credit* sales account. It can be seen that individual entries in personal ledger accounts are no longer part of the double-entry system. They are now *memoranda* accounts. Control over the individual accounts is maintained by regularly balancing them and agreeing the total with the balance on the control account.

Since transactions are entered only once in a computer system and all further entries are automatic, it would appear that the total of entries in individual accounts at any time should always be the same as the total posted to the control account. A list of balances should still be printed out and checked with the control account as part of period end procedures as inconsistencies may arise, for example:

(1) timing differences in updating the personal ledger and the nominal ledger,
(2) a whole batch omitted from the control account,
(3) adjustments made to one ledger without the normal procedures for routine transactions.

8.3 The trial balance

At the end of an accounting year (or at any time during the year when a balance sheet or profit and loss account is needed) the accounts in a manual system must be balanced, as described in the previous chapter. The balances are then listed with debits in one column and credits in another (this procedure is called *extracting a trial balance*) before the balances are transferred to the profit and loss account or recorded on the balance sheet. If the totals of the columns do not agree, this signifies an error (or errors), for example:

(1) *errors of posting*, where one part of the double entry is lost or recorded on the wrong side when transferring information from books of prime entry to ledgers;

(2) *arithmetic errors,* where the addition and balancing processes are inaccurate;

(3) *omission of an account,* where the balance on an account is not recorded in the trial balance;

(4) *misreading a balance,* where the wrong amount is transferred to the trial balance, or the correct balance written to the wrong column.

It is clear that these types of error should not arise in a computer system. A system should reject partial entries which do not maintain the double-entry system, and all the calculations are automatic. However, a trial balance is still an essential step in the process of producing a profit and loss account and balance sheet as computers (and their operators) are not infallible. An imbalance must be immediately investigated as it indicates a serious breakdown of the accounting system.

Table 8.1. contains a possible trial balance extracted from the books of the business of F. Montefeltro on 31 December . . . 99. Any errors revealed by imbalance have already been corrected in the trial balance.

A trial balance which balances is not a guarantee that there are no errors, and checks have to be built in to an accounting system to try to avoid errors (see Section 11.6 on auditing).

8.4 The journal

The *journal* used to be a book of account through which passed entries for *all* transactions that did not affect the other books of prime entry. Like the other books of prime entry, the journal was outside the double-entry

Table 8.1   Trial balance extracted from the books of F. Montefeltro as at 31.12.99 (£)

Item	Debits	Credits
Capital		20,000
Freehold premises	10,000	
Fixtures and fittings at cost	4,500	
Depreciation provision at 1.1.99		900
Opening stock at 1.1.99	4,800	
Purchases	11,600	
Sales		16,500
Drawings by Montefeltro	2,400	
Debtors	2,100	
Creditors		1,600
Wages and salaries	800	
Lighting and heating	100	
Rent and rates	300	
Miscellaneous expenses	200	
Cash and bank balances	2,200	
	39,000	39,000

system. As a result not only could every entry in the accounts be traced to the corresponding entry that made up the double entry, but also every double entry could be traced (using its date) to a book of prime entry.

It then became normal practice to omit journal entries for routine entries to the accounts which were recorded elsewhere (e.g. salary information which can be found in the payroll). However, a journal is still very useful for keeping a record of unusual transactions (e.g. the purchase of fixed assets, or the correction of errors in the accounts). When such entries are made to a computer system, a printout of the amounts posted and the accounts used takes the place of a journal. It is useful to enter as complete a *narrative* as possible so that an explanation for each entry is permanently recorded. In many businesses a written journal is prepared first so as to record the authorization for the adjustment. Figure 8.1 shows an example of a journal sheet. The total debits in each journal must equal the total credits.

At the end of the year there will be a variety of entries that are necessary before the accounts can be properly drawn up. These closing and adjusting entries are sufficiently unusual that, in order to trace them and understand them later on, it will be sensible to pass them through the journal. In the case of F. Montefeltro's business (the trial balance of which is shown in Table 8.1) the year-end entries may result from the following information:

(1) 10 per cent depreciation for the year should be provided on the cost of fixtures and fittings.
(2) Rates have been paid in advance to the extent of £50.
(3) Specific bad debts of £100 are to be written off.
(4) A provision for future bad debts of 10 per cent of debtors is to be set up for the first time.
(5) Closing stock is valued at £5,000.

Date:		Journal No.
	Debit	Credit
Machines a/c	1,500	
Urbino Engines Ltd a/c		1,500
Purchase of a sprocket cruncher on credit		
Total	1,500	1,500
Authorised by:		

Figure 8.1 Example of a journal sheet

These entries are shown in Figure 8.2. They can now be added to the previous trial balance of Table 8.1. The result is shown as Table 8.2, where the new entries have affected the asterisked balances. The adjustments that have been made are shown in the right-hand columns. The trial balance still works. The next stage is to transfer all the revenue and expense balances to a profit and loss account by closing the accounts, using the double entry method as seen in Chapter 7. As the balances are transferred, the record in the trial balance can be ticked. (The revenue and expense balances have already been ticked in Table 8.2.) In this case the account in Table 8.3 will result.

All the remaining unticked balances in the trial balance (Table 8.2) will be asset, liability or capital balances. These can now be recorded on the balance sheet. As noted at the end of Chapter 7, the balance sheet is not part of the double-entry system. Therefore, these unticked accounts are not closed down, nor are their balances transferred.

JOURNAL SHEET NO: 302		
Date: 31.12.99	£ Debits	£ Credits
Depreciation charge	450	
Depreciation provision		450
Being 10% depreciation for the year on £4,500 cost		
Rates (opening balance for next year)	50	
Rates		50
Being the recognition of £50 paid in advance		
Bad debts	100	
Debtors		100
Being the writing-off of specific bad debts		
Bad debts	200	
Provision for bad debts		200
Being the setting up of a provision, 10% of £2,000		
Stock	5,000	
Trading acocunt		5,000
Being the recording of the closing stock		
Total	5,800	5,800

Figure 8.2 Journal sheet of F. Montefeltro for 31.12.99

Table 8.2 Trial balance of F. Montefeltro as at 31.12.99 after journal sheet adjustments (£)

Item	Debits	Credits	Adjustments already made Debits	Adjustments already made Credits
Capital		20,000		
Freehold premises	10,000			
Fixtures	4,500			
*Depreciation provision at 31.12.99		1,350		+450
√*Depreciation charge	450		+450	
√Opening stock (in trading account)	4,800			
√*Closing stock (in trading account)		5,000		+5,000
*Closing stock (in asset account)	5,000		+5,000	
√Purchases	11,600			
√Sales		16,500		
Drawings	2,400			
*Debtors	2,000		−100	
Creditors		1,600		
√Wages and salaries	800			
√Lighting and heating	100			
√*Rent and rates	250		−50	
√*Rates (opening balance for next year)	50		+50	
√*Bad debts	300		{ +100 +200	
*Provision for bad debts		200		+200
√Miscellaneous expenses	200			
Cash and bank balance	2,200			
	44,650	44,650	+5,650	+5,650

When all the balances in the trial balance have been used, the balance sheet in Table 8.4 will result. Double entry has ensured that it balances.

A computer system will produce a profit and loss account and balance sheet whenever required, without necessarily closing off those accounts whose balances make up the profit and loss account. At the end of the accounting period a separate period end process will be carried out, during which the balances on revenue and expenditure accounts increase or decrease the accumulated capital account. The balances on these accounts, and the transactions which made them up, are then deleted as discussed in Appendix 8.1.

Table 8.3 Trading and profit and loss account of F. Montefeltro for the year ending 31.12.99 (£)

Opening Stock	4,800	Sales	16,500
Purchases	11,600		
	16,400		
less Closing stock	5,000		
	11,400		
Gross profit c/d	5,100		
	16,500		16,500
Wages and salaries	800	Gross profit b/f	5,100
Lighting and heating	100		
Rent and rates	250		
Depreciation	450		
Bad debts	300		
Miscellaneous expenses	200		
	2,100		
Net profit c/d	3,000		
	5,100		5,100
		Net profit b/f	3,000

Table 8.4 Balance sheet of F. Montefeltro as at 31.12.99 (£)

	Cost	Cumulative depreciation	Net Book value		
Fixed assets:				Owner's interest:	
Freehold premises	10,000		10,000	Capital (at 1.1.99)	20,000
				Net profit for the year	3,000
Fixtures and					23,000
fittings	4,500	1,350	3,150		
	14,500	1,350	13,150		
				less Drawings	2,400
				Capital (at 31.12.99)	20,600
Current assets:				Current liabilities:	
Stock		5,000		Creditors	1,600
Debtors	2,000				
less Provision	200	1,800			
Prepaid expenses		50			
Cash at bank		2,200	9,050		
			22,200		22,200

8.5 Incomplete records

Some businesses do not operate a full double-entry accounting system. A small trader may not understand the advantages of such a system or may think that the expertise and time needed will be too costly for a business with a relatively small number of transactions each year. This situation should not arise in a limited company because the Companies Act 1985 requires proper accounting records to be kept (further discussed in Chapter 11). However, it is possible that, due to damage or loss, some of the accounting records of a limited company may be missing.

In all these cases profit will still need to be calculated for the information of managers and owners and for the purpose of the Inland Revenue. Depending on the extent of the incompleteness of the records, it will be necessary for an accountant to do work ranging from the logical deduction of missing figures to guesswork based on the memories of the proprietor and a knowledge of the business. The accountant is aided by knowing that any increase in the net assets of the business must be due to profit, assuming that there has been no net introduction of capital. This has been looked at in Chapter 3.

At worst, then, a closing balance sheet can be prepared from information about the assets and liabilities. The balancing item in it will be the closing capital. This closing balance sheet is compared with the opening balance sheet (i.e. last year's closing balance sheet); if there is none, it will have to be estimated. The difference between the earlier and the later capital figures is the profit. If there have been drawings or capital introductions, the following familiar equation can be used:

$$\text{opening capital} + \text{profit} + \text{introductions} - \text{drawings} = \text{closing capital}$$

Clearly, this method provides very little information for owners and managers to enable them to make decisions about investment, pricing, expense control and so on. Also, the risks of undetected theft and fraud are much higher when there is no complete accounting system. So, in all cases, attempts should be made to calculate profit by comparison of revenues and expenses, leaving comparison of opening and closing capitals as a check.

One particular example of incomplete records where this may be possible is called *single entry*. Here the small trader may be merely maintaining a cash book. However, starting with this, double entries can be created. Suppose that, after the receipts and payments have been combined together by type, the cash book of S. Malatesta's business appears as in Table 8.5.

Table 8.5   Cash account of S. Malatesta as at 31.12.96 (£)

(1) Opening balance 1.1.96	1,000	(5) Drawings by Malatesta	1,500
(2) Cash sales	7,500	(6) Fixtures bought	1,200
(3) Payments by debtors	4,000	(7) Purchases in cash	3,500
(4) Extra capital introduced	2,500	(8) Payments to creditors	5,000
		(9) Rent and rates	900
		(10) Wages	1,400
		(11) Closing balance 31.12.96	1,500
	15,000		15,000
(11) Opening balance 1.1.97	1,500		

By analysing the outstanding invoices (sent and received) and by making a physical stock check, the accountant finds that at 31 December . . . 96:

Debtors are	£1,500
Creditors are	£1,250
Stock is	£2,400

Let us assume that a balance sheet as at 31 December . . . 95 is also available (Table 8.6). From all this information the accountant can construct double entries for the year and then produce a profit and loss account.

This will now be done, using the reference numbers in the cash account (Table 8.5) to identify the other parts of each double entry. Entry (1) in the cash account has a double entry in the previous year's cash account; entry (2) will have its partner in the sales account, and so on.

Debtors control account (£)

Balance 31.12.95	1,300	(3) Cash	4,000
∴ Sales	4,200	Balance 31.12.96	1,500
	5,500		5,500
Balance 31.12.96	1,500		

Sales account (£)

Trading a/c	11,700	(2) Cash	7,500
		Debtors	4,200
	11,700		11,700

The credit sales have been worked out to be £4,200 by deduction, by making the debtors account balance. These sales have a double entry in the sales account. The balance on the sales account (£11,700) is transferred to the trading account (below). Let us continue:

Table 8.6 Balance sheet of S. Malatesta as at 31.12.95 (£)

	Cost	Cumulative depreciation	Net book value		
Fixed assets:					
Premises	15,000		15,000	Capital (at 1.1.95)	20,000
Fixtures	4,000	1,000	3,000	Profit (year to 31.12.95)	1,500
					21,500
	19,000	1,000	18,000	less Drawings	700
Current assets:				Capital (at 31.12.95)	20,800
Stock		1,600			
Debtors		1,300		Current liabilities:	
Cash		1,000	3,900	Creditors	1,100
			21,900		21,900

Creditors control account (£)

(8) Cash	5,000	Balance 31.12.95	1,100
Balance 31.12.96	1,200	∴ Purchases	5,100
	6,200		6,200
		Balance 31.12.96	1,200

Purchases account (£)

(7) Cash	3,500	Trading a/c	8,600
Creditors	5,100		
	8,600		8,600

The purchases have been calculated as £5,100 because that makes the creditors account balance. The double entry for this is in the purchases account. The remaining accounts below also follow from the cash account:

Rent and rates account (£)

(9) Cash	900	Profit and loss a/c	900
	900		900

Wages account (£)

(10) Cash	1,400	Profit and loss a/c	1,400
	1,400		1,400

Capital account (£)

Balance 31.12.96	23,300	Balance 31.12.95	20,800
		(4) Cash	2,500
	23,300		23,300
		Balance 31.12.96	23,300

Drawings account (£)

(5) Cash	1,500	

There should also be accounts for the fixed assets and stock. Suppose that straight line depreciation for fixtures should be provided at 10 per cent each year on cost:

Premises (£)

Balance 31.12.95	15,000	

Fixtures (at cost) (£)

Balance 31.12.95	4,000	Balance 31.12.96	5,200
(6) Cash	1,200		
	5,200		5,200
Balance 31.12.96	5,200		

Provision for depreciation (£)

Balance 31.12.96	1,520	Balance 31.12.95	1,000
		Depreciation charge	520
	1,520		1,520
		Balance 31.12.96	1,520

Depreciation charge (£)

Depreciation provision	520	Profit and loss a/c	520
	520		520

Stock account (£)

Balance 31.12.95	1,600	Trading a/c	1,600
	1,600		1,600
Trading a/c	2,400		

The profit and loss account will now have been prepared (Table 8.7). It contains the other halves of various entries in the accounts above.

The year-end balance sheet shown in Table 8.8 will be compiled by collecting together all the remaining balances. The reader should check that these (and only these) balances can be found on the preceding accounts.

Table 8.7 Trading and profit and loss account of S. Malatesta for the year ending 31.12.96 (£)

Opening stock	1,600	Sales	11,700
Purchase	8,600		
	10,200		
less Closing stock	2,400		
Cost of goods sold	7,800		
Gross profit c/d	3,900		
	11,700		11,700
Wages	1,400	Gross profit b/f	3,900
Rent and rates	900		
Depreciation	520		
Net profit c/d	1,080		
	3,900		3,900
		Net profit b/f	1,080

Table 8.8 Balance sheet of S. Malatesta as at 31.12.96 (£)

	Cost	Cumulative depreciation	Net book value		
Fixed assets:					
Premises	15,000		15,000	Capital (at 1.1.96)	23,300
				Net profit (year to	
Fixtures	5,200	1,520	3,680	31.12.96)	1,080
	20,200	1,520	18,680		24,380
				less Drawings	1,500
Current assets:				Capital (at 31.12.96)	22,880
Stock		2,400			
Debtors		1,500		Current liabilities:	
Cash		1,500	5,400	Creditors	1,200
			24,080		24,080

8.6 Summary

The double-entry system is the basis of all accounting up to the preparation of the profit and loss and balance sheet. It is important to understand the double-entry system even where a computer accounting system is used. Techniques such as control accounts help to detect errors. The journal has been described and used in this chapter to illustrate the process of moving from a trial balance, through year-end adjustments, to a set of final accounts.

The accountant may have to assist in the preparation of accounts in cases where less than full double-entry records are available. It may be possible to create double entries from a cash book and certain year-end information. A last resort (other than for purposes of checking other methods) is a comparison of opening and closing balance sheets to reveal an implied profit figure.

Appendix 8.1
The audit trail in a computerized system

All businesses must maintain an *audit trail*, i.e. cross-referenced records which enable each transaction to be traced to its final destination in the financial statements, and also allow each constituent part of figures in these statements to be traced back to its source.

It is common for computer systems periodically to delete details of transactions which are no longer current, such as purchase invoices which have been paid. Some systems create an electronic *archive* which can be read when required. Some leave it to the user to create a *back-up copy* of the data files before deletions, but it is often inconvenient to access these files later. It is common therefore to print out all transactions on paper before the electronic records are deleted. This may be a complete list of all transactions in the order in which they are entered, or separate listings for different types of transaction, taking the place of the day books of a manual system. In either case there must be a method of linking these to the final figures in the financial statements to show that a complete record of all transactions exists.

Appendix 8.2
An example of the wider uses of accounting information

Bookkeeping and accounting have wider uses than producing periodic financial statements for a business. Employees need accurate information in order to carry out operations, and management need summaries of business activities in order to make decisions. An example follows of an information system covering customers' orders, invoicing and stock control in a wholesale stationery business.

An order arriving from a customer triggers serveral events:

(1) before the order is accepted, the customer's credit standing is checked,
(2) delivery instructions are sent to the warehouse,
(3) stock control records are updated,
(4) a sales invoice is sent to the customer,
(5) the debtors ledger is updated.

If the stock control system shows a low stock level, a further sequence of events is triggered:

(6) supplier records are checked to find the best price and quality,
(7) a purchase order is sent,
(8) the warehouse is informed of goods expected.

When goods are received:

(9) quantity ordered is checked,
(10) actual amount received is recorded,
(11) the stock control records are updated with quantity.

When the purchase invoice is received:

(12) quantity received is checked,
(13) price agreed with supplier is checked,
(14) the creditors ledger is updated,
(15) the stock records are updated with price information.

Each process requires information and all relevant data must be gathered before processing can be done. Data is gathered in the correct format by preprinted forms, or screens on computer terminals.

If the information required by a process will also be required elsewhere, it can be circulated by using copy documents. For example, copies of sales invoices may be sent to the warehouse (process 2 above), stock control (3), and debtors ledger (5). Alternatively information can be circulated electronically and processed to update the warehouse system, the stock control system, and the debtors ledger system, all of which can be accessed through terminals. A third method is to store all data once only in a central database, where different people can access it through remote terminals when required. This reduces the amount of storage space required and also reduces the time spent in entering data. For example, customer names and addresses can be stored once and used whenever required, perhaps for a delivery note, an invoice, a reminder, or a mailshot.

Similarly, data which is held on computer can be processed in different ways to provide information for many purposes, for example, sales data may provide information for identifying debtors whose payments are overdue, customers who have not ordered recently and slow moving stock items, and for preparing cash flow forecasts.

Self-assessment questions

Suggested answers to the self-assessment questions are given at the end of the book.

1. The Capital account, Withdrawals account, and the Summary of Profit and Loss account for Baker's Repair Shop for the accounting period are presented below in T account form. All the entries are for the same year.

Baker, Capital	
31 Dec. 400	1 Jan 800
31 Dec. 300	

Baker, Withdrawals	
1 Mar. 100	31 Dec. 300
1 Jun. 100	
1 Sep. 100	

Summary of profit and loss		
31 Dec.	1,000	31 Dec. 600
		31 Dec. 400

The amount of net profit (or net loss) for the period was:

(a) £400 net loss.
(b) £600 net profit.
(c) £400 net profit.
(d) None of the above.

2. Consider the information given in Question 1. The amount of withdrawals for the period was:

(a) £100.
(b) £500.

(c) £300.
(d) None of the above.

3. Consider the information given in Question 1. Baker's opening Capital balance was:

(a) £200.
(b) £300.
(c) £800.
(d) None of the above.

4. Consider the information given in Question 1. The closing balance of Baker, Capital, was:

(a) £100.
(b) £800.
(c) £200.
(d) None of the above.

5. If a debtors account has debits of £26,000, credits of £28,000, and a closing balance of £24,000, which of the following was its opening balance?

(a) £26,000.
(b) £24,000.
(c) £2,000.
(d) £50,000.

6. Which of the following errors will *not* cause the debit and credit columns of the trial balance to be unequal?

(a) A debit was entered in an account as a credit.
(b) The balance of an account was incorrectly computed.
(c) The account balance was carried to the wrong column of the trial balance.
(d) A debit entry was recorded in the wrong account.

7. The following information pertains to the K Corporation.

(i) The corporation's stationery supplies account showed an opening balance of £300 and had purchases of £900. The closing balance in the account was £200.
(ii) Depreciation on buildings is estimated to be £7,000.
(iii) A one-year insurance policy was puchased for £2,400. Three months have passed since the purchase.
(iv) Accrued interest on a commercial bill receivable amounted to £75.

The profit and loss account would contain:

(a) A debit for Stationery Expense of £900.
(b) A credit for Stationery Expense of £900.

(c) A debit for Stationery Expense of £1,000.
(d) None of the above.

8. Consider the information given in Question 7. The year-end entry for depreciation on buildings would include:

(a) A debit to Accumulated Depreciation for £7,000.
(b) A credit to Accumulated Depreciation for £7,000.
(c) A credit to Depreciation Expense for £7,000.
(d) None of the above.

9. Consider the information given in Question 7. The year-end entry for the insurance policy would include:

(a) A debit to Prepaid Insurance for £600.
(b) A credit to Prepaid Insurance for £600.
(c) A credit to Insurance Expense for £600.
(d) None of the above.

10. Consider the information given in Question 7. The year-end entry to record the accrued interest on the commercial bill would include:

(a) A credit to Interest Receivable for £75.
(b) A debit to Interest Receivable for £150.
(c) A credit to Interest Income for £75.
(d) None of the above.

Tutorial questions

1. Using the symbols *A, L, OE, R* or *E* (see Tutorial Question 1, Chapter 7) identify each of the following balances in a trial balance:

	Answers
(a) Closing stock	_____
(b) Creditors	_____
(c) Rent expense	_____
(d) Prepaid rent	_____
(e) Depreciation expense	_____
(f) Interest received	_____
(g) Buildings	_____

2. A trial balance for Brent Property at the end of its accounting year is as follows:

Brent Property
Trial Balance
31 December 1997

Cash	4,275	
Debtors	2,325	
Prepaid insurance	585	
Office supplies	440	
Equipment	5,300	
Accumulated depreciation, Equipment		765
Car	6,750	
Accumulated depreciation, Car		750
Accounts payable		1,700
Unearned management fees (1998)		1,500
Diego Brent, Capital		14,535
Diego Brent, Withdrawals	14,000	
Sales commissions earned		31,700
Office salaries expense	12,500	
Advertising expense	2,525	
Rent expense	1,650	
Telephone expense	600	
	50,950	50,950

You also know that:

(a) Office supplies on hand at 31.12.97 are £135.
(b) Insurance unexpired amounts to £270.
(c) Estimated depreciation for 1997 of office equipment is £375.
(d) Depreciation for 1997 on the car is estimated at one-ninth of its cost.
(e) At the year end, the rent of £150 for December had not been paid.

You are required to:

(i) Adjust the trial balance for the information in (a) – (e).
(ii) Prepare a profit and loss account and balance sheet for 1997 in the conventional form.
3. John Hawkwood Co. had the following Balance Sheet as at 31 December 19x8, after the company's first year of trading.

Unfortunately a number of transactions have been completely omitted from his financial records; these transactions being as follows:

(i) Sales of goods costing £6,000 for £10,000 in cash.
(ii) Purchases of fixed assets (plant and machinery) costing £10,000 on credit.
(iii) Inventory existing at the year end. The inventory cost £9,500, although the market value of the inventory was £7,500.
(iv) Payments to creditors have not been recorded. These payments total £6,500.
(v) Payment of expenses during the year. These expenses totalled £4,500 for the year.

	£	£
Fixed Assets		
Land and Buildings	100,000	
Plant and Machinery	60,000	
		160,000
Current Assets		
Inventory	41,000	
Debtors	3,000	
Bank	10,000	
	54,000	
Current Liabilities		
Creditors	30,000	
		24,000
		184,000
Capital		
Share Capital		150,000
Reserves		34,000
		184,000

Amend the Balance Sheet of John Hawkwood Co. to take into account all the omitted transactions.

4. On 1 January 19x9 Thomas Aquinas starts business as a coal merchant and opens a business bank account with £18,000. The following is a summary of his transactions for 19x9:

(a) Bought a lorry for £10,000 in January.

(b) Coal purchased and received during the year, £82,000. Aquinas had paid invoices for £79,800 and still owed his suppliers £2,200 on 31 December 19x9.

(c) Aquinas estimates that the stock of coal in the yard at 31 December 19x9 is worth £2,400.

(d) Sales value of coal delivered and charged to customers during the year was £119,000. Of this, £112,000 had been received in cash. £400 was irrecoverable (a bad debt) and it was expected that the balnce would be paid in full.

(e) Fuel and oil, maintenance and taxation for the lorry cost £3,100 for the year, all of which had been paid.

(f) Wages of assistant, earned and paid during the year, £7,800.

(g) Rent of yard – £1,200 was paid in January, covering the period to 30 June and a further £2,400 paid in July covered one year's rent.

(h) Other expenses all relating to the year, and paid for during the year, £1,700; and a further £200 expense was incurred but not yet paid for.

(i) During the year Aquinas withdrew from the business bank account for his personal use, £20,000.

From this information draw up a summary of changes in the bank balance, prepare a Profit and Loss Account for the year, and a Balance Sheet at 31 December 19x9. Assume all money received was paid into the bank and all payments made by cheque.

PART II

ACCOUNTING FOR

BUSINESS ENTITIES

The chapters in Part II deal with the legal and taxation background of businesses and with published financial statements. Chapter 9 looks at the legal, tax and accounting aspects of partnerships. The next two chapters discuss companies. Chapter 10 covers the purpose of incorporation and some of its legal, economic and tax effects. In Chapter 11 the objectives and nature of corporate published accounts are examined. Also, two other stewardship concerns, namely, auditing and dividend policy, are discussed.

Then the effects of price changes on financial accounting, and the methods of adjusting published accounts for these effects, are looked at in Chapter 12. Finally, the subject matter of this part is studied again on a comparative international basis in Chapter 13.

PARTNERSHIPS 9

So far, the businesses of *sole traders* have been used for illustration of various accounting conventions and formats. This is because sole traders have the simplest form of capital structure and accounts. The basic conventions remain exactly the same for *partnerships* and for *companies*.

9.1 The partnership form

Sole traders may see substantial advantages in that form of business. They can organize the business as they wish and need not share the profit with anyone. However, there are substantial disadvantages in some circumstances. These may lead a sole trader to take part in the formation of a partnership. Several advantages may be gained by a sole trader who joins with other sole traders or who invites an employee or friend to form a partnership. Sole traders may wish to expand the business but not to acquire extra creditors or lenders who must be paid back. By forming a partnership they may find partners who can provide the capital for expansion. Also, they can now share the risks (and losses) of the business with partners, who are all jointly and severally liable for the debts of the partnership.

The partners will also share the burden of running the business, which is particularly useful at time of holiday or sickness. Indeed, on retirement the business need not be closed down with the consequent loss of work for loyal employees and the loss of the value of customers' goodwill and the value in use of the assets. The partnership can continue with the remaining partners plus replacement partners, who can buy out the retiring partner's share of the business. Further, in a large business it may be quite impossible for one person to find time to manage all aspects of the business or to have sufficient skills to do so. Consequently, it is very useful to have other partners, who are committed to the success of the business and can contribute management skills as well as capital.

There are, of course, several disadvantages to partnerships compared to being a sole trader. Partners must live with the possibility that other partners may be making bad decisions or acting dishonestly. This may reduce the profit shares of the partners or leave them with large debts for which they are jointly and severally liable. In any case, a partner has to yield both a share of control and a share of profit to the other partners.

Usually, the partners will draw up a partnership deed to regulate the running of the partnership and the rights and duties of the partners. It is not strictly necessary to have a deed, but clearly it may help to avoid or settle later disagreements. If there is no deed, or if the deed is silent on a certain point, recourse may be had to the Partnership Act, which sets out standard rules. The deed will usually contain an agreement as to how the profit will be shared, whether any partners are to draw salaries before the profit shares are calculated and whether interest is to be paid on capital amounts. The Act provides for profits to be shared equally among the partners and for there to be no salary or interest on capital.

The reason for paying salary to some partners may be that they work harder to contribute more valuable skills than others. If one partner works much harder than others, he or she may nevertheless be unable to persuade the others to reduce their profit shares, but they may think it reasonable to pay him a salary before profit shares are calculated. Similarly, if some partners contribute much more capital than others, it seems reasonable that they should benefit from this by receiving interest from the partnership before profit shares are calculated.

The fact that a partner earns interest, salary and profit from his business does not mean that any or all of this must be withdrawn in the form of cash. If it is not, it remains to the credit of the partner in a current account. The current accounts of the partners are maintained separately from the capital account, which usually holds a steady amount of the capital. This figure is of legal relevance in certain cases.

9.2 Taxation and disclosure

Taxation on the profits of an unincorporated business is borne by the owners, not by the business. This is because, at least under English law, partnerships are not seen as legal entities separate from their owners. The tax borne by the partners is income tax and it is levied on the profit share, salary, interest and other benefits, whether or not these are withdrawn from the business. The accounting profits are adjusted in various ways in order to find taxable profits, in a similar way to that for company profits (see Chapter 10). Income from these sources is added to a sole trader's or partner's other income and becomes part of the personal income tax assessment. The Inland Revenue sends the tax bill to the partnership because, if one partner cannot pay the tax on the partnership profits, the others will be liable. However, this is only a practical matter of extracting payment; the business does not pay tax. This may mean that an unincorporated business is a more attractive form of organization in certain cases than a company, which pays corporation tax. The choice will depend on the tax rates paid by the sole trader or partners (James and Nobes, 1997).

Another factor that may influence a business's decision is that companies have to disclose substantial amounts of financial information in yearly accounts that can be inspected by the public, including competitors. This does not apply to sole traders or partnerships.

9.3 Accounting implications

There will be two extra accounts for partnerships in addition to those already met when accounting for sole traders. These accounts are the *appropriation account*, which is an extension of the profit and loss account and deals with the splitting up of the net profit; and the *current accounts* of the partners, which may be presented in columnar form in one account, as seen below. Also, there will be some effects on the capital entries on the balance sheet. A good way to illustrate this is to work through an example.

Alpha and Beta is a partnership whose two partners share profits and losses on a 2:1 basis. Interest on capital is agreed at 5 per cent per annum, and Beta is credited with a salary of £800 per annum. At 31 December 1998 the trial balance is as shown in Table 9.1. Also,

(1) the closing stock is valued at £7,900;
(2) depreciation on fixtures and fittings is allowed at 10 per cent per annum; and
(3) insurance has been paid in advance to the extent of £34.

The journal entries for these three notes will be used to adjust the accounts in the trial balance (see Figure 9.1).

In order to simplify the trading account, the purchases figure will be stated as £32,317 (purchases − returns out + carriage in) and the sales figure as £44,093 (sales − returns in). The profit and loss account will look as in Table 9.2.

Table 9.1 Trial balance of Alpha and Beta as at 31 December 1998 (£)

Item			Debits	Credits
Capital account:	Alpha			5,000
	Beta			3,000
Current accounts at 1.1.98:	Alpha			300
	Beta		150	
Drawings:	Alpha		2,500	
	Beta		2,400	
Purchases and sales			32,070	44,173
Returns in and out			80	33
Carriage in			280	
Salaries			4,050	
Rent			590	
Insurance			60	
Bad debts			70	
Opening stock			7,100	
Fixtures and fittings (cost)			3,400	
Debtors and creditors			3,020	4,464
Cash			1,880	
Provision for depreciation 1.1.98				680
			£57,650	£57,650

JOURNAL SHEET	£ Debit	£ Credit
Date:		
(1) Debit stock account	7,900	
Credit trading account		7,900
Being the recording of closing stock		
(2) Debit depreciation account	340	
Credit provision account		340
Being the provision of 10% depreciation for the year		
(3) Debit insurance account (opening balance of next year)	34	
Credit insurance account		34
Being the recognition of a prepayment		
Total	8,274	8,274

Figure 9.1 Journal Sheet for Alpha and Beta at 31.12.98

Table 9.2 Trading and profit and loss account of Alpha and Beta for the year ending 31 December 1998 (£)

Opening stock	7,100	Sales	44,093
Purchases	32,317		
	39,417		
less Closing stock	7,900		
Cost of goods sold	31,517		
Gross profit c/d	12,576		
	44,093		44,093
Salaries	4,050	Gross profit b/f	12,576
Rent	590		
Insurance	26		
Bad debts	70		
Depreciation	340		
Net profit c/d	7,500		
	12,576		12,576
		Net profit b/f	7,500

The net profit brought forward is the first entry in the appropriation account, which is where the interest, salary and profit shares are appropriated to the partners. The credit parts of the double entries are in the partners' current accounts, which already have the opening entries from the trial balance. After these two accounts, it is possible to produce the balance sheet (see Tables 9.3, 9.4 and 9.5).

Table 9.3 Appropriation account of Alpha and Beta (£)

Current account Alpha (interest)	250	Net profit b/f	7,500
Current account Beta (interest)	150		
Current account Beta (salary)	800		
Current account Alpha (profit)	4,200		
Current account Beta (profit)	2,100		
	7,500		7,500

Table 9.4 Current accounts of Alpha and Beta (£)

	Alpha	Beta		Alpha	Beta
Opening balance		150	Opening balance	300	
Drawings	2,500	2,400	Appropriation:		
			Interest	250	150
			Salary		800
Closing balance	2,250	500	Profit	4,200	2,100
	4,750	3,050		4,750	3,050
			Opening balance		
			1.1.99	2,250	500

Table 9.5 Balance sheet of Alpha and Beta as at 31 December 1998 (£)

				Alpha	Beta
Fixed assets:			Capital account	5,000	3,000
Furniture and fittings	3,400				
less Depreciation	1,020		Current account	2,250	500
		2,380		7,520	3,500
Current assets:			Owners' interests		10,750
Stock	7,900				
Debtors	3,020				
Prepayments	34				
Cash	1,880	12,834	Current liabilities		4,464
		15,214			15,214

9.4 Summary

There are several advantages that may be gained by forming a partnership. These include the pooling of resources and skills and the sharing of risks and the burdens of running the business. Also, partnerships need not have an audit or disclose financial information, and they may benefit from the fact that they are taxed to income tax.

For accounting purposes an appropriation account becomes necessary to record the splitting up of profits; and the capital and current accounts of the partners need to be maintained separately. Otherwise, bookkeeping and accounting remain much the same as for sole traders. There are several more complex problems relating to retirements and introduction of partners, which are dealt with in more detailed texts.

Self-assessment questions

Suggested answers to the self-assessment questions are given at the end of the book.

1. The partnership form might be useful to the owners of small business in order to:

   (1) Reduce risks.
   (2) Gain limited liability.

(3) Reduce taxable income.
(d) Share profits.

2. Partnership profit is taxable:

(a) Under corporation tax.
(b) Under partnership tax.
(c) Under personal income tax at a partnership rate.
(d) Under personal income tax in the hands of individual partners.

3. Accountancy firms usually operate as partnerships instead of companies because:

(a) They cannot find enough owners.
(b) They wish to limit their liability.
(c) They wish to advertise.
(d) It makes it easier to open offices overseas.
(e) None of the above.

Tutorial questions

1. Explain the various possible advantages to a group of sole traders in joining together as a partnership.
2. Why do accountancy firms traditionally operate as partnerships?
3. How does partnership accounting differ from sole trader accounting?

Reference

James, S.R. and Nobes, C.W. (1997) *The Economics of Taxation*, Hemel Hempstead: Prentice Hall, ch. 12.

COMPANIES: LAW, TAX AND FINANCE 10

A business will find that severe limitations are put on its ability to raise capital for growth after it has reached a certain size, unless it becomes a limited company. Since it is also usual for all partners to have unlimited liability for the firm's debts and thus to require a say in the management, the practical limit may be small. Therefore capital (which will be used here to mean long-term finance provided by owners or by lenders) can usually only be raised from the partners or their associates. A partnership is not allowed to advertise for capital, nor is there an exchange market in its securities. So, it would be very difficult to persuade complete strangers to lend money to it, let alone to contribute ownership capital and accept the unlimited liability arising from it.

10.1 The need for capital

After moving from sole trader to partnership the next step in solving the problem of capital raising is to adopt the form of a *private limited company*, although some sole traders become private companies without passing through the partnership stage. As the owners of the company have limited liability for the company's debts, it will be acceptable to some of them not to be managers. These two reasons should mean that more capital can be raised. However, there can still be no advertising for capital nor public issue or exchange.

Two other effects of incorporation may be less attractive to the capital-hungry partnership that is thinking of becoming a private company. First, information about the performance and financial standing of the company must be disclosed in the form of yearly accounts, which must be sent to the Registrar of Companies. (Disclosure will be considered in Chapter 11.) This may be an unacceptable price to pay for limited liability.

Second, private companies pay corporation tax, rather than each partner paying income tax on his share of business profits as in the case of partnerships. This may be disadvantageous (see later). Nevertheless, despite these two reasons the number of private companies has steadily risen to nearly a million.

Most of the companies whose names would be widely recognized are *public limited companies* (plc). This form of organization may enable the company to raise very much larger amounts of capital than a private company can. Disclosure requirements and taxation are similar to those for private companies. However, the public company is allowed to advertise for capital, and there can be an exchange market in its shares, by arranging for the share price to be quoted on a registered stock exchange and published in daily newspapers. There were about 15,000 public companies until greater differentiation between public and private companies was introduced in 1980. There are now about 12,000 companies in plc form, about one-fifth of which are listed on the Stock Exchange.

Companies must satisfy the requirements of the Companies Acts. The previous Acts were replaced by the Companies Act 1985, which has since been amended by the Companies Act 1989. This has provisions relating to the powers of directors, the disclosure of information, safeguards for shareholders and so on. In addition, there are many accounting and auditing rules (see Chapter 11). There are also Stock Exchange requirements to satisfy before a quotation will be allowed, and an audited prospectus must be published before the first public issue of any type of share. For all these reasons, and particularly because shares in public companies can be resold fairly easily to other investors, a public company should be attractive to a large potential market for shares in its ownership. Much the same reasoning can be applied to loan finance (i.e. debentures and bonds) as to share finance.

10.2 The corporate entity

A sole trader's business is not a separate legal entity from the sole trader as a person. The business's debts are legally those of the sole trader. He must sue or be sued in his own name. He pays income tax on the profits of the business; the business does not pay tax, because it is not a separate entity for revenue law purposes. The same applies to partnerships, except that the partners become jointly and severally liable for all debts of the business, which is still not a separate entity from them (at least, in English law).

However, a company *is* a separate legal entity. It can sue and be sued, has perpetual succession (although ownership may change) and is taxed independently from its owners. The accounting practice of showing capital on the same side of the balance sheet as the liabilities becomes more than a convenient balancing act, since the business is thereby acknowledging past contributions by its legally separate shareholders.

All companies are bound by the rules briefly mentioned in the previous section. Each company has its own rules too, set out in its *Memorandum* and *Articles of Association*. The Memorandum states the name, domicile and objects of the company, what its authorized capital is and whether its members have limited liability. So, this document is of relevance for outsiders in their relationships with the company.

The Articles of Association are concerned with such internal matters as the powers of directors, the management of meetings, the relationship of different classes of shareholders and so on. If a matter is not included in a company's Articles, resort may be made to standard Articles in the Companies Acts.

10.3 Types of capital

Although there are several other ways of raising finance (which will be discussed later), it can be said that there are two categories of issued capital: share (or equity or owners') capital and loan (or debt or lenders') capital.

10.3.1 Share capital

Share capital is provided by those who wish to become part owners of the company. These shareholders share in profits and losses. They bear the risks, and so they have some decision-making power. This is usually exercised only once a year at the company's annual general meeting, when directors are elected, dividends for the year are proposed and annual accounts are presented. The shareholders' involvement in management is usually limited to this, just as their liability is limited (to their share contribution). Various consequences follow from this, which will be examined in Section 10.4. Shares can be of several types, as shown in Figure 10.1 and discussed below.

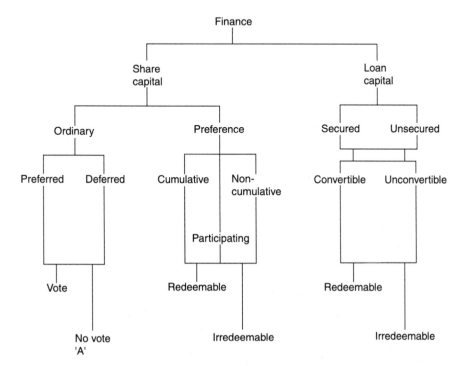

Figure 10.1 Types of external long-term finance

Preference shares usually carry a fixed percentage dividend, although *participating* preference shares (which entail rights to a share in profit if it exceeds a certain amount) earn more under some circumstances. Usually preference shareholders have no votes at general meetings, unless their shares are *cumulative* (i.e. any unpaid dividends remain to their credit) and in arrears. If there is insufficient profit or cash to pay dividends to both preference and ordinary shareholders, the latter can be paid nothing until the former are paid in full. Preference shares will also usually be in front of ordinary shares in the queue for repayment of capital in the event of the company being wound up. They are sometimes *redeemable*, like debentures (see below).

Ordinary shares do not carry a fixed dividend and are not cumulative. However, in normal circumstances companies try to keep the level of dividends more even than profits, and they endeavour to declare a dividend every year. As we have seen, it is usual for the ordinary shareholder to receive income and capital after the preference shareholder. Some companies split ordinary shares further into *preferred* and *deferred* (i.e. owners') shares. The latter may be the original shares representing the money put into the company to set it up. These deferred shares will only pay dividends if the preferred ordinary shareholders have received their dividends at some set rate. It can be seen, therefore, that the order of size of profit-sharing is the reverse of that for security of income and capital.

Usually, the owner of an ordinary share has a *vote* at the general meetings of the company. Control of more than half the votes means control of the company. Some shares have no votes (often called 'A' ordinary shares) and are issued and exchanged at slightly lower prices than their voting equivalents. These are now discouraged by the Stock Exchange.

10.3.2 Loan capital

Loan capital is provided by those who wish to lend money to the company without sharing profits and losses or bearing as much risk as shareholders. The company issues paper to acknowledge indebtedness, called *debentures* or *bonds*. The debenture holders receive fixed interest payments and usually have a redemption date when the capital will be returned. They are not owners of the company and can sue for any unpaid interest, thereby possibly causing the company to be wound up. Their main concern is with the security of capital and income and thus with the stability and liquidity of the company. The riskier is the business, the less attractive will the company be to a fixed interest investor, and therefore the higher will be the interest rate that he will require.

Further variety of loan capital is worth pointing out (see Figure 10.1).

(1) Security can vary from a fixed charge on specific assets (e.g. a building or plot of land), to a floating charge on the companies' assets, to no charge at all. The words 'debenture' and 'loan stock' have been used

interchangeably. An *unsecured* loan may be called a *naked* debenture. Debentures are normally *secured*.

(2) Debentures can be issued with the option that, at the wish of the holders, between certain dates and at certain values they can be converted into shares. (*Convertible* debentures will be considered further below.)

(3) Debentures are usually *redeemable*, in which case their value depends on future interest flows and the ultimate repayment of capital. The real value will approach the face (nominal) value more closely as the redemption date approaches. However, some debentures are *irredeemable* and have value only for future interest flows.

10.4 The separation of ownership from management

It has been mentioned that many of a company's owners (i.e. the shareholders) do not demand daily management control because their liability for the company's debts is limited. Therefore the company's capital is not restricted to the number of directors that it could have. The power to appoint the directors lies with the voting owners (i.e. the holders of voting ordinary shares and usually the holders of preference shares that are in arrears). Power to appoint the directors means power to appoint the company's other managers. It may be possible for a major shareholder to control the company with much less than 50 per cent of the voting shares if the other shareholders have very small holdings and do not exercise their rights to vote. Small shareholders may find it easier to sell their shares than to complain if a company disappoints them. This leaves control in many cases to family groups or to such financial institutions as life assurance companies and pension funds.

Although the managers may have some shareholding, their main reward for management is their salary, not the benefits from their shares (and thus directly from profit). Consequently, although it may be true that the *owners* of the company are looking for maximum long-run profit, it is very likely that the *managers*, who make the economic decisions, have additional aims, which may be more important to them. For example, the siting of an expensive head office administration may remain in London or move to a major south-coast town because the directors would prefer it, rather than because the siting is economically the most sensible. Decisions may well be made in order to maximize sales or directors' income or managers' leisure, or to have an even flow of profit rather than maximum profit.

There are several other results of the separation of ownership from management that directly affect the accountant and the accounts. In particular the need for published accounts, which must disclose certain accounting and other facts about the company, follows partly from the fact that most owners have no day-to-day connection with the company. As noted before, audit is also required for this reason. Other accounting implications will be looked at in Chapter 11.

10.5 Taxation

As has been said, the company is a separate legal entity and is required to pay taxation as such. Until 1965 the tax system for companies was similar to that for individuals. In 1965 corporation tax was introduced in order to tax companies separately from individuals, in a way that would allow for future differential manipulation in rates, controls and incentives between individuals and companies. The introduction of corporation tax (with rates set each year in the Finance Act) led to a disincentive to pay dividends. There was a further reform in 1973. This is discussed below; here is a brief summary:

Pre-1965: *income tax* at standard rate on all profit (gross of interest), *plus profits tax* (10½–15 per cent on profit net of interest).

1965–73: *classical system of corporation tax* at rates of 40–45 per cent on profit net of interest, *plus* income tax on dividends.

After 1973: *imputation system of corporation tax* on profit net of interest; part is imputed to shareholders as an *income tax credit*. Rates: 52 per cent (1973–82), falling gradually to 33 per cent for 1991–1997. There is also a lower rate for companies with small profits.

10.5.1 Dividends

One of the most important areas of difference between corporation tax systems has been the treatment of dividends. From 1965 to 1973 distributed profit was taxed more highly than undistributed profit. This was because all profits bore corporation tax, and then dividends bore income tax at their recipients' marginal rates. There was clearly a disincentive to distribution.

For a country whose economists and politicians ascribed many of its economic problems to chronic lack of investment, a tax system that encouraged retention and so, presumably, investment should surely have been perpetuated. However, economists argued that capital should flow towards those companies which could best use it – that is, in general the most profitable companies. The most profitable companies would be those most concerned with expansion and those which could most easily attract investors. Therefore, it was argued that if all companies paid maximum dividends there would be more money in the hands of profit-maximizing investors, who would use their money to buy issues of capital in the companies that could best use more capital.

This argument, the feeling that double taxation of dividends was inequitable and the wish to harmonize with other EU tax systems all played their parts in the decision to introduce the imputation system of corporation tax in 1973. The important change is that recipients of dividends do not pay full income tax because they receive a tax credit, which in 1996/7 was 25 per cent of the size of dividends. In effect, basic rate taxpayers pay no income tax on dividends. Shareholders who pay no income tax can claim the tax credit as a refund; higher rate taxpayers pay income tax at their top marginal rates on the 'gross' distribution, but may use the tax credit; corporate shareholders pay no tax on UK dividends received, and so they cannot use the tax credit for this purpose.

As the proportion of profit paid in dividends rises, so the imputation system becomes more favourable in terms of the total tax borne by the company and shareholders together. The effect of this is to reduce the bias against dividend payments. For basic rate taxpayers the total tax paid by the company and shareholders does not increase as dividends increase. Therefore the system is neutral in these cases.

There is a complicating feature in the UK imputation system which is not present in other EU imputation systems. This is a tax called *advance corporation tax* (ACT), which is payable by a company on a quarterly basis. The amount of the tax is 25 per cent of the dividends paid in the quarter. Dividends received can be set off against dividends paid in order to reduce the liability to ACT.

ACT is not an extra tax under normal circumstances. It is a prepayment of part of the corporation tax liability. The balance, called *mainstream corporation tax*, is paid nine months after the company's financial year end. One of the purposes of the ACT is to improve the government's cash flow to replace the loss of the classical system's income tax deduction at source.

10.5.2 Interest

Payment of an amount of interest is cheaper than payment of the same amount of dividend. Under the imputation system let us look at two similar companies, one of which pays £1,500 cash dividend and the other of which pays £2,000 gross interest, which is equivalent to £1,500 after basic rate tax of 25 per cent, for example (Table 10.1).

Table 10.1 Effect of paying interest or dividend (£)

	Company paying interest	Company paying dividend
Net profit before interest and tax	10,000	10,000
less Interest	2,000	–
Net profit before tax	8,000	10,000
less Corporation tax at 35% (e.g.)	2,800	3,500
Net profit after tax	5,200	6,500
less Dividend	–	1,500
Undistributed profit	5,200	5,000

The £2,000 interest paid really costs the company only £1,300 (i.e. £6,500 − £5,200) in post-tax profit, because tax is reduced by the other £700. Consequently, companies that wish to issue 'fixed interest' capital will seldom choose preference shares, because dividends are paid out of post-tax profit. Instead, more attractive interest rates can be offered on debentures and this will still leave more profit after tax.

However, if the recipient is a company, the comparison of interest costs with dividend costs is more complicated. A company does not pay income tax on any income, but it does pay corporation tax on interest received, although not on dividends received. The former income has not already borne corporation tax in the paying company; the latter has. Therefore a company will prefer to receive £1,500 dividends to £2,000 gross interest, on which it must pay corporation tax.

10.5.3 Adjustments to profit

Another factor that affects economic decision-making is that the profit for taxation purposes is not the accounting profit. The latter is adjusted in a variety of ways to calculate the former. First, there are several items of income that are included in the accounts but not fully brought in to charge for corporation tax. For example, all UK dividends received (i.e. franked investment income) and part of any capital gain are excluded. There is also a longer list of items that are treated as expenses for accounting purposes but are not allowable as deductions in the calculation of taxable profit. Examples of these items are entertaining customers, increasing a general bad debts provision, the costs of defending the company in tax cases, fines where the company or its employees have committed illegal acts, and most charitable or political donations. For example, with the present rates of corporation tax it can be seen that £100 spent on wages is really about two-thirds as expensive as £100 spent on entertaining customers in terms of post-tax profit.

Perhaps the most important feature of this type is the disallowance of depreciation and the granting instead of *capital allowances*. The latter are a standardized system which allows the judgement of accountants to continue for the financial accounts, but not to affect taxable income. Also, for many years capital allowances served as investment incentives, because they were very generous. For example, between 1970 and 1984, capital allowances for plant and machinery were 100 per cent of the cost in the year of purchase. These capital allowances were gradually phased out, partly because they might not encourage the creation of jobs, which was seen as more important than investment *per se*. From 1986, expenditure on plant and machinery, cars, patents and 'know how' attracts 25 per cent 'writing down allowances' (on the reducing balance basis); and industrial buildings receive a 4 per cent straight line allowance. These still represent faster depreciation than that normally charged in the accounts. This continues to create the possibility of recognition of this 'deferred tax liability' in the accounts. In UK accounts, such potential liabilities are normally mentioned in the notes.

10.5.4 Further points

There are very many detailed aspects of corporation tax that are of great importance in practice. For example, there is a special low rate of tax (24 per cent) for small profits, and there are special provisions to control small 'close' companies that are run like partnerships. There are particular rules relating to the taxation of capital gains and to the treatment of losses. These matters are left for more detailed texts (James and Nobes, 1997).

10.6 Raising finance

When a company plans to raise finance, it may be faced with a choice between a large number of possible methods. One way of categorizing these is into short-term and long-term. It is possible in the short term for a business to obtain more finance by not paying its bills, by chasing debtors and by not replacing stock. It may also be possible to increase an overdraft. Bank finance of this sort is usually regarded as short-term. Even if overdrafts tend to remain outstanding for several years, they may theoretically be recalled.

This section is concerned with long-term finance: self-finance, share issues, debenture issues and one-off financial adjustments. It is a rule of thumb that fixed assets and working capital (i.e. the excess of current assets over current liabilities) should be covered by this long-term finance.

In making a choice between methods of finance a company must have some criteria. The basic criterion may reasonably be the long-run benefit to the present shareholders. The various effects of raising capital can then be seen in the context of this criterion. The possible effects include a change in the control of the company due to more shareholders, an increase in the interest burden, a dilution of profit among more shareholders, costs of issue, and many others.

It has already been suggested that the separation of ownership from management may affect the goals of a company. It may be that a company's management aims to maximize the company's total profits rather than to maximize future profits per share of existing shareholders. For the rest of this chapter, however, the assumption will be that decision-making will be carried out for the benefit of the existing shareholders.

10.6.1 Self-finance

Retained profits are the largest source of company finance in the United Kingdom. This is particularly true for private companies, which find that lack of a public quotation makes it difficult for them to attract investors or lenders. Fast-growing companies tend to rely less on self-finance, even though they tend to be earning high profits and to be retaining larger-than-average proportions of them. These fast-growing companies have such appetites for capital that they need to raise a higher than average proportion of capital from outside sources. This is made possible because of their attractiveness as earners of good profits.

The small new private company finds it difficult not only to attract investors and lenders for securities of various sorts but also to raise bank loans, because of its lack of assets to mortgage and lack of profit history. Consequently, the reliance on self-finance may be very heavy.

The amount of profit ploughed back into a company is clearly directly related to the amount of dividend paid. The consensus is that the dividend decision is generally made first, leaving the retained profit as a residue. This complicated problem will be discussed in Chapter 11. Having decided upon the amount of undistributed profit it may be tempting to regard this as costless capital. However, considering the simple case where the company would have to borrow from outside if it did not use the undistributed profit internally, there is an opportunity cost of not doing the most profitable external alternative. It may be more profitable to pay off all loans or to invest in government securities than to plough back the profits. It is possible that the managers of some companies use all the undistributed profits without considering the opportunity cost, through ignorance or because they want a larger company rather than a more profitable one.

10.6.2 External finance and gearing

The two categories of external finance are shares and debentures (see Figure 10.1). If a company needs substantial amounts of extra capital that cannot be provided from its own profits, it will normally have to turn to public issues. The choice between more shares and more debentures will be affected by the existing relationship between these types of capital in the company. Before examining shares and debt in more detail, we shall look at their relationship with the aid of the concept of *gearing*.

If a company is highly geared, it means that there is a high proportion of fixed interest capital, which may or may not be defined to include preference shares on which the dividend is fixed but can be cancelled or postponed. Preference shares will be ignored for the rest of this chapter because of their declining importance since the advent of corporation tax. Suppose that an extract from company X's balance sheet were to show a long-term capital position such as that in Table 10.2. The gearing of this company could be measured in a variety of ways; for example,

$$\frac{\text{Debenture capital}}{\text{Ordinary capital}} = \frac{800,000}{100,000} = 800\%$$

$$\frac{\text{Debenture capital}}{\text{Shareholders' interests}} = \frac{800,000}{300,000} = 267\%$$

$$\frac{\text{Debenture capital}}{\text{Total long-term capital}} = \frac{800,000}{1,100,000} = 73\%$$

Different users may have preferences for different measures of gearing. The important point is that a consistent measure should be used when comparing one company with another, or a company in one year with the same company in a previous year. In the case of company X the gearing can be seen to be very high. The effect of this on the rewards to the shareholders is considerable. Let us look at the profit of this company over two years (Table 10.3). In the first year its net profit before interest and taxation is £100,000. In the second year the profit doubles to £200,000. Because of the very high gearing a doubling in operating profit has led to earnings that are six times larger. In a company that can be sure of covering its heavy interest charges and expects increases in profit, the shareholders will benefit greatly from high gearing.

An alternative measure of gearing (which can be called *income gearing* as opposed to *capital gearing* above) is useful as a measure of the interest burden resulting from high capital gearing. In company X the income gearing ratios are as follows:

Table 10.2 The long-term capital position of company X (£)

Oridinary shares, nominal value £1	100,000
Reserves of past profits	200,000
	300,000
Debentures, 10%, 1999	800,000
Net capital employed	1,100,000

Table 10.3 Profits of company X over two years (£)

Item	Year 1	Year 2
Net profit before interest and tax	100,000	200,000
less Interest	80,000	80,000
Net profit before tax	20,000	120,000
less Taxation (at 50%, say)	10,000	60,000
Net profit after tax (earnings)	10,000	60,000

$$\frac{\text{interest paid}}{\text{net profit before interest and tax}} = \frac{\overset{\textit{Year 1}}{80{,}000}}{100{,}000} = 80\% \quad \frac{\overset{\textit{Year 2}}{80{,}000}}{200{,}000} = 40\%$$

A company with income gearing anywhere near as large as 80 per cent is clearly very vulnerable to financial disaster if profits fall. The reciprocal of the income gearing ratio is a *times interest covered* figure. These ratios and many others will be further discussed in Chapter 14.

10.7. New issues

10.7.1 Shares

The attractiveness of shares can be looked at from the point of view of the company and the investor. The company may find the issue of shares more attractive than the issue of debentures if it is a new company that expects to be unprofitable for its first few years or if it is a company that has fluctuating profits. In these cases it may dislike having to pay regular amounts of interest, preferring to pay high dividends when it can afford them.

The company will take account of the cost of issuing shares, which is very high if the shares are to be sold to the public. The costs include advertising, administering the issue, obtaining advice from a merchant bank, preparing an audited prospectus containing large amounts of information about the company and paying an underwriter in case the issue is undersubscribed. Alternatively, if the company already has many shareholders, it may decide to try to issue its new shares to those existing shareholders in proportion to their holdings. This is known as a *rights issue*. If there are 100,000 shares before the issue and the company wishes to issue 50,000 more, there will be a '1 for 2' rights issue. The shares are offered at slightly below their market price in order to persuade the existing shareholders to take up the issue. This method of issuing shares is much cheaper than offering them to the public because the advertising, prospectus and other costs are saved. With merchant banker, stockbroker and printing costs the costs of a rights issue normally amount to 3 or 4 per cent of the gross sum raised.

The control of the company may be affected by the issue of new shares. A company may not be prepared to issue more shares if the controlling group of shareholders will stand to lose control. Also, there will be dilution of profits to go with any dilution of ownership. Existing shareholders may not be happy to share future profits with new shareholders. However, a rights issue that is fully subscribed has the benefit of maintaining the importance of all the shareholders. For this reason and their lower costs, rights issues are by far the most popular form of equity issues. The dilution problems are also avoided by issuing debentures instead of shares.

From the point of view of the investor, buying ordinary shares involves greater risk of loss of earnings and loss of capital, but it also involves greater control of the company and participation in profits through dividends or capital gain. Investors will be more prepared to buy shares if the company shows signs of continuing to be profitable and if its sector of industry and the economy as a whole are buoyant.

10.7.2 Debentures

Debentures are attractive to the company because they are cheaper to issue than offering shares to the public and because there is no dilution of ownership or profit-sharing. However, there is a constant burden on profit because of the inevitable payment of interest. This will be less serious if the company expects to make stable and high profits.

Companies will find it easier to persuade lenders to take up their debentures if there are substantial amounts of fixed assets that can be offered as security. Breweries that own many public houses and warehouses, hotel groups and retailers owning many department stores are examples of companies that are likely to be able to offer security to debenture holders. From the lender's point of view this security of capital, coupled with security of income from the fixed interest debentures, may be important.

Inflation is of great significance when considering fixed interest loans. From the point of view of the company, if inflation continues, both the interest payments and the repayment of capital will be less onerous year by year. If inflation runs at 10 per cent per annum, a loan of £1,000 made today for ten years will result in an eventual repayment of only £385 in today's terms. From the point of view of the lender this is a high price to pay for so-called 'security' of income and capital. An investor may find shares more attractive, because they are backed by real assets and participate in real profit.

10.7.3 Factors determining the choice

We have looked at a number of factors that a company seeking capital should consider. If the directors have the best interests of the shareholders in mind, they may seek to raise the gearing to as high a level as is consistent with ability to pay the interest comfortably. Therefore, before more debentures are issued, the company must examine the present gearing and future profit forecasts. The ability to offer more debentures may also depend on the availability of assets that have not already been offered as security on previous loans. If the economy is depressed, it may be easier to raise money by loans than by shares. The company will also consider that given amounts of interest payments are cheaper than the same amount of dividend, because the former are chargeable against income for taxation purposes (see Section 10.5).

It may be that a company wishes to issue more shares but considers that the state of the company or of the economy makes this difficult. In this case the issue of convertible debentures may be attractive. The prospective investor may be pleased to buy debentures that have the option of conversion into ordinary shares at a future date.

10.8 Financial adjustments

There are many ways in which a company may benefit from one-off adjustments to its financial arrangements:

(1) *Factoring of debts* involves the passing over of a company's debtors to a financial institution, which administers the collection of the debts and may provide immediate funds that are equivalent to some large proportion of the total debtors. This and internal methods of better credit control should reduce the total debt outstanding and provide cash instead. Credit control will be discussed in Chapter 15.

(2) *Sale and lease-back* arrangements with financial institutions involve the sale of a company's fixed assets for immediate cash, followed by the leasing of them for periodic payments.

(3) *Financial surgery and asset-stripping* involve the sale of certain fixed assets or parts of companies that are thought to be worth more on the open market than in their present use. The resulting capital can be put to better use.

(4) *Trade credit* taken from suppliers can be extended by some companies, who can exert pressure on their suppliers to increase the length and limits of credit permanently. A company may be able to increase substantially the finance provided by its creditors by exerting this pressure and by never paying its bills until the last minute.

10.9 Summary

Large-scale enterprise is very much facilitated by a variety of legal provisions (e.g. the allowance of limited liability and public issue and exchange of shares, and the insistence on audited published accounts). These make long-term investment in publicly quoted companies sufficiently popular for major private enterprise organizations to evolve.

The owners (only a few of whom will be involved in management) are the holders of ordinary and preference shares. Other suppliers of capital are debenture holders, who are long-term creditors of the company, not owners. They receive interest, which must be paid. There are several types of share and debenture. The rights of the various holders and the company (which has a separate legal identity) are specified in the Articles of Association of the company and the documentation produced at the time of issue.

Since 1965 companies have paid corporation tax, which is a quite separate tax from income tax. The corporation tax system makes debenture interest (which is tax allowable) cheaper than an equal amount of dividend. It may also affect decision-making in other areas, where some expenses are not allowable for tax purposes. The granting of accelerated depreciation in the form of capital allowances is intended to be an investment incentive. Taxation also affects the timing of cash flows. The imputation system reduces the former bias in corporation tax against the distribution of profit.

The largest source of company finance is ploughed-back profits. This is particularly the case for small young private companies. Fast-growing companies may have to seek outside sources of extra capital. When deciding how to raise long-term capital, companies need to have a clear idea of their objectives. An objective may be to maximize the long-term benefits to the existing shareholders. A number of relevant factors must be considered in the light of this criterion.

One important factor is the existing gearing of a company from the point of view both of capital and of income. Other things being equal, a low-geared company can more safely issue more debentures. Another factor is the cost of issues. 'Rights' issues of ordinary shares or issues of debentures are cheaper than issues of shares to the public. Further, a company should consider the effects of issuing more shares on the dilution of profits and control. The availability of unmortgaged fixed assets to offer as security to debenture holders and the general state of the economy are relevant factors. The cost of servicing the issue of debt or shares should also be considered. A number of factors are important here (e.g. the effects of taxation and the expected rate of inflation).

In addition to the company's own past profits, share issues and debenture issues, there are a number of one-off financial manipulations that have the effect of raising capital.

Self-assessment questions

Suggested answers to the self-assessment questions are given at the end of the book.

1. Corporations generally have the following *differences* from partnerships (please read through the complete question before answering):

    (a) The owners have limited liability for the debts of the business.
    (b) The corporation is a separate legal entity.
    (c) The corporation is accounted for as separate from the owner.
    (d) The corporation pays less tax than the partnership.
    (e) Corporations are cheaper to form.
    (f) Corporations have fewer rules to obey.

    Circle as many letters as you think are differences.

2. What is the meaning of the word 'limited' in the name of a limited company?

   (a) The number of shareholders is limited to 50.
   (b) The liability of the company for its own debts is limited.
   (c) The liability of shareholders for the company's debts is limited.
   (d) There is a limit on the amount of debts that the company can contract.

3. A company might prefer to raise more debt capital rather than equity capital in order to:

   (a) Get more owners.
   (b) Minimize tax.
   (c) Reduce the risk of bankruptcy.
   (d) Reassure its creditors.

4. In a rights issue, shares are sold as follows:

   (a) New shares are sold to existing shareholders.
   (b) Existing shares are sold by some shareholders to others.
   (c) Existing debentures are sold to shareholders.
   (d) New shares are sold to new shareholders.

Tutorial questions

1. Explain the various advantages and disadvantages of moving to a corporate form instead of operating as a partnership.
2. Distinguish between debt capital and equity capital, and suggest which is likely to be favoured by a company raising finance in a high-tax environment.
3. How might a company seek to raise extra finance in ways other than issuing new debt or equity securities?

Reference

James, S.R. and Nobes, C.W. (1997) *The Economics of Taxation*, Hemel Hempstead: Prentice Hall, ch. 13.

COMPANIES: FINANCIAL REPORTING

11

The directors of a company are appointed by the shareholders to operate the company in the best interests of the shareholders. The directors are stewards of the shareholders' wealth invested in the company. Since the majority of shareholders in a large company have no day-to-day connection with the company, they will need reports from the directors showing how well they have discharged their stewardship role. Independent auditors act on behalf of the shareholders to verify these reports. The government has enacted various provisions from time to time to protect the shareholders and creditors of companies.

In this chapter we shall look at the regulatory framework, the objectives and the formats of published company reports and then at the work of auditors. There is also a section on the stewardship of directors with respect to dividend policy.

11.1 Regulatory framework

There has already been mention in previous chapters of Companies Acts and of accounting standards. The regulatory framework for the financial reporting of companies is explained in some more detail here.

The tradition in the United Kingdom is that the detail of accounting rules is made by committees of accountants rather than by parliament. The Companies Acts provide a structure for this by imposing certain reporting and auditing requirements. The Companies Act 1985 brought together the provisions of many previous Companies Acts, including those of 1948, 1967, 1980 and 1981. The Act requires the publication of audited balance sheets and profit and loss accounts. As a result of the implementation of EU Directives in the 1980s, UK law now contains detailed accounting rules on some issues, for example the formats of published financial statements. A long list of disclosures is also required, though the list in accounting standards is longer. The Act also lays down the labels for companies (public limited company (plc) and private limited company (Ltd)) and includes minimum capital requirements for public companies (£50,000 issued share capital). Some smaller private companies are exempted from some disclosures, as examined in Section 11.3.

From 1970 to 1990, accounting standards were prepared and issued by committees of the accountancy profession. However, the system was revised in 1990 in order to increase the independence of standard-setters from large companies and audit firms, and in order to strengthen compliance. The Financial Reporting Council, set up in 1990, is an independent body, relying on donations from companies, accountancy firms, the government etc. Its mission is to set accounting standards in the public interest, and to work for compliance by companies. The Accounting Standards Board (ASB) and the Financial Reporting Review Panel are its main operating arms.

The ASB sets accounting standards. It has adopted the previous standards (Statements of Standard Accounting Practice, SSAPs) and issues new or revised standards (Financial Reporting Standards, FRSs). Before the issue of an FRS, there is research and consultation, including the issue of an exposure draft (FRED) for comment by interested parties.

The Companies Act 1989 introduced a requirement whereby directors of public companies and some other large companies must state in the annual report whether or not they have complied with standards. The ASB's 'Foreword to Accounting Standards' explains that legal counsel's opinion is that it will normally be necessary to comply with accounting standards in order to obey the legal requirement to give a 'true and fair view'. Auditors are required to give their opinion on whether a true and fair view has been given.

The Financial Reporting Review Panel (FRRP) is allowed by the 1989 Act to take companies to court for issuing 'defective accounts'. This would include failure to give a true and fair view. So far, the FRRP has brought no such cases, but has made many investigations, leading to several examples of companies changing their accounting policies.

In conclusion, there is now some legal backing for standards, there is a presumption that compliance with accounting standards is legally required, and there is an enforcement mechanism.

11.2 Objectives of company reports

In the nineteenth century, one of the main concerns of accountants and the government with respect to published accounts was the protection of creditors and lenders. Such people were mainly interested in the ability of the company to pay its debts. Consequently, the balance sheet was the most important accounting document, and the conventions of conservatism and objectivity were strongly applied. There has been a shift in the twentieth century towards a greater emphasis on financial decision-making by shareholders. Therefore, the profit and loss account has become more important than the balance sheet, and recently efforts have been made to inject more realism into company accounts.

Another tendency of recent importance has been the recognition of the needs of customers, suppliers, the government, employees and pressure groups of various sorts. All these different groups require different information and different slants to the same information. The objective of company reports is clearly a matter that must be decided before it can be agreed what information they should contain.

In 1975 a working party set up by the Accounting Standards Committee (ASC) published a discussion paper called the Corporate Report. This document recommended that company reports cover a wider range of information. It suggested that the information be given to those having 'reasonable rights' to such information. These include employees, financial analysts, the government and the public, as well as shareholders and creditors. The company would have to bear the cost of supplying extra information to all these groups. This is justified by the argument that companies have the benefit of limited liability and have important effects on the economy and society; therefore they should act responsibly. This includes supplying information.

At present published accounts include a balance sheet, a profit and loss account, a cash flow statement (called for by accounting standard rather than company law) and some non-financial information about the company. This will be discussed in greater detail in Section 11.3 onwards. The Corporate Report suggested that six additional statements be included:

(1) a value added statement;
(2) an employment report;
(3) a statement of money exchanges with government;
(4) a statement of transactions in foreign currency;
(5) a statement about future prospects;
(6) a statement about corporate objectives.

These reports would be interesting, but they would also involve considerable cost and effort to prepare. Some companies began to experiment with such statements soon after the publication of the Corporate Report. The costs of annual reports are considerable and would rise if they had to contain much more information. These costs include printing, postage and auditing as well as preparation.

In addition to the high costs of annual reports, there is also evidence that the reports are under-used and poorly understood by most readers (Lee and Tweedie, 1978). These facts led some large companies to propose that companies should be allowed to send summary reports to their shareholders. The proposal was taken up in the Companies Act 1989, so that listed companies can now send summary reports to shareholders. The full reports can be requested by any shareholder and are still filed for public inspection.

The Corporate Report usefully listed the attributes that annual reports should possess. Reports should be relevant, understandable, reliable, complete, objective, timely and comparable. Sadly, those qualities may not be consistent. Historical cost accounts are reasonably understandable (perhaps speciously) and objective, but they are not very relevant for decision-making, nor truly comparable. Inflation accounting may be more difficult to understand and will be less reliable, in the sense of being more subjective.

Also, completeness tends to operate against timeliness, understandability and relevance.

Similar work was carried out from the mid-1970s in much more detail by the Financial Accounting Standards Board in the United States, under the title of the Conceptual Framework Project. This led to Statements of Financial Accounting Concepts which set out the objectives of financial statements (mainly seen as financial decision-making), propose qualitative characteristics (particularly relevance and reliability) and define key elements such as assets and liabilities. A smaller-scale work by Solomons (1989) was prepared for the guidance of UK standard-setters. Some definitions of asset and liability produced in the United Kingdom in FRS 5 are:

Assets:　　Rights or other access to futures economic benefts controlled by an entity as a result of past transactions or events.

Liabilities:　An entity's obligations to transfer economic benefits as a result of past transactions or events.

Such items should be recognized in balance sheets if there is sufficient evidence of their existence and they can be measured with sufficient reliability. If these are accepted, it is possible to confirm the conclusions of Chapter 3 that the following are not assets of a company:

(1) motorway (not controlled);
(2) totally worn out machine (no future benefits);
(3) unfruitful development expenditure (no future benefits).

Also, the following may be assets but are not *recognized* as such in a balance sheet:

(1) research expenditure (not sufficiently certain);
(2) internally generated brand names (no identifiable cost or value);
(3) customer loyalty (no identifiable cost or value).

On the other hand, assets leased from a finance company for the whole of their useful lives do seem to satisfy the criteria. Although they are not legally owned by the lessee, they are controlled as a result of past transactions, the use gives rise to probable benefits, and the initial cost can be measured in terms of (i) what it would have cost to buy the asset or (ii) the present value of the expected lease payments. Under the provisions of SSAP 21, such leased assets should be recognized (and depreciated) in the accounts of the lessee.

As far as liabilities are concerned, the FRS definition would seem to include an employers' pension obligations if not properly funded by an independent scheme, and even if the obligations result only from normal commercial expectations rather than from legally enforceable rights. Also, the expected payments of the lessee discussed above appear to be liabilities.

In 1991, the Accounting Standards Board began to publish drafts of chapters in its conceptual framework, the *Statement of Principles*. This suggests that the basic purpose of financial reports is to enable users to make financial decisions. The definitions of assets and liabilities in FRS 5 are confirmed. Equity is then the difference between the two. Revenues are defined as increases in assets or decreases in liabilities; and vice versa for expenses.

11.3 Disclosure in annual reports

We have seen that the traditional justification for disclosure (in terms of its being the price to be paid for limited liability) has been joined by the recognition that disclosure is necessary because of the economic, social, environmental and other effects that companies of significant size have on the community. However, there are many large businesses that do not operate as companies and do not have to obey disclosure rules. Examples of these are large firms of accountants, which may have important economic and other effects. In many ways it seems more important that these firms, which may be multinationals with tens of thousands of employees, should be forced to disclose than that the corner grocery store, which may be a private limited company, should be so obliged. Some criterion relating to size should perhaps be added to disclosure rules to include such businesses.

There *are* size criteria in the Companies Acts relating to the exemption of smaller private companies from certain accounting and publication requirements. For this purpose, companies are small or medium-sized, according to whether they fall below two of three criteria, as below:

	Small	Medium
Turnover (£)	2.8m	11.2m
Balance sheet (total assets) (£)	1.4m	5.6m
Employees	50	250

Other companies are large.

Small companies are exempted from publishing the profit and loss account and the directors' report, and are allowed to publish an abbreviated balance sheet and notes. Medium-sized companies have some lesser exemptions. Section 11.6 deals with exemption from audit on the grounds of size.

In addition, for quoted companies there are those requirements of the Stock Exchange which relate to disclosure, most obviously the requirement to publish half-yearly interim reports. Also, there are disclosure requirements in many Statements of Standard Accounting Practice (SSAPs) and Financial Reporting Standards (FRSs).

A considerable amount of information that must be disclosed in the annual report of a company is not directly connected with the balance sheet or the profit and loss account. This information (mainly factual matters relating to the past year) is put into the report of the directors. Most large companies also include a report of the chairman (general statements about the company's performance, intentions and prospects). The annual report must contain the names of the directors, information about their financial interests in the company, the average number of employees (if 100 or more), total political and charitable donations, any issue of shares or debentures, any significant changes in fixed assets and much else.

11.4 Financial statements

There are four compulsory accounting statements in UK annual reports: the balance sheet, the profit and loss account, the statement of total recognized gains and losses, and a cash flow statement. A version of the latter statement was introduced by SSAP 10 in the 1970s. The current rules are in FRS 1. This will be discussed more fully in Section 15.3.

11.4.1 Disclosure of accounting policies

With the published balance sheet and profit and loss account there should be a 'statement of accounting policies'. The disclosure of these policies became normal practice after the issuing of the standard on accounting policies, SSAP 2, in 1971. This fundamental standard suggests that there are four basic concepts in accounting: going concern, consistency, accruals and prudence. These are sufficiently widespread that companies need only disclose any deviation from them. The Companies Act 1985 also requires a statement of accounting policies and lays down the four concepts of SSAP 2.

The standard goes on to state that each company will then decide upon a number of accounting policies. Because these may differ from company to company, they need to be disclosed in order that the accounts of different companies can be compared more sensibly. Examples of accounting policies include the method of valuing stock, the methods of depreciation used, the treatment of research and development expenditure and the policy with regard to deferred tax.

11.4.2 The balance sheet

For centuries the two-sided balance sheet, as seen in several earlier chapters, was the normal method of presentation for both private and (later) published financial information. In recent decades, however, published balance sheets have increasingly been presented in vertical form, for reasons mentioned below. The Companies Act requires companies to choose one of the two detailed balance sheet formats which it sets out. The Act's accounting provisions result from the EU's Fourth Directive on company law, which was heavily influenced by German uniform practices. The Act sets out one vertical format (see Table 11.1) and one two-sided format, although there is some flexibility for companies in the use of the formats. The full formats are reproduced in an appendix to this chapter.

In addition to the balance sheet there will be a large number of notes, which provide information made necessary by Companies Acts or accounting standards. To include all the information on the face of the balance sheet would clutter it considerably. The following are examples of information usually contained in notes: gross values of fixed assets, cumulative depreciation figures, market value of investments, loans to company officers, provisions for bad debts, the nature of share capital and debentures, the constituent parts of the reserves figure, any contingent liabilities and any commitments to capital expenditure.

Table 11.1 An abbreviated vertical balance sheet

D. & D. Pirana and Co. Ltd			
Balance sheet as at 31.12.1999 (£000)			
Fixed assets			
Tangible assets			
Land and buildings			4,000
Plant and machinery			2,000
Fixtures and fittings			1,000
			7,000
Investments			800
			7,800
Current assets			
Stocks	1,500		
Debtors			
Trade debtors	1,700		
Prepayments	150		
Cash at bank and in hand	300		
		3,650	
Creditors: falling due within one year			
Bank loans and overdraft	800		
Trade creditors	1,200		
Corporation tax	800		
Proposed dividends	600		
Accruals	100		
		3,500	
Net current assets			150
Total assets less current liabilities			7,950
Creditors: falling due after one year			
Debentures			3,000
Capital and reserves			
Called-up share capital		2,000	
Profit and loss account		2,950	
Shareholders' interest			4,950
Long-term liabilities and capital			7,950

One set of information required by the Companies Acts that would normally be shown on the face of the balance sheet (although it is not in Table 11.1) is the series of comparative figures for the previous year. These are useful for putting this year's figures into context. Another way of trying to improve the clarity and usefulness of published accounts is to round figures to the nearest £1,000. In 1980–1, 77 per cent of a surveyed 300 UK companies were doing this throughout their published accounts. Even greater rounding was performed by a further 18 per cent of the companies (ICAEW 1981: 139, latest available data).

The purpose of vertical formats for balance sheets is also to improve their clarity for the majority of shareholders, who have little accounting knowledge. One traditional problem used to be the placing of the shareholders' interests on the 'liabilities' side of the two-sided balance sheet. This possible source of confusion to shareholders is avoided by using the vertical format. Also, the calculation and presentation of working capital and net assets are made possible. By 1980–1, nearly all of the 300 surveyed UK companies were using the vertical format for their balance sheets. In 1968–9, only 76 per cent had been doing so (ICAEW, 1981: 138).

11.4.3 Profit and loss accounts

The twentieth century has seen the slow passage of the profit and loss account from its traditional obscurity to compulsory publication in outline form (by the Companies Act 1929), to an expanded form (in the Companies Act 1967), to a uniform format (chosen from four available in the Companies Act 1981, now the 1985 Act). Its increasing importance marks the shift away from preparing published accounts primarily for creditors and lenders, who may be more interested in conservative balance sheet information. Shareholders and financial analysts are more interested in a 'true and fair view' of profit.

Of the four formats available in the Companies Act (see the appendix to this chapter), the two vertical formats are by far the most popular for the published accounts of large companies. The format illustrated in Table 11.2 fits most comfortably with UK traditional practice. It involves the specific disclosure of cost of sales and gross profit and some companies prefer the Act's alternative vertical format which avoids this.

The notes to the profit and loss account will show necessary information such as the depreciation charge, auditors' fees and the make-up of the dividends. As with the balance sheet, comparative figures must be shown, and rounding is normal.

FRS 3 requires companies to show separately the turnover and operating profit from continuing and discontinuing operations. This may be done in various ways, including columnar presentations. Table 11.2 is drawn up on the basis that there are no discontinuing operations. The exceptional items shown separately in Table 11.2 include such amounts as gains or

Table 11.2 A possible published profit and loss account

<table>
<tr><td colspan="3" align="center">D. & D. Pirana and Co. Ltd
Profit and loss account for the year ending
31.12.1999 (£000)</td></tr>
<tr><td>Turnover</td><td></td><td align="right">9,000</td></tr>
<tr><td>Cost of sales</td><td></td><td align="right">5,800</td></tr>
<tr><td>Gross profit</td><td></td><td align="right">3,200</td></tr>
<tr><td>Distribution costs</td><td align="right">400</td><td></td></tr>
<tr><td>Administrative expenses</td><td align="right">800</td><td></td></tr>
<tr><td>Interest payable</td><td align="right">500</td><td align="right">1,700</td></tr>
<tr><td></td><td></td><td align="right">1,500</td></tr>
<tr><td>Exceptional losses</td><td></td><td align="right">50</td></tr>
<tr><td>Profit before tax</td><td></td><td align="right">1,450</td></tr>
<tr><td>Tax on profit</td><td></td><td align="right">700</td></tr>
<tr><td>Profit for the year</td><td></td><td align="right">750</td></tr>
<tr><td>Dividends paid and proposed</td><td></td><td align="right">200</td></tr>
<tr><td>Retained profit</td><td></td><td align="right">550</td></tr>
</table>

losses on the disposal of fixed assets or businesses. Table 11.2 does not show any 'extraordinary items' because these are very rare under FRS 3.

The corporation tax figure may contain some amount that does not actually have to be paid in the immediate future but has been temporarily postponed, as a result of such matters as capital allowances. In the United Kingdom, according to SSAP 15, amounts of 'deferred tax' need only be charged to profit (the debit) and treated as liabilities (the credit) if they are expected to be paid in the foreseeable future. Often, this means that no deferred tax is accounted for because each year there are new capital allowances to cause tax to be further postponed.

The meaning of 'earnings' is profit after tax but before dividends. SSAP 3 requires the disclosure of earnings per share by companies with publicly traded securities.

The next financial statement, which is often very brief, is the statement of total recognized gains and losses (STRGL). This begins with the profit for the year (the '750' in Table 11.2) and then shows any gains or losses that are not included in the profit and loss account, for example unrealized gains on the revaluation of fixed assets. The STRGL is a bridge between the profit and loss account and the change in size of the shareholders' funds during the year. Of course, shareholders' funds will also have changed due to transactions with the owners, such as dividend payments and any receipts from the issue of new shares.

11.5 Groups

Most of the accounts that members of the public see are those of listed companies. A great number of these are groups of companies. The shares listed on the Stock Exchange will be those of the *parent company*, which may be a non-trading holding company. The parent company may own a number of *subsidiaries*, which are companies in which more than 50 per cent of the voting shares are owned by the parent or whose board of directors is controlled for some other reason by the parent. Subsidiaries may be private or public companies. Many subsidiaries may be fully owned; partly owned subsidiaries may even be listed companies themselves.

If the accounts of the group were only to show the detailed assets and liabilities of the parent company, including its investment in subsidiaries at cost, this would be very misleading. Therefore, in addition to the accounts of the parent company, which are calculated on this basis, there are *consolidated accounts* for the whole group, which show the aggregate totals of the different types of assets and liabilities. The Companies Act and FRS 2 demand consolidated accounts from groups.

There is a large variety of possible techniques of consolidation. Different techniques are used in different countries (Nobes and Parker, 1995). In the UK subsidiaries are consolidated using the *parent company method*. For the balance sheet this involves adding together the assets and outside liabilities by category. Any indebtedness between companies within the group is cancelled out during aggregation.

The share capital in the consolidated balance sheet is only that of the parent company. In the process of consolidation the share capital and pre-acquisition reserves of subsidiaries are set against the price paid for the shares, which are shown as an investment in the parent company's balance sheet. Any excess of the investment over the value of capital and reserves at the date of acquisition is called *goodwill* and is shown as an asset in the consolidated balance sheet. Any undistributed profit earned by subsidiaries after acquisition is aggregated with the reserves of the parent company for consolidation purposes.

Let us look at a simple example as an illustration of this. Suppose that P Ltd bought all the shares of S Ltd on 31 December 1997 for £2,000. At that date the share capital of S Ltd was £1,000, and its reserves were £300. One year later, there having been no payment of dividends, the balance sheets of P Ltd and S Ltd are as shown in Tables 11.3 and 11.4.

Table 11.3 P Ltd abbreviated balance sheet as at 31.12.98 (£)

Fixed assets:			Share capital		2,500
Land		3,000	Reserves		2,000
Machines		1,000			
		4,000			4,500
Investment in S Ltd		2,000	Loans		2,000
Current assets:			Current liabilities:		
Stock	800		Overdraft	1,000	
Debtors	900		Loan from S Ltd	200	
Cash	300	2,000	Creditors	300	1,500
		8,000			8,000

Table 11.4 S Ltd abbreviated balance sheet as at 31.12.98 (£)

Fixed assets:			Share capital		1,000
Land		1,000	Reserves		400
Machines		500			
		1,500			1,400
			Loans		800
Current assets:			Current liabilities:		
Stock	500		Overdraft	200	
Debtors	400		Creditors	300	500
Loan to P Ltd	200				
Cash	100	1,200			
		2,700			2,700

Eliminating the inter-company loan and setting the £2,000 'investment in S Ltd' against the original net asset value of £1,300, the consolidated balance sheet may be drawn up as in Table 11.5. The reserves figure is the total of those of the parent comapny (£2,000) and the post-acquisition profit of the subsidiary (i.e. £400–£300).

For the purposes of consolidation all the assets and outside liabilities are included, irrespective of whether the subsidiaries are wholly owned. Where there are outside shareholders, the value of their proportion of net assets is separately shown as *minority interests* in the consolidated balance sheet. If, in the above example, only 80 per cent of the shares had been bought for the £2,000, there would be a minority interest of 20 per cent of the orignial net asset value (i.e. 20% × £1,300 = £260) plus 20 per cent of the year's profit (i.e. £20). The consolidated goodwill figure would be larger in this case, because £2,000 was paid for net assets of £1,040 (i.e. 80% × £1,300) (see Table 11.6).

In practice, there is a further complication in that the assets and liabilities of the subsidiary must be reassessed at 'fair values' at the date of acquisition. This affects their values in the group accounts, and affects the size of goodwill. The fair value is usually equivalent to the replacement cost. It is an estimate of the current cost of the assets to the purchasing group.

Turning to the consolidated profit and loss account, this contains the aggregated turnover, profit and tax figures for the group. The share of post-tax profit due to the minority shareholders in subsidiaries is shown as

Table 11.5 Abbreviated consolidated balance sheet of P Ltd and subsidiary as at 31.12.98 (£)

Fixed assets:			Share capital		2,500
Land		4,000	Reserves (2,000 + 100)		2,100
Machines		1,500			
		5,500			4,600
Goodwill (2,000 − 1,300)		700	Loans		2,800
Current assets:			Current liabilities:		
Stock	1,300		Overdraft	1,200	
Debtors	1,300		Creditors	600	1,800
Cash	400	3,000			
		9,200			9,200

Table 11.6 Abbreviated consolidated balance sheet of P Ltd and subsidiary (80% share of S Ltd) as at 31.12.98 (£)

Fixed assets:			Share capital		2,500
Land		4,000	Reserves (2,000 + 80)		2,080
Machines		1,500			
		5,500			4,580
Goodwill (2,000 − 1,040)		960	Minority interests		280
			Loans		2,800
Current assets:			Current liabilities:		
Stock	1,300		Overdraft	1,200	
Debtors	1,300		Creditors	600	1,800
Cash	400	3,000			
		9,460			9,460

Table 11.7 Abbreviated consolidated profit and loss account of P Ltd and subsidiary for the year ending 31.12.98 (£)

Group turnover	4,300
Group profit before taxation (after providing for expenses as in note)	810
less Taxation	390
Group profit after taxation	420
less Extraordinary items	30
Group profit after extraordinary items	450
less Share of minority interests	110
Profit attributable to the company	340
less Dividends	100
Undistributed profit	240

a deduction before the 'profit attributable to the company'. An abbreviated example of a consolidated profit and loss account is given in Table 11.7.

There may be other companies in which the group has a significant but less than controlling interest. 'Significant influence' is normally deemed to exist when the group holds over 20 per cent of the voting share of another company. Such companies are called *associated companies*. For these, it seems inappropriate to consolidate the assets of the companies but sensible to take credit for more than just the dividend payments. Standard practice in this area is outlined in SSAP 1 which requires that the appropriate share of the post-tax profits of associates be brought into the consolidated profit and loss acount of the group. Therefore, in the consolidated balance sheet the appropriate proportion of the post-acquisition retained profits is added to the consolidated reserves, and it is also added to the figure for investments in associated companies.

When examining the published accounts of a company, it is important for most purposes to ensure that one is looking at the consolidated accounts for the group, not at the accounts of the parent company. The latter accounts are usually included in the same document but are highly misleading as indicators of the economic position of the group as a whole. The parent company of a vast group may comprise merely an office with a few legal and financial staff, for example.

11.6 Auditing

The published accounts of a company are the responsibility of the directors of the company. The accounts are partly an exercise in *accountability* or *stewardship*. The directors make a report in this way to the shareholders who have provided the company's funds and who are the owners. As seen before, this reporting is necessary because of the separation of ownership from management, which is essential in all but small companies and is facilitated by limited liability.

In order to protect the interests of the shareholders it seems reasonable that the directors' accounts be checked. This will also be useful for the creditors. The process of checking the truth and fairness of the accounts and their underlying values is called *auditing*. Auditing became legally necessary for banks in 1879 and for other companies in 1900. Originally, auditors were a group of shareholders chosen by the other shareholders in general meeting to look after the interests of all. Now, auditors are independent experts who, in the case of some firms of accountants, do not even allow themselves to be shareholders.

One of the important activities of major accountancy firms is the auditing of the published accounts of companies. The Companies Act 1985 requires companies above a certain size to appoint auditors who must be qualified independent experts who are on the register of auditors kept by the professional accountancy bodies. Companies with annual turnover below £50,000 are exempt from audit.

The auditors check that the assets exist and are properly 'valued' and that the accounts follow the law and standards. Much of the time of an audit is spent confirming that the procedures of the company are strong enough to record properly the transactions of the year and to prevent mistakes and fraud. This is called an *audit of internal control*. To a large extent auditors now rely upon sampling techniques in this work. If the auditors are not happy with the strength of the internal control systems, they will make recommendations to the directors and check the transactions of the business more thoroughly to ensure that they have been correctly recorded.

It is normal, especially in large companies, for there to be a number of 'internal auditors', whose work includes the examination and improvement of the systems of internal control. This may reduce the work that the external auditors have to do, although it does not reduce their responsibilities.

If the auditors are satisfied on all the above matters, they will give an opinion that the accounts comply with the Companies Act 1985 and give 'a true and fair view' of the activities and financial standing of the business. If they are not satisfied with the books of account, the underlying assets, the use of law or standards or the accuracy of the records of transactions, they will refuse to offer an opinion or will offer an opinion that is 'qualified' in some way.

If the directors and the auditors seriously disagree, the latter may resign or be sacked. However, this may lead to a stormy annual general meeting of the shareholders, who are responsible for ratifying the directors' choice of auditors. Also, it is etiquette among accountancy firms not to accept an audit unless they are satisfied with the reasons for the departure of the previous auditors. There is also the threat of investigation by the Financial Reporting Review Panel. Consequently, the auditors are usually in a fairly strong position, and it should not be assumed that they are necessarily rendered ineffective because they are paid by the company and need the co-operation of the directors.

Acting as the spur to the responsibility of the auditors is their knowledge that they might be sued for damages by parties who have suffered by relying upon any misleading information that the auditors have certified. Such actions for professional negligence have become fairly common in the United States, partly because lawyers there receive a percentage of the benefits of successful actions. Firms of accountants take out indemnity insurance to protect themselves. However, the premiums on these policies become very expensive after successful actions against auditors.

In addition to their auditing activities, firms of accountants may also be involved with the preparation of accounts, taxation, management consultancy and other advice to companies.

11.7 Dividend policy

One of the traditional purposes of the calculation of yearly profit has been to help to determine a suitable level of dividend. Profit, as we have seen, is supposed to be an estimate of the excess of revenues over expenses in a year, after maintaining the capital intact. Consequently, it should be possible to distribute all the profit without eating into the capital of the business. The definition of distributable profit for practical purposes was slowly put together, not by economists or accountants, but by lawyers. There were many court cases on this subject until the Companies Act 1980 (now the 1985 Act) introduced a statutory definition of distributable profit as:

accumulated, realised profits . . . less its accumulated, realised losses

This is not unambiguous, but for most purposes the normal accounting rules for profit determination are used. For example, gains on revaluing land and buildings are not taken to the profit and loss account until sale, nor are they legally distributable until then.

Rather than distributing profit, the directors may decide that profit would be more sensibly used for expansion or that there are insufficient liquid resources to pay a dividend. It is part of the stewardship role of the directors to make these decisions and to recommend the level of dividends to the shareholders. The shareholders may vote for less than the recommended dividend, but they may not vote for more. They can, of course, vote to remove the directors and substitute more amenable ones.

The company's dividend policy is its general stance towards the payment of dividends in the long term. Study of dividend policy and the factors affecting it is an interesting but complicated matter. Detailed study requires the use of more advanced textbooks. However, it seems appropriate here to list some of the factors that may affect dividend policy. First, observation of the movement of dividends suggests that stability is an important factor. Companies dislike lowering dividends because they wish to avoid disappointing their shareholders and giving them cause to worry about the financial strength of the company. Both these factors may depress share prices, which the directors may regard as important. Companies consequently also dislike *raising* their dividends, unless they can be fairly sure of maintaining the higher level in future. In addition, some shares are sought for their combination of low income and high capital gains, perhaps for tax reasons. Other investors seek shares with the opposite characteristics. Therefore, to exhibit unstable behaviour may cause both types of investor to steer clear.

Second, the long-run profit performance of the company should affect its willingness and ability to pay higher dividends. The importance of the previous factor suggests that dividends will only increase after a clear trend towards higher profit has been established. A third factor is the constraint of liquidity. In difficult economic circumstances, with high interest rates and controlled money supply, companies may feel unable to find the cash to pay dividends. There are also arguments in favour of the importance of a fourth factor, which is the needs of the company for capital for expansion.

Underlying all this is the theory that directors, by their dividend policy, should be trying to maximize the long-run benefits to the shareholders. This could mean that the decision about how much dividend to pay should rest on such factors as the relative tax rates of the shareholders for dividends and capital gains, and the rate of return on investment inside the company compared with that on the investment that the shareholders would make if they received dividends.

11.8 Summary

Financial reporting by companies is regulated by Companies Acts, although the most detailed regulations on valuation and disclosure are to be found in accounting standards issued by an independent body. Directors are required to state whether they have complied with standards, and legal opinion suggests that compliance is necessary in order to give a 'true and fair view'.

An analysis of the objectives of published accounting must rest upon the discovery of the needs of those who have rights to be provided with information. The groups who have been thought to have reasonable rights have expanded in recent years. The problems of supplying accurate and useful information to all these groups at a reasonable cost are very great.

Disclosure in published accounts is the concern of Companies Acts, of accounting standards and of the Stock Exchange. Information is disclosed in report form and in four types of financial statement: the balance sheet, the profit and loss account, the statement of total recognized gains and losses, and the cash flow statement. The formats of the first two of these accounts are specified by law. In general vertical formats have now been adopted for the presentation of the accounts of companies. Many published accounts relate to companies that own subsidiaries. In these cases the consolidated accounts of the parent and its subsidiaries added together are much more informative than the accounts of the parent company alone.

The accounts of all limited companies need to be audited by qualified accountants, who check on behalf of the shareholders that the accounts provided by the directors give 'a true and fair view'. Such auditing is the most important activity of large firms of accountants.

One particular aspect of the general 'stewardship' role of the directors concerns their responsibility for recommending the level of dividends to the shareholders. Dividend policy is influenced by a number of complicated factors. As with most of the topics in this chapter, it has been necessary to be tantalizingly brief on this subject. All the topics will be developed by more advanced courses in accountancy than those for which this book is intended.

Appendix 11: formats for British annual financial statements from Schedule 4 of the Companies Act 1985, as amended by the Companies Act 1989

Balance sheet formats

Format 1

A. Called up share capital not paid
B. Fixed assets
   I   Intangible assets
       1. Development costs
       2. Concessions, patents, licences, trade marks and similar rights and assets
       3. Goodwill
       4. Payments on account
   II Tangible assets
       1. Land and buildings
       2. Plant and machinery
       3. Fixtures, fittings, tools and equipment
       4. Payments on account and assets in course of construction
   III Investments
       1. Shares in group undertakings
       2. Loans to group undertakings

    3. Participating interests
    4. Loans to undertakings in which the company has a participating interest
    5. Other investments other than loans
    6. Other loans
    7. Own shares

C. Current assets
  I   Stocks
      1. Raw materials and consumables
      2. Work in progress
      3. Finished goods and goods for resale
      4. Payments on account
  II Debtors
      1. Trade debtors
      2. Amounts owed by group undertakings
      3. Amounts owed by undertakings in which the company has a participating interest
      4. Other debtors
      5. Called up share capital not paid
      6. Prepayments and accrued income
  III Investments
      1. Shares in group undertakings
      2. Own shares
      3. Other investments
  IV Cash at bank and in hand

D. Prepayments and accrued income
E. Creditors: amounts falling due within one year
      1. Debenture loans
      2. Bank loans and overdrafts
      3. Payments received on account
      4. Trade creditors
      5. Bills of exchange payable
      6. Amounts owed to group undertakings
      7. Amounts owed to undertakings in which the company has a participating interest
      8. Other creditors including taxation and social security
      9. Accruals and deferred income

F. Net current assets (liabilities)
G. Total assets less current liabilities
H. Creditors: amounts falling due after more than one year
      1. Debenture loans
      2. Bank loans and overdrafts
      3. Payments received on account
      4. Trade creditors
      5. Bills of exchange payable
      6. Amounts owed to group undertakings

7. Amounts owed to undertakings in which the company has a participating interest
8. Other creditors including taxation and social security
9. Accruals and deferred income

I. Provisions for liabilities and charges
    1. Pensions and similar obligations
    2. Taxation, including deferred taxation
    3. Other provisions

J. Accruals and deferred income

K. Capital and reserves
    I Called up share capital
    II Share premium account
    III Revaluation reserve
    IV Other reserves
        1. Capital redemption reserve
        2. Reserve for own shares
        3. Reserves provided for by the articles of association
        4. Other reserves
    V Profit and loss account

Format 2

ASSETS

A. Called up share capital not paid
B. Fixed assets
    I Intangible assets
        1. Development costs
        2. Concessions, patents, licences, trade marks and similar rights and assets
        3. Goodwill
        4. Payments on account
    II Tangible assets
        1. Land and buildings
        2. Plant and machinery
        3. Fixtures, fittings, tools and equipment
        4. Payments on account and assets in course of construction
    III Investments
        1. Shares in group undertakings
        2. Loans to group undertakings
        3. Participating interests
        4. Loans to undertakings in which the company has a participating interest
        5. Other investments other than loans
        6. Other loans
        7. Own shares
C. Current assets
    I Stocks
        1. Raw materials and consumables
        2. Work in progress

        3. Finished goods and goods for resale
        4. Payments on account
  II Debtors
        1. Trade debtors
        2. Amounts owed by group undertakings
        3. Amounts owed by undertakings in which the company has a
           participating interest
        4. Other debtors
        5. Called up share capital not paid
        6. Prepayments and accrued income
  III Investments
        1. Shares in group undertakings
        2. Own shares
        3. Other investments
  IV Cash at bank and in hand
D. Prepayments and accrued income

LIABILITIES*

A. Capital and reserves
  I   Called up share capital
  II   Share premium account
  III Revaluation reserve
  IV Other reserves
        1. Capital redemption reserve
        2. Reserve for own shares
        3. Reserves provided for by the articles of association
        4. Other reserves
  V   Profit and loss account
B. Provisions for liabilities and charges
        1. Pensions and similar obligations
        2. Taxation including deferred taxation
        3. Other provisions
C. Creditors
        1. Debenture loans
        2. Bank loans and overdrafts
        3. Payments received on account
        4. Trade creditors
        5. Bills of exchange payable
        6. Amounts owed to group undertakings
        7. Amounts owed to undertakings in which the company has a
           participating interest
        8. Other creditors including taxation and social security
        9. Accruals and deferred income
D. Accruals and deferred income

* This is the word used in the Act, but 'shareholders' funds and liabilities'
would be a better term.

Profit and loss account formats

Format 1
1. Turnover
2. Cost of sales
3. Gross profit or loss
4. Distribution costs
5. Administrative expenses
6. Other operating income
7. Income from shares in group undertakings
8. Income from participating interests
9. Income from other fixed asset investments
10. Other interest receivable and similar income
11. Amounts written off investments
12. Interest payable and similar charges
13. Tax on profit or loss on ordinary activities
14. Profit or loss on ordinary activities after taxation
15. Extraordinary income
16. Extraordinary charges
17. Extraordinary profit or loss
18. Tax on extraordinary profit or loss
19. Other taxes not shown under the above items
20. Profit or loss for the financial year

Format 2
1. Turnover
2. Change in stocks of finished goods and work in progress
3. Own work capitalised
4. Other operating income
5. (a) Raw materials and consumables
   (b) Other external charges
6. Staff costs:
   (a) Wages and salaries
   (b) Social security costs
   (c) Other pension costs
7. (a) Depreciation and other amounts written off tangible and intangible fixed assets
   (b) Exceptional amounts written off current assets
8. Other operating charges
9. Income from shares in group undertakings
10. Income from participating interests
11. Income from other fixed asset investments
12. Other interest receivable and similar income
13. Amounts written off investments
14. Interest payable and similar charges
15. Tax on profit or loss on ordinary activities

16. Profit or loss on ordinary activities after taxation
17. Extraordinary income
18. Extraordinary charges
19. Extraordinary profit or loss
20. Tax on extraordinary profit or loss
21. Other taxes not shown under the above items
22. Profit or loss for the financial year

Format 3

A. Charges
    1. Cost of sales
    2. Distribution costs
    3. Administrative expenses
    4. Amounts written off investments
    5. Interest payable and similar charge
    6. Tax on profit or loss on ordinary activities
    7. Profit or loss on ordinary activities after taxation
    8. Extraordinary charges
    9. Tax on extraordinary profit or loss
    10. Other taxes not shown under the above items
    11. Profit or loss for the financial year
B. Income
    1. Turnover
    2. Other operating income
    3. Income from shares in group undertakings
    4. Income from participating interest
    5. Income from other fixed asset investments
    6. Other interest receivable and similar income
    7. Profit or loss on ordinary activities after taxation
    8. Extraordinary income
    9. Profit or loss for the financial year

Format 4

A. Charges
    1. Reduction in stocks of finished goods and in work in progress
    2. (a) Raw materials and consumables
       (b) Other external charges
    3. Staff costs:
       (a) Wages and salaries
       (b) Social security costs
       (c) Other pension costs
    4. (a) Depreciation and other amounts written off tangible and intangible fixed assets
       (b) Exceptional amounts written off current assets
    5. Other operating charges
    6. Amounts written off investments
    7. Interest payable and similar charges

      8. Tax on profit or loss on ordinary activities
      9. Profit or loss on ordinary activities after taxation
     10. Extraordinary charges
     11. Tax on extraordinary profit or loss
     12. Other taxes not shown under the above items
     13. Profit or loss for the financial year
  B. Income
      1. Turnover
      2. Increase in stocks of finished goods and in work in progress
      3. Own work capitalized
      4. Other operating income
      5. Income from shares in group undertakings
      6. Income from participating interests
      7. Income from other fixed asset investments
      8. Other interest receivable and similar income
      9. Profit or loss on ordinary activities after taxation
     10. Extraordinary income
     11. Profit or loss for the financial year

Self-assessment questions

Suggested answers to the self-assessment questions are given at the end of the book.

1.   Withdrawals by the owner of a sole proprietorship are similar in nature to which of the following for corporations?

   (a) Investments by shareholders.
   (b) Payments to creditors.
   (c) Retained earnings.
   (d) Dividends.

2.   A company's profit and loss account would normally include which of the following items that would *not* be found on an income statement of a sole proprietorship?

   (a) Tax expense.
   (b) Interest income.
   (c) Interest expense.
   (d) Income from operations.

3. The draft balance sheet for Chaton Auto Parts appears as follows:

Chaton Auto Parts		
Balance sheet		
31 December 19xx (£)		

Assets

Cash		50,000	
Short-term investments		40,000	
Debtors		20,000	
Other debts (receivable in one year)		30,000	
Merchandise stock		70,000	
Land held for future use		80,000	
Land		100,000	
Building	100,000		
Less Accumulated depreciation	20,000	80,000	
Trademark		70,000	
Total assets			540,000

Liabilities

Bills payable (due in one year)	50,000	
Creditors	20,000	
Salaries payable	10,000	
Mortgage payable (due in 7 years)	100,000	
Total liabilities		180,000

Owner's equity

Bob Chaton, Capital		360,000
Total liabilities and owner's equity		540,000

The total of current assets is:

(a) £160,000.
(b) £210,000.
(c) £180,000.
(d) None of the above.

4. Consider the balance sheet in Question 3. The total net book value of tangible fixed assets is:

(a) £200,000.
(b) £180,000.
(c) £250,000.
(d) None of the above.

5. Consider the balance sheet in Question 3. The working capital is:

(a) £360,000.
(b) £30,000.
(c) £130,000.
(d) None of the above.

6. The primary source of new accounting rules in the United Kingdom is:

(a) Parliament.
(b) Department of Trade and Industry.
(c) Accounting Standards Board.
(d) Financial Reporting Review Panel.

7. What was the main purpose of financial reporting in the United Kingdom until the second half of the twentieth century:

(a) To aid investors to make financial decisions?
(b) To be the basis for governments to levy taxation?
(c) To make directors accountable for their use of corporate resources?
(d) To keep hundreds of thousands of accountants employed?

Tutorial questions

1. What are the advantages and disadvantages of making rules by Companies Acts as opposed to making them by professional standards?
2. What categories of accounting subject-matter are covered by Companies Acts now? What categories were new in 1981?
3. Who is supposed to obey Accounting Standards? Are they followed in practice?
4. Which sort of standards are most likely to be controversial? Use examples of UK standards to illustrate your answer.
5. What are the fundamental principles that accounts should use when valuing assets and measuring profits? Give specific examples of the use of these principles and their direct effects.
6. The Burnt Norton Co. Ltd was founded on 1 January 19x1 with an authorized share capital of £50,000 made up of ordinary shares of 25p each.

The following trial balance was extracted from its books on 31 December 19x4:

	£	£
Share capital, fully paid		20,000
10% debentures		10,000
Share premium account		5,000
Profit and loss account		5,000
Other reserves		4,000
Debtors and creditors	8,500	7,000
Freehold premises (cost £24,000)	22,000	
Office furniture (cost £5,000)	3,500	
Stock at 1 January	9,500	
Salaries and wages	6,850	
Lighting and heating	500	

Rates	650	
Selling and distribution expenses	2,250	
Other administration expenses	750	
Purchases and sales	22,500	44,500
Cash at bank	18,500	
	95,500	95,500

Additional information:

(a) Stock on hand at 31 December 19x4 was valued at £9,300.
(b) Depreciation is to be provided on the straight-line method as follows:

Freehold premises	5 per cent p.a.
Office furniture	10 per cent p.a.

(c) There is an electricity bill for £50 outstanding.
(d) A full year's interest is due on the debentures.
(e) A provision for bad debts is to be created equal to 5 per cent of debtors.
(f) Rates have been prepaid by £50.
(g) The directors propose that the profits be appropriated as follows:
    (i)   in payment of final dividend of 20 per cent on ordinary shares;
    (ii) the balance to be carried forward.

You are required to:
Prepare the profit and loss account for the year 19x4 and a balance sheet as at 31 December 19x4.

References

Institute of Chartered Accountants in England and Wales (ICAEW) (1981) *Survey of Published Accounts, 1981–2*, London: ICAEW, p. 85.
Lee, T.A. and Tweedie, D.P. (1978) *The Private Shareholder and the Corporate Report*, London: ICAEW.
Nobes, C.W. and Parker, R.H. (1995) *Comparative International Accounting*, Hemel Hempstead: Prentice Hall, ch. 14.
Solomons, D. (1989) *Guidelines for Financial Reporting Standards*, London: ICAEW.

ACCOUNTING UNDER INFLATION

12

The objective of this chapter is to outline some of the problems involved in adjusting accounting information for general and specific price changes. We shall look first at inflation, then at the reasons why inflation causes traditional profit figures to be unrealistic for some purposes and then at the problems that follow from this lack of realism. After that, there is an examination of the possible adjustments to correct accounts for general and specific price changes, and of actual accounting systems proposed in the United Kingdom and elsewhere to deal with the problems caused by changing prices.

12.1 Inflation

Inflation is a general increase in prices that causes a fall in the purchasing power of money. The causes of inflation are widely discussed and disputed, but they are not the province of this book. The average of prices faced by a particular consumer will change at a different rate from the average faced by another. Again, there will be a difference between price changes faced by consumers and those faced by producers. However, it is generally agreed that one useful and easily available general measure of UK inflation is the *index of retail prices*. The index for the average prices in the years 1968–77, with 1970 set at 100, is shown in Table 12.1. This is the period when inflation reached a peak in the United Kingdom.

Such a series of indices as that in Table 12.1 can be used to estimate, for example, how much money was needed by a consumer in 1977 to equal the value of £1,000 in 1973. The answer is about £2,065 (i.e. £1,000 × 254.4/123.2). Also, a measure of the rate of inflation can be calculated from these figures, as shown in Table 12.2. These high rates of inflation help to explain the great interest taken during the 1970s in systems to adjust accounting for the effects of inflation. By contrast the inflation rate for 1995 was 3.4 per cent.

The index of retail prices is produced on a monthly basis by the Department for Education and Employment. There are many technical problems relating to the choice of items involved, their weighting and delays in the collection of information. As far as the input costs and output prices relating to a particular business are concerned, such a general index is not likely to be very informative. The costs of different raw materials and capital equipment may move up (and down) at very different rates.

It is obvious that specific price information is relevant to the planning and

Table 12.1 Index of retail prices, 1968–77

Year	Index
1968	89.2
1969	94.0
1970	100.0
1971	109.4
1972	114.8
1973	123.2
1974	152.0
1975	188.7
1976	219.6
1977	254.4

Sources: Central Statistical Office (1977) *Economic Trends*, No. 3, London: HMSO, p. 96; Central Statistical Office (1978) *Monthly Digest of Statistics*, London: HMSO, May, p. 157.

Table 12.2 Increase in yearly average of the general index of retail prices, 1968–77

Year	Change in index (%)
1968–9	5.4
1969–70	6.4
1970–1	9.4
1971–2	7.1
1972–3	9.2
1973–4	16.0
1974–5	24.2
1975–6	16.6
1976–7	15.8

Source: Calculated from Table 12.1

budgeting of a business. How to take account of it in the reporting of past financial results is not so clear.

12.2 Effects on accounting

The effects of price changes are at their clearest when the valuation of assets in a conventional balance sheet is considered. For example, freehold properties may be recorded and added together at a variety of values, including historical cost and subsequent valuations. Similar properties may be recorded and added together at very different values because they were bought at different times. For those users of a balance sheet who are expecting to gain information about the value of a business, such a balance sheet may be very misleading. Proposed solutions for this problem will be examined later.

The effects on profit measurement are more complicated. Normally, three main deficiencies are identified. In each case the problem concerns *matching* – one of the conventions introduced in Chapter 4 as an important rule in the calculation of profit by the comparison of revenue with expenses. The point here is that, unless adjustments are made to correct for changing prices, some expenses based on *past* costs will be matched against revenues based on *current* sales prices.

The first of the three deficiencies concerns depreciation charges, which may be inadequate because they are based on past costs (i.e. historical costs of fixed assets). This was mentioned at the end of Section 5.1. For example, one year's usage of a machine with no scrap value and a five-year life may more realistically be said to incur a charge of one-fifth of the replacement cost of the asset rather than one-fifth of its historical cost.

Second, it has been mentioned in Section 6.7 that the value of stocks may reasonably be considered to be their replacement cost, because this is what the business would have to pay if it did not already own the stocks or if it were deprived of them. Similarly, the using up of stocks can be said to involve an expense that is equal to their replacement cost rather than their historical cost. This will necessitate a *cost of sales adjustment* to historical cost profit, since the latter only allows for the historical cost of stocks used.

The third deficiency concerns gains and losses on monetary items. A company that borrows money long-term in inflationary periods is making a gain, in the sense that the money that it will eventually pay back will be worth less in real terms. The same factor affects those short-term assets and liabilities which are fixed in money terms. If there is inflation a 'gain' will be made on holding overdrafts and creditors, and a 'loss' will result from holding debtors and cash. Deciding upon the correct treatment of these long-term and short-term monetary items has given rise to the most controversy of the three deficiencies discussed here.

It is generally agreed that, if profit is used to measure the economic performance of a company, historical cost profit is greatly overstated owing to the lack of depreciation and cost of sales adjustments. For most companies an adjustment for net monetary items will work in the opposite direction to the other two adjustments but will be smaller (see below).

Unless this net overstatement of profit is recognized, the usefulness of accounting data for decision-making will be seriously impaired. For example, decisions about what dividends to pay or what pay rises can be afforded may be seriously in error. Even if the company understands the problem, shareholders and employees may not and may press for payments based on historical cost results.

There is a similar problem with corporation tax (and indeed with income tax on the profits of unincorporated businesses). Taxation is levied on taxable profit, which is based on historical cost accounting profit, which is in some sense overstated. Therefore, the effective rate of tax on a more realistic measure of profit will be very high. However, as shown in Chapter 10, there are substantial adjustments involved in the calculation of taxable profit. From the early 1970s to the middle 1980s, two of these adjusted the taxation system for inflation: high first-year capital allowances and stock appreciation relief. The former allowed the full cost of plant and machinery to be deducted in the calculation of taxable profit in the first year, when the replacement cost *was* the historical cost. The latter relief approximated to an adjustment for the cost of sales.

Problems that are perhaps even more serious concern the effects on the decision-making of management. In decisions about prices, type of production, the assessment of the performance of managers and so on, accounting information will be used. Correct decisions require relevant information, which includes adjustments for the effects of inflation.

12.3 General or specific adjustment

The major divide between different systems of accounting for inflation is the divide between those systems which adjust primarily for the changes in prices of the specific assets owned by the business and those which adjust for a general price movement. The latter can be called *current purchasing power accounting* systems. Those current value systems which do not include adjustment for general price changes have been said by some not to be systems of *inflation* accounting at all because they do not take account of the falling value of money. The type of adjustment for depreciation and cost of sales depends upon which system is being used.

The underlying difference between the two systems concerns the concept of *capital maintenance*. In the opening chapters of this book it has been mentioned that one way of measuring profit for a year is to compare the net worth of a business at the beginning of the year with that at its end. Any increase will be the profit, assuming that no capital has been introduced or withdrawn. That is, profit is any excess left over after maintaining the capital of the business.

When there are specific and general price changes, the concept of capital maintenance involves several possible results. Consider a simple business which buys one property for £10,000 with cash introduced by the owner. It may be represented thus:

Balance sheet (£)			
Property	10,000	Capital	10,000
	10,000		10,000

After several years the business sells the property for £15,000. In the meantime the general price index has risen from 100 to 130, and the specific property index has risen from 100 to 145. The business intends to buy a very similar replacement for £14,000 in a more convenient location. What profit does the business make on the sale of the property? The answer depends upon which concept of capital maintenance is being used.

The historical cost concept is that the original nominal money capital should be maintained. Immediately after the original building has been sold, the balance sheet will appear as below, showing a profit of £5,000, which is the current sales revenue *less* the original historical cost. (It has been assumed for the moment that the property has been sold, since this avoids the problem of unrealized profit.)

Historical cost balance sheet (£)			
		Capital	10,000
Cash	15,000	Profit	5,000
	15,000		15,000

An alternative concept is that the business should maintain the purchasing power of the original capital and treat any excess over this as profit. In this case to maintain the real value of the capital to the owners will require £13,000 (i.e. £10,000 × 130/100). This will lead to a profit of £2,000, as shown in the restated balance sheet:

Current purchasing power (CPP) balance sheet (£)			
		Original capital	10,000
		Purchasing power adjustment	3,000
		Current purchasing power capital	13,000
Cash	15,000	Profit	2,000
	15,000		15,000

A further possibility is to hold that the business only makes profit after it has maintained its physical capital intact. This is a current value concept. It need not mean that the exact original assets are maintained, but it does mean that there is the same productive potential. Since the capital figure in this case is represented by the single property, it can be said that to maintain the physical capital will require a figure of £14,500 (i.e. £10,000 × 145/100). This will lead to a profit of £500. The 'specific adjustment' to capital may be called a *capital maintenance reserve*:

Current value balance sheet (£)			
		Original capital	10,000
		Specific adjustment	4,500
		Current value capital	14,500
Cash	15,000	Profit	500
	15,000		15,000

However, it should be noted that the specific property price index is only used as a proxy for more detailed information about the actual replacement cost of the business's asset. In this case the business has decided that it can maintain its productive potential by buying a replacement costing £14,000. When this transaction is completed, it is very clear that the physical capital has been maintained and that the profit on a current value basis should be regarded as £1,000. An alternative way of looking at this is that current 'expense' (replacement cost) has been compared with current sales revenue:

Current value balance sheet (£)

Property	14,000	Original capital	10,000
		Specific adjustment	4,000
		Current value capital	14,000
Cash	1,000	Profit	1,000
	15,000		15,000

These various possibilities are summarized in Table 12.3. There are arguments in favour of each of them. The historical concept is simple to use and avoids the need for subjective estimates. Also, for the purposes of strict accountability there is an advantage in the sense that the accounting system deals only with actual amounts of money received or spent. This makes it easily verifiable.

From the point of view of the owners it may be said that the effect of inflation on the spending power of their capital is more relevant than the specific price changes of the business's assets. If this were the case, a current purchasing power system would be preferred. However, it is more usual in accounting to use the *entity convention*, whereby the business is viewed as being quite separate from the shareholders. It is also a fundamental accounting concept that the business is usually assumed to be a going concern. Therefore it does not intend to return to the owners the assets that represent the capital. Normally (including this case), the business will intend to replace the original property with another of similar productive potential. Since the assets are not to be returned to the owners but to be replaced by similar assets, their specific current value is surely of greater relevance than their general purchasing power.

If this argument is followed, it will lead to the adoption of a current value approach. The use of the specific replacement cost is clearly more accurate than a specific index. However, obtaining the former information before the asset is sold may often be too difficult or too expensive to be practical.

Critics of current value systems have pointed out that, although there are obvious advantages of such systems irrespective of any general movement in prices, they do not take account of *inflation* as previously defined in terms of a general decline in the purchasing power of money. In order to meet this criticism it is possible to combine adjustments for both general and specific price changes. The original capital of the owners can be adjusted for inflation by using a general index. However, the need for the going concern to

Table 12.3 Capital maintenance concepts

Concept	Capital to be maintained	Profit (£)
Historical cost	Historical cost capital	5,000
Current purchasing power	Capital adjusted by general index	2,000
Current value (approximate)	Capital adjusted by specific index	500
Current value (actual)	Capital adjusted by specific replacement cost	1,000

take account of specific price changes can also be recognized. This is done by ensuring that any part of current purchasing power 'profit' that relates to the specific increase in the value of assets is treated as an undistributable holding gain. Returning to the earlier example, the balance sheet will appear thus:

Balance sheet (£)			
Property	14,000	Original capital	10,000
Cash	1,000	Purchasing power adjustment	3,000
		CPP capital	13,000
		Undistributable reserve	1,000
			14,000
		Distributable reserve	1,000
	15,000		15,000

Such a system may be considerd to be too complex for many users of accounts. However, it has the obvious advantage of adjusting the assets for specific price changes and the capital for changes in purchasing power.

Once an approach to capital maintenance has been chosen, the detailed problems of adjusting the accounting system for price changes can be looked at. In practice, balance sheets and profit and loss accounts are required yearly without the above simplifying assumption that the property has been sold. Therefore the assets as well as the capital must be adjusted for specific or general price changes. The adjustments to profit follow from this. For example, the type of adjustment for depreciation will depend upon whether a fixed asset is restated using a general or specific index. If a current value approach is adopted, a fixed asset will be restated using a specific index, and depreciation for a year will be based on this restated amount. This is discussed in the next sections, where actual proposals for new systems of accounting to replace or supplement historical cost are examined.

12.4 Current purchasing power systems

Current purchasing power (CPP) or *general purchasing power* accounting systems are based on historical cost accounts, adjusted with general price index numbers. Such systems were being discussed as long ago as the 1930s. In the early 1970s, when interest in inflation accounting was very strong because of the high levels of inflation mentioned in Section 12.1, many accountancy bodies in the English-speaking world investigated CPP systems. In 1974 a provisional standard (PSSAP 7) was issued by the UK accountancy bodies. This did not become standard practice because of the intervention of the government-sponsored Sandilands Committee in favour of current cost accounting (see Section 12.6). However, about 150 UK companies produced supplementary CPP information in their annual accounts.

The basic task of a CPP system is to translate pounds of different periods into current pounds of uniform purchasing power. Current items in the balance sheet are already in end-of-year pounds, but fixed assets need to be analysed by age and adjusted accordingly, using the general price index.

The profit and loss account adjustments are the three discussed earlier: depreciation, cost of sales and monetary items. In each case the general price index is used, so that all figures are adjusted for *inflation* rather than for specific price changes.

The work involved in producing CPP accounts need not be prohibitive. There are fewer difficulties than those involved with the specific adjustments of current value systems, and CPP accounts remain fairly objective. However, the major reason for the failure of CPP accounting to be adopted in the United Kingdom is the serious doubt about whether the information that it provides is particularly useful. Criticisms have been made about the difficulty of comprehending accounts not produced in 'physical money' terms, about the lack of relevance of adjusting fixed assets, depreciation and stocks by a general index and about the inclusion of monetary gains in published profit figures.

Although CPP accounting has been adopted in some South American countries where rates of inflation have been very high, there seems no chance of its being introduced anywhere in the English-speaking world.

12.5 Current value accounting

The current value of an asset can be considered to be based on one of the three concepts briefly introduced in Chapter 2: *economic value* (EV), *net realizable value* (NRV), and *current replacement cost* (CRC). It would be possible to establish complete accounting systems based on each of these concepts or, alternatively, to combine them in such a system as current cost accounting (see Section 12.6).

12.5.1 Economic value

A current value accounting system based on EVs would have a strong theoretical basis, because the real value of an asset depends upon the discounted future net flows of money from it. However, there are serious practical problems in estimating such future flows and establishing suitable discount rates. The resulting costs would be very high. Also, the attendant subjectivity would make an auditor's job very difficult and reduce the reliability of accounting information. In addition, if the individual assets and liabilities of a business were all to be separately valued using an EV basis, there would be the theoretical problem that cash flows result from assets working in combination. The estimation of the flows resulting from one asset alone is perhaps not a sensible task.

For these reasons no country proposes, or has seriously considered proposing, a system of accounting based mainly on EVs. Nevertheless, EV has been included as a basis to be used in exceptional circumstances within systems such as *current cost accounting*.

12.5.2 Net realizable value

Another possibility is to have a current value system based on NRVs. An example of such a system is *continuously contemporary accounting* (CoCoA), proposed by the Australian academic R.J. Chambers (1975). Under such a system assets are adjusted to NRV, and depreciation is the fall in the NRV of a fixed asset over an accounting period.

This approach may well provide useful information for management making decisions about the future use of assets, for creditors and for banks. However, it is fairly complex and difficult to use. For example, it is not possible to rely on the use of index numbers in the calculation of second-hand values of many fixed assets or partially completed stocks. Therefore individual values must be calculated. Also, major criticisms concern the subjectivity involved and the fact that most businesses have no intention of selling most of their fixed assets in the near future, which casts doubt on the relevance of NRVs. However, as an exceptional basis NRV is included in the proposals for current cost accounting examined in the next section.

12.5.3 Current replacement cost

A third basis for a current value system is CRC. Here the values of fixed assets, for example, are their depreciated CRCs. The gross CRC may be determined by valuers, by suppliers' catalogues or by age analysis of fixed assets followed by the application of specific indices. Suppose that a company buys a machine for £10,000 on 1 January 1995. The machine is expected to have a useful life of five years and no scrap value. It is to be depreciated at 20 per cent per year on a straight line basis. After three years on 31 December 1997, a CRC balance sheet is drawn up. The specific index has risen over the three years from 100 to 140. Therefore the gross CRC, in the absence of more exact information, will be £14,000 (i.e. £10,000 × 140/100). The net CRC will be £5,600 (i.e. £14,000 *less* 60 per cent cumulative depreciation of £8,400). The value of stocks will also be based on their CRC, although this may be difficult to determine in the case of partially worked or finished goods.

One of the problems with CRC for any assets is the difficulty that there may be in finding the cost of an identical replacement. This is particularly obvious in the case of obsolete fixed assets. It is necessary to establish the concept of the *modern equivalent asset*, the current cost of which is adjusted for any improvements that it embodies compared with the asset that it replaces. When the CRCs have been established, the excesses over historical costs are reflected in an asset revaluation reserve.

As far as the profit and loss account is concerned, there are two important adjustments. Depreciation is based on the current cost of fixed assets. It is generally proposed for simplicity that the end-of-year rather than the average-for-the-year CRC of a fixed asset be used. The second adjustment is to eliminate the stockholding gains from profit by increasing the value of stocks used by a cost-of-sales adjustment. This is done by using a company's detailed records or a set of specific indices. It is generally thought that these holding gains should not be regarded as distributable. An adjustment for gains and losses on monetary items is not usually included in CRC systems, which concentrate on specific price changes of physical resources.

CRC is the main basis involved in those current value systems which have been seriously considered or partially introduced in many English-speaking countries and the Netherlands. Such a system is current cost accounting, which will be discussed in the next section. The advantages and disadvantages of CRC will be mentioned there.

12.6 Current cost accounting

During the period in which the accountancy profession was considering a supplementary CPP system, leading up to the issue of PSSAP 7 in 1974, the government became sufficiently concerned about inflation accounting to appoint its own committee of inquiry. The Sandilands Committee, consisting of twelve members, including only three accountants, was appointed in July 1973 and reported in September 1975. It suggested that 'if UK company accounts are to show more adequately than at present the effect of changes in prices, it is accounting practices that must be changed, not the unit of measurement in which accounts are expressed' (Sandilands Committee, 1975: para. 415). The recommendation was that, instead of the supplementary CPP accounts provisionally proposed by the profession, historical cost accounts should be replaced for all companies by a system of current cost accounting (CCA). This would involve the continued use of money as the unit of measurement, the expression of assets and liabilities in the balance sheet at a current valuation, and the measurement of profit after allowing for the *value to the business* of resources consumed.

The profession reacted reasonably well to this opposing point of view. It appointed the Inflation Accounting Steering Group (Morpeth Committee) in January 1976 to examine the Sandilands proposals. The Morpeth Committee adopted these proposals to a large extent and produced an exposure draft, ED 18, in November 1976. The details outlined below apply to both the Sandilands recommendations and ED 18, unless a difference is pointed out.

One of the fundamental proposals in CCA is that assets be shown at their 'value to the business' which means 'the maximum amount of the loss that would be suffered by the company if it were deprived of the assets concerned' (ED 18, para. 183). This *deprival value* concept had been advanced as early as the 1930s for property valuation. Depending on the circumstances the deprival value will be either the CRC, the NRV or the EV of the asset.

Suppose that a business intends eventually to replace a particular machine with an identical new asset. The deprival value of the machine will be the maximum amount that would be lost if the machine were stolen, blew up or disappeared in some other way. In this case the business would buy a replacement, so that the deprival value would be the depreciated CRC. This is the normal case, in which the EV of the machine is greater than the CRC, and the NRV is smaller than the CRC (i.e. EV > CRC > NRV). Thus it would be sensible to replace it and not sensible to sell it. The deprival value is not as high as the EV; this is because the EV would not be lost because the asset would be replaced.

On the other hand, if the business is about to sell the asset because CRC > NRV > EV, the deprival value will be what will be gained from the sale (i.e. the NRV). If the business intends to continue using the asset but not to replace it because CRC > EV > NRV, the deprival value of the asset will be the loss of future revenues from it (i.e. the EV).

Logically, there are six possibilities of arrangement for these three current values, but the above three are the most likely to occur, and that which leads to CRC should apply to the great majority of fixed assets (Gee and Peasnell, 1976). These possibilities can be arranged in diagrammatic form, as in Figure 12.1 overleaf.

The profit and loss account would contain current cost figures for cost-of-sales and depreciation charges. There would be no adjustment for monetary items. Estimates of the effects of CCA on profit figures suggest that there would be a fall of over 50 per cent on average across all industries in a high inflation year such as 1975 (Philips and Drew, 1975). CPP would produce no fall on average, although there would be large sectoral differences.

The advantages of a system of CCA compared with historical cost accounting are said to be that it provides a balance sheet that gives a much better indication of the value of individual assets and a whole business and that CCA profit figures can reasonably be used as measures of distributable profit and business performance and for decisions about prices and output. CCA as proposed in ED 18 was welcomed with reservations by the councils of the accountancy bodies, many of the leading accountancy firms, academics, the government and the Stock Exchange. It was implemented on an experimental and voluntary basis by many large UK companies in the late 1970s.

However, opposition from the bulk of practising accountants and from many companies was strong. Vociferous objections were raised concerning the great complexity of the system and the consequent cost, the impracticability of the EV basis for fixed assets and the expense of finding CRC for stocks, the 'enormous' burden and doubtful value of CCA for small companies, the 'disastrous' effects on profit figures and the planned disappearance of familiar historical cost accounting. This opposition led to a call for a

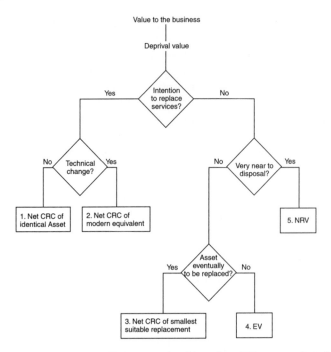

CRC, current replacement cost; NRV, net realizable value; EV, economic value (future earning potential). The information represented on this diagram has been drawn from paras 183–5 and 227–86 of ED18.
Note: The top diamond represents the decision whether to replace the services of the asset fairly exactly. 'Yes' will be the usual answer.
Source: Nobes (1977).

Figure 12.1   ED 18's valuation of plant

vote by the membership of the Institute of Chartered Accountants in England and Wales (ICAEW), which was held in July 1977 and showed a majority against the compulsory replacement of historical cost accounting by CCA.

After this, several further documents were produced by the Accounting Standards Committee (ASC), leading to SSAP 16 in 1980. This required supplementary CCA financial statements from all large and listed companies. However, by the mid-1980s there was increasing non-compliance with this standard as inflation fell. The standard ceased to be mandatory and was eventually formally withdrawn in 1988.

12.7 **Revaluations in the 1990s**

Despite the demise of CCA, there remain worries about the effects of price changes on financial statements. Examples of reactions to these are that:

● Many large British companies revalue their land and buildings from time to time, in order to show a more impressive balance sheet.

- When a new subsidiary's assets are brought into the group accounts for the first time, they are measured at fair value as an estimate of current cost (see Chapter 11).

- Investment properties must be revalued each year in the United Kingdom, according to SSAP 19.

- Financial institutions such as banks revalue many of their investments to market value for each balance sheet, taking gains or losses to income. This is called 'marking to market'. There are proposals to extend this sort of treatment to the financial instruments of all companies.

- In some countries (e.g. the United States, Germany, Italy, Japan), LIFO is used as a way of taking inflationary gains on stocks out of income.

- As noted earlier, CPP systems survive in some South American countries.

- Utility companies in several countries use a version of replacement cost accounting, particularly for the purpose of establishing whether price rises should be allowed.

12.8 Summary

Inflation ran at a very high level in the United Kingdom in the mid-1970s, thus encouraging attempts to adjust historical cost accounting for general or specific price changes. Indices for both are available on a monthly basis. The effects of price changes cause deficiencies in historical cost balance sheets and profit calculations. The effects on profit are the more complex and may involve adjustments for depreciation, for cost of sales and for gains and losses on monetary items. Unless adjustments are made, users of accounts may be seriously misled about the value of a business and about what may be suitable levels of dividends, wages or prices.

Adjusted systems of accounting fall into two groups: those which adjust for general price changes and those which adjust for specific price changes. The underlying difference concerns the concept of capital maintenance. General adjustment aims to maintain the inflation-adjusted value of the owners' capital. Specific adjustment aims to maintain the productive capacity of the business. The choice determines how assets are to be restated, and in each case profit is what remains after the appropriate measure of capital has been maintained. It is possible to combine the two approaches, so that both inflation and specific price changes are taken into account.

A supplementary system of current purchasing power accounting was provisionally proposed in the United Kingdom in 1974. It was adopted by several companies in the following two years. However, the government-sponsored Sandilands Report of 1976 recommended a system of current cost accounting based on adjustments for specific price changes.

Current value systems could be based purely on economic values, on net realizable values or on current replacement costs. Current cost accounting is a system that uses all three bases, although mainly current replacement cost. The Sandilands recommendations for current cost accounting were adopted by the accountancy bodies in ED 18. However, this was rejected by a majority of practising accountants in July 1977 as being too complex, subjective and expensive for a compulsory system for all companies. In 1980, the ASC issued requirements about supplementary current cost accounts, but these soon fell into disuse.

However, several partial adjustment systems remain in use in the United Kingdom and other countries.

Self-assessment questions

Suggested answers to the self-assessment questions are given at the end of the book.

1. Which of the following terms or phrases is most closely associated with current value accounting?

   (a) Specific price changes.
   (b) General price changes.
   (c) Inflation.
   (d) A change in the purchasing power of the pound.

2. Current purchasing power accounting is most closely associated with:

   (a) Specific price changes.
   (b) General price changes.
   (c) Changes in replacement cost.
   (d) Changes in net realizable value.

3. An asset purchased for £1,000 in 1980, when the consumer price index was 116 (1977 = 100) would be restated to what amount today in constant currency terms, assuming today's consumer price index is 200?

   (a) £2,000.
   (b) £1,160.
   (c) £1,724.
   (d) £1,000.

4. During a period of inflation, a company whose monetary liabilities exceed its monetary assets has:

   (a) A net loss in purchasing power.
   (b) A net gain in purchasing power.
   (c) Either a net gain or a net loss in purchasing power.
   (d) Neither a net gain nor a net loss in purchasing power.

Tutorial questions

1. Explain the meaning of 'capital maintenance'.
2. Explain and define the concept of the deprival value of an asset.
3. Arsenale Properties is a small family owned company that only has equity share capital. It has no debt capital. Its net assets at 1 January 19x8 were £1,000, and on the 31 December 19x8 the net assets were £1,400. There have been no issues or withdrawals of share capital during the year. The general rate of inflation, as measured by the Retail Price Index is 10 per cent, whereas the specific rate of inflation for the type of goods sold by the company is 15 per cent.

   Calculate three alternative measurements of profit for the company using:

   (i)   the money maintenance concept,
   (ii) the real capital maintenance concept, and
   (iii) the maintenance of specific purchasing power.

References

Chambers, R.J. (1975) *Accounting for Inflation*, Sydney: University of Sydney Press.
Gee, K.P. and Peasnell, K.V. (1976) 'A pragmatic defence of replacement cost', *Accounting and Business Research*, Autumn.
Institute of Chartered Accountants of England and Wales (ICAEW) (1952) *Accounting in Relation to Changes in the Purchasing Power of Money*, N.15, London: ICAEW, para. 31.
Nobes, C.W. (1977) 'CCA: valuation by intent', *Accounting and Business Research*, Spring.
Phillips and Drew (1975) *Reports*, September and October.
Sandilands Committee (1975) *Inflation Accounting*, London: HMSO.

INTERNATIONAL FINANCIAL ACCOUNTING

13

Study of matters connected with accounting in other countries has usually been omitted from introductory textbooks. However, it is becoming increasingly important and relevant to the study of accounting and so deserves to be examined in a separate chapter. We shall look at the most important countries from the point of view of the United Kingdom, namely the United States, Japan and the principal member states of the European Union (EU).

We noted briefly in Chapter 7 that the development of accountancy over the last seven centuries initially involved several European countries and later became even more international. It has also been seen many times in this book that the pace of change in accountancy has been rapid and accelerating over the last few decades. In such circumstances there is more scope for influences from outside. The development of standard practice in various areas has become much more international. The great expansion in the number of UK subsidiaries overseas and of overseas subsidiaries in the United Kingdom also adds relevance to any study of international accounting.

The effects of all this on UK companies is particularly obvious when moves towards harmonization are examined. The International Accounting Standards Committee (IASC) has become an important body, which affects multinational companies in particular. Also, some of the Directives of the EU on company law have had powerful effects on UK accounting practice.

In this chapter we shall look first at the background areas to accounting, and then more closely at the legal entities, the accounting rules and the published accounts in six countries: the United Kingdom, the United States, France, Germany, Japan and the Netherlands. Finally, there is a section on harmonization.

13.1 Background factors

Over the centuries, various factors have shaped accounting differently throughout the world. As a result, differences in financial reporting are major, deep-seated and long-lasting. The factors related to these differences include the legal system, users of financial statements, the tax system, the profession, the influence of theory, inflation, and accidents. These are discussed briefly in turn below.

There are two major legal systems in the Western developed world: the Roman (generally codified) legal system and the English common law system. The former operates throughout most of continental Europe and usually involves extensive prescription from government. In accounting, this tends to mean that Roman countries have many rules in law or in commercial codes or accounting plans.

In the cases of the Netherlands, France, Germany and Japan, the laws amend the commercial codes; additionally, in the case of France, much of the detail is found in the accounting plan (*plan comptable général*) which is prepared by a government committee and is enforced by law. By contrast, common law countries, such as the United Kingdom and the United States, tend to survive on limited amounts of government-controlled rules. The United Kingdom, for example, has traditionally relied upon professional judgement, although this has increasingly been written down as accounting standards. Rather unfortunately for the neatness of this analysis, the Netherlands is the main continental exception. It has a Roman legal system but, traditionally, there has been little detail in law. With a *laissez-faire*, maritime, mercantile history like that of England it has managed to maintain a 'hands off' approach by government.

The second influential factor is the nature of corporate owners and financiers, and hence users of financial statements. In the United Kingdom and the United States, there is a long history of widespread ownership of shares, and hence the need for published and audited financial statements. By contrast, in much of continental Europe and Japan, corporate finance has traditionally come from banks, governments or family members. This means that the major financiers are board members who can obtain up-to-date detailed information as directors. Consequently, there has traditionally been no great demand for publication of financial reports or for external audit. The small size of the profession in France and Germany is evidence of this, as is the small number of listed companies (see Tables 13.1 and 13.2). Furthermore, many of those comparatively few French and German companies that are listed are extensively held by financial institutions, governments or families. Again, the Netherlands seems a slight anomaly. It has fairly few listed companies; yet it has the longest history of public shares (the Dutch East Indies Company), and many of its companies look very Anglo-American in style (such as Unilever, Philips, Royal Dutch, Akzo).

The third factor is the tax system. Simply put, taxation rules are a strong influence on many of the details of normal continental European or Japanese accounting, such as the valuation of assets, the measurement of depreciation and the calculation of bad debt and other provisions. The principle is at its most obvious in Germany, where the *Massgeblichkeitsprinzip* requires that the figures in the financial accounts form the basis for those in the tax accounts. This is not the case in the United Kingdom, the United States or

Table 13.1 Some professional bodies

Country	Body	Founded[a]	Size (000)
United Kingdom and Ireland	Institute of Chartered Accountants in England and Wales	1880 (1870)	107
	Association of Chartered Certified Accountants	1939 (1891)	47
	Institute of Chartered Accountants of Scotland	1951 (1854)	13
	Institute of Chartered Accountants in Ireland	1888	9
Netherlands	Nederlands Instituut van Registeraccountants	1895	9
France	Ordre des Experts Comptables et des Comptables Agréés	1942	13
Germany[b]	Institut der Wirtschaftsprüfer	1932	7
United States	American Institute of Certified Public Accountants	1887	315
Japan	Japanese Institute of Certified Public Accountants	1948	13

Notes: [a] Date of founding of earliest predecessor is in parentheses. [b] A second tier body, of vereidigte buchprüfer, became important from the late 1980s as auditors of GmbHs.

Table 13.2 Major stock exchanges at 31 December 1995

Country	Exchange	Domestic listed companies	Market capitalization of domestic equities £bn	Market capitalization as % of United Kingdom
Europe				
France	Paris	710	321	35
Germany	Federation of exchanges	437	373	41
Netherlands	Amsterdam	217	185	20
Switzerland	–	216	256	28
United Kingdom	London	2,303	907	100
North America				
Canada	Toronto	1,196	237	26
United States	NASDAQ	4,760	747	82
	New York	2,428	3,714	410
Asia				
Hong Kong	Hong Kong	518	197	22
Japan	Tokyo	1,714	2,284	252
Australasia				
Australia	Australian	1,129	159	18
Africa				
South Africa	Johannesburg	614	181	20

Source: Based on *London Stock Exchange Fact Book 1996*, p.49.

the Netherlands, where taxation rules are different from accounting rules for several matters, sometimes giving rise to substantial amounts of deferred tax.

Fourth, the accountancy profession is old and strong in the United Kingdom, the United States and the Netherlands, where it has played a major part in setting and enforcing the standards for accounting and for auditing. In France, Germany and Japan the profession is newer, smaller and weaker. Governments or government-run committees control most of the rules of accounting and auditing. French, German and Japanese professional pronouncements have much less status than those of the United Kingdom, the United States and the Netherlands.

Theory has been an influence on the uniformity of French accounting and on the use of replacement cost in Dutch accounting. By contrast, until recently UK and US accounting rules have seemed virtually theory-free, developing as they do in a practical *ad hoc* manner.

Differential amounts of inflation have affected accounting. The unpleasant German encounter with hyper-inflation in the 1930s has led to deep opposition to inflation or inflation accounting there. The French have had compulsory revaluation through tax laws. The Dutch have experimented with replacement cost. The British and the Americans have toyed with several different systems, but have no standard response to accounting for price changes.

Lastly, 'accidents' have played their part in causing or lessening differences. The German occupation of France influenced the foundation of the French accountancy profession and the development of uniformity. The American administration of Japan after the Second World War had a major effect on accounting there. The accounting practices of the United Kingdom and the Netherlands are being pulled towards legal prescription because of membership of the EU, although these countries did not join for that purpose!

13.2 Forms of business organization

In the United Kingdom and throughout the EU there are two main types of company legally: public and private. Only the public company is allowed to create a market in its securities. The difference between public and private companies is larger in other countries than in the United Kingdom, where the rules for accounting and other matters are very similar for both types of company. In Japan, there is also a distinction, which is particularly similar to the German company types. These company names are set out in Table 13.3.

In the United States, there are not two legal forms of company, but only the corporation, as was the case in the United Kingdom in the nineteenth century. If an American corporation wishes there to be a market in its

Table 13.3 Company names

	Public	Private
United Kingdom	Public limited company (PLC)	Private Limited Company (Ltd)
France	Société Anonyme (SA)	Société à Responsibilité Limitée (Sàrl)
Germany	Aktiengesellschaft (AG)	Gesellshaft mit beschränkter Haftung (GmbH)
Netherlands	Naamloze Vennootschap (NV)	Besloten Vennootschap (BV)
Japan	Kabushiki Kaisha (KK)	Yugen Kaisha (YK)

securities, it must register with and follow the rules of a government body, the Securities and Exchange Commission (SEC).

13.3 Accounting practices

The causes of differences discussed earlier in this chapter are major, deep-seated and long-lasting. The differences that result must therefore be expected to be considerable. In general terms, for example, one would expect Anglo-Saxon accounting to be less conservative and more interested in providing information specifically for shareholders. The purpose of this chapter is not, of course, to be a detailed practice manual on international accounting. Therefore it may be useful to examine a summary of the typical differences between the two types of country dealt with in the chapter. Table 13.4 presents this.

The effects of the differences summarized in Table 13.4 are that a British profit figure cannot directly be compared with a German one; nor an American price/earnings ratio with a Japanese one, and so on.

These sorts of problems create major difficulties for multinational companies, auditors, investors etc. Not surprisingly, effort has been put into reducing the differences, as discussed below.

13.4 Harmonization

One driving force in the international harmonization of accounting practices is the International Accounting Standards Committee (IASC), formed in 1973 by accountancy bodies of nine countries. It issues Exposure Drafts and Standards in a similar way to the UK's Accounting Standards Board. It is, of course, very difficult to reach agreement on international standards (IASs), and some of them are therefore compromises that allow flexibility. However, the IASC is very useful in promoting international understanding of the problems of harmonization, and many developing countries are able to use the standards as a ready-made package of generally accepted principles.

In 1993 the IASC published ten revised standards from which most of the options had been removed. This was part of a programme of improvements

Table 13.4 A two-group classification

Anglo-Saxon	Continental
Background	
English law	Roman law
Large, old, strong profession	Small, young, weak profession
Large stock exchange	Small stock exchange
General accounting features	
Fair	Legal
Shareholder orientation	Creditor orientation
Disclosure	Secrecy
Tax rules separate	Tax dominated
Substance over form	Form over substance
Professional standards	Government rules
Specific accounting features	
Percentage of completion method	Completed contract method
Depreciation over useful lives	Depreciation by tax rules
No legal reserves	Legal reserves
Finance leases capitalized	No lease capitalization
Funds/cash statements	No funds flow statements
Earnings per share disclosed	No earnings per share disclosure
No secret reserves	Secret reserves
No tax-induced provisions	Tax-induced provisions
Preliminary expenses expensed	Preliminary expenses capitalizable
Taking gains on unsettled foreign currency monetary items	Deferring gains on unsettled foreign currency monetary items
Some examples of countries	
United Kingdom	France
Ireland	Germany
United States	Austria
Canada	Sweden
Australia	Italy
New Zealand	Portugal
Singapore	Japan
Denmark	Belgium
Netherlands	Greece

agreed with the world's stock market regulators (IOSCO). The objective is that, after further improvements (scheduled for completion in 1988/9), IOSCO will accept IASs for the financial statements of foreign companies listed on any stock exchange. So, IASs will become the international language of accounting.

Already, by the mid-1990s a number of large companies in continental Europe were preparing their group accounts using IASs. Group accounts are not relevant for tax, so there is more room for manoeuvre. This trend is increasing, and it seems that IASs may supplant national standards in the long run, even in the United Kingdom.

A more direct source of harmonization in terms of its effects on UK accounting practice so far is the EU, which issues Directives to member governments that must be implemented by legislation through national parliaments. The Directives on company law include several which deal with accounting. In particular the Fourth Directive (of 1978) covers the presentation and content of accounts and methods of valuation (Nobes, 1983), and the Seventh Directive (of 1983) deals with consolidated accounts (Gray and Coenenberg, 1993; Nobes and Parker, 1995).

The arguments for harmonized accounting practices throughout the EU are strong. They include the desire to impose the same legal requirements for all companies that have similar legal forms and operate in competition, and the need to encourage the free flow of investment, trade and labour by ensuring the transmission of reliable homogeneous financial information from all EU companies.

The Fourth Directive owes a considerable debt to German law, but it was redrafted in 1974 and 1978 to include many changes argued by the United Kingdom and Ireland, and supported by the Netherlands. It now demands a number of rules which have involved changes to continental practice. For example, the 'true and fair view' must override accounting rules. Also, SSAP 2's conventions of consistency, prudence, accruals and going concern are clearly established. Exceptional depreciation claimed in the financial accounts and other effects of tax-based accounting must be disclosed. Also, in order to reduce the importance of secret reserves, all value movements must be passed through the profit and loss account. Current liabilities must be separated from non-current liabilities. Extra notes are required about valuation methods, capital commitments, turnover by category and location, directors' emoluments and research and development costs.

UK and Irish practice has been altered by the need for companies to adopt one of two basic formats for the profit and loss account and one format for the balance sheet (in each case, horizontal or vertical styles are allowed). Liabilities, expenses and revenues have to be shown in greater detail and in a more uniform order than previously.

One other important change in the United Kingdom is the division of companies into three groups by size. Private companies that fall below certain 'medium size' or 'small size' criteria are allowed to publish less information. In the case of small companies, they are exempted from publication of profit and loss accounts, from many balance sheet figures and from most notes. However, all companies must still prepare full audited accounts for their shareholders (as opposed to the Registrar of Companies and the public).

In the case of the United Kingdom, all these provisions were introduced in the Companies Act 1981 which has been consolidated into the Companies Act 1985. Table 13.5 shows the dates of implementation in other EU states. It should be noted that the dates of coming into force for companies are after the implementation dates.

The Seventh Directive requires that subsidiaries, both domestic and foreign, be consolidated using the parent company concept and that associated companies be treated by the equity method. This appears to be very similar to UK practice, but there are some important differences, including the

Table 13.5 Implementation of Accounting Directives as laws

	Fourth	Seventh
Denmark	1981	1990
United Kingdom	1981	1989
France	1983	1985
Netherlands	1983	1988
Luxembourg	1984	1988
Belgium	1985	1990
Germany	1985	1985
Ireland	1986	1992
Greece	1986	1987
Spain	1989	1989
Portugal	1989	1991
Italy	1991	1991
Sweden	1995	1995

definition of control. In the case of the United Kingdom, implementation was via the Companies Act 1989 (see Table 13.5).

Harmonization objectives have led not only to Directives but also to proposals for a 'European company' that would be supranational for all purposes, including company law and taxation. This *Societas Europea* is an idealistic approach to the solution of the problems involved in harmonization, but it will be difficult to get national governments to agree about it.

13.5 Summary

The study of international accounting is becoming increasingly relevant to UK accounting, and the effects of harmonization are becoming increasingly noticeable. This explains the attempts of this chapter to introduce an understanding of the effects of different company forms, taxation and legal systems on accounting rules and formats.

We have seen that for many purposes it is useful to divide the countries that are of most importance to the United Kingdom into Anglo-Saxon (including Dutch) and continental. The importance of law and taxation and the lack of importance of public quoted companies and individual shareholders in continental countries and Japan help to explain the difference in aims of accounting.

Consequently, when trying to interpret accounts of continental companies, several problems are met. For example, the accounts are likely to be much more conservative, partly due to what Anglo-Saxon accountants would describe as excessive provisions. Some of this excess is due to the legal necessity to include extra provisions in the published accounts if they are to be claimed for tax.

Harmonization is proceeding with the aid of the IASC and the Directives of the EU. The effects of the Fourth and Seventh Directives are particularly important for published accounts.

There are many interesting problems concerned with international accounting which there is not the space to deal with in this book. For example, there is much debate about whether it is better to translate the accounts of foreign subsidiaries by using the historical rates of exchange or the current year-end rate of exchange.

Self-assessment questions

Suggested answers to the self-assessment questions are given at the end of the book.

1. Professional accountancy bodies were invented by:

    (a) The Romans.
    (b) Fourteenth-century Italians.
    (c) Nineteenth-century Britons.
    (d) Twentieth-century Americans.

2. In which of the following countries are depreciation charges most closely tied to tax rules?

    (a) United States.
    (b) United Kingdom.
    (c) Germany.
    (d) Netherlands.

3. Which country generally has the most conservative income calculations?

    (a) United States.
    (b) United Kingdom.
    (c) Netherlands.
    (d) Japan.

4. Which country has the smallest number of listed companies?

    (a) United States.
    (b) United Kingdom.
    (c) Australia.
    (d) Germany.

5. Which country has the smallest number of auditors?

    (a) United States.
    (b) United Kingdom.
    (c) Canada.
    (d) Japan.

6. International differences of financial reporting might cause difficulties for:

(a) Investors.
(b) Bankers.
(c) Auditors of multinational companies.
(d) Managers of multinational companies.
(e) All of the above.

7. In which of the following countries did consolidated accounts arrive most recently?

(a) United States.
(b) United Kingdom.
(c) Australia.
(d) France.

Tutorial questions

1. Explain for whom international differences in financial reporting are a problem. Are those who suffer doing something about the problem?
2. Are international differences in the accountancy professions the cause or the result of accounting differences?
3. Give examples of the effects on accounting that the dominance of tax rules might have in certain countries.
4. 'In the absence of a strong profession and/or a large stock market, it is the government (via fiscal and legislative agencies) that takes control of accounting regulation.'

Discuss the above in the context of the East European countries.

References

Gray, S.J. and Coenenberg, A.G. (1993) *International Group Accounting*, London: Routledge.
London Stock Exchange Fact Book 1996, London: LSE.
Nobes, C.W. (1983) 'The origins of the harmonising provisions of the 1980 and 1981 Companies Acts', *Accounting and Business Research*, Winter.
Nobes, C.W. and Parker, R.H. (1995) *Comparative International Accounting*, Hemel Hempstead: Prentice Hall, ch.13.

PART III
INTERPRETATION OF FINANCIAL INFORMATION

The three chapters of Part III examine the ways in which the information presented in financial statements may be interpreted. Chapter 14 introduces asset ratios and profitability ratios. Chapter 15 examines a business in terms of cash flows, discussing the measurement and control of liquidity. Finally, Chapter 16 looks at balance sheet and income measures of the value of a business.

PROFITABILITY 14

It has been shown how accounting information is recorded, processed and produced as balance sheets and profit and loss accounts. These financial statements need to be interpreted by their readers, who include the company's existing shareholders, prospective investors and financial and other managers. The exact nature of the problems of interpretation depends upon whether a historical cost or an inflation accounting system has been used to prepare the accounts.

If a company's balance sheet contains historical cost assets and therefore historical cost capital figures, it may well be meaningless to compare its profit-to-capital ratio with that of another company. We have also seen that inflation not only causes historical cost profit to become unrealistic for many purposes but also affects different companies in different ways. Consequently, to compare profitability ratios using conventional profit and asset figures will lead to results that are somewhere between not very useful and highly misleading. Part of the reason for this is, of course, the traditional importance of the stewardship role of accounting, which is not primarily concerned with investment decision-making. Another issue to beware of is that comparisons of accounting figures or ratios across countries are likely to be misleading because of all the international differences outlined in Chapter 13.

With these warnings, in this chapter we start by looking at ways of combining accounting figures for use in analysis. Then, various ratios connected with the profitability of a company will be discussed.

14.1 Definitions of accounting aggregates

Published balance sheets and profit and loss accounts have been illustrated and discussed in Chapter 11. Various totals and subtotals within such accounts will be useful both by themselves and as parts of ratios for comparison with other years and other companies. Depending on the format of a set of accounts, different totals will become obvious. With a horizontal format, the totals for fixed assets, current assets, all assets, shareholders' funds, long-term funds, current liabilities and all liabilities and capital should be clear. This is illustrated in Table 14.1.

Clearly, total assets (TA) equals total capital and liabilities (TK). However, various other relationships, such as those involving working capital (WK) and net assets (NA), are not made clear. Using a vertical format, as in Table 14.2, it is easier to do this. This time comparative figures for the previous year are included, as they should be for published accounts.

Table 14.1 Abbreviated balance sheet of Ay Ltd as at 31 March 1998 (£000)

Land and buildings		900	Ordinary shares	1,000
Plant and machinery		800	Share premium	500
Fixtures and fittings		200	Reserves	500
Total fixed assets		1,900	Shareholders' funds	2,000
			Debentures	1,000
Stock	600		Long-term sources of funds	3,000
Debtors	600		Overdraft	200
Cash	400		Creditors	300
Total current assets		1,600	Total current liabilities	500
Total assets		3,500	Total capital and liabilities	3,500

Table 14.2 Abbreviated balance sheet of Ay Ltd as at 31 March 1998 (£000)

		1998			*1997*
Fixed assets:					
Land and buildings		900			800
Plant and machinery		800			700
Fixtures and fittings		200			200
Total fixed assets		1,900			1,700
Current assets:					
Stock	600		400		
Debtors	600		400		
Cash	400	1,600	200	1,000	
Current liabilities:					
Overdraft	200		200		
Creditors	300	500	200	400	
Working capital		1,100			600
Total assets less current liabilities		3,000			2,300
Debentures		1,000			500
Net assets		2,000			1,800
Ordinary shares		1,000			1,000
Share premium		500			500
Reserves		500			300
Shareholders' funds		2,000			1,800

Using *FA* for fixed assets, *CA* for current assets, *CL* for current liabilities, *SF* for shareholders' funds and *D* for debentures and other loans, the following relationships can be seen in one of the two formats of balance sheet:

$$TA = FA + CA$$
$$WK = CA - CL$$
$$NA = FA + WK - D$$
$$NA = SF$$
$$TA = TK$$
$$TK = SF + D + CL$$
$$SF = TA - D - CL$$

If we wished to compare the size of one company with its previous size or with the size of another company, we might use the total assets or the net assets figure. However, this would be a misleading measure if, say, a heavy engineering company were being compared with a financial institution. Other measures (e.g. turnover, staff employed) should be used as well to obtain a broader picture.

If more complicated comparisons (e.g. profitability, liquidity) are to be performed, straightforward comparisons of single figures are totally inadequate. For example, a very large company may have a bad year and make only £50,000 profit. This may be the same profit as a small company employing just a few people. It would clearly be ridiculous to suggest that they are similarly profitable. It is for this type of reason that the above aggregates are used by incorporating them into ratios.

14.2 Asset ratios and gearing

Some ratios can be calculated without using turnover or profit figures from the profit and loss account. For example, the ratio of current assets to total assets can be calculated for Ay Ltd:

$$\frac{CA}{TA} = \frac{1998}{3,500} = 46\% \qquad \frac{1,000}{2,700} = 37\%$$

This shows that a growing proportion of the company's assets is being held in the form of current assets. This may mean that the current assets could be used more productively. An extremely large number of ratios can be calculated, but the analyst should take care to ensure that all the ratios actually mean something. For example, the ratio CL/FA is of doubtful worth.

There are many ratios that contribute to the measurement of a company's liquidity. For example, the *liquidity ratio* compares current assets and current liabilities (CA/CL), and the *quick ratio* compares current assets *less* stock (which is not very current) with current liabilities. These ratios, and other liquidity ratios concerned with turnover of debtors, stock and creditors, will be discussed in Chapter 15.

The concept of *gearing* has already been met in Chapter 10, where it was useful in discussing sources of long-term company finance. This is a further case where ratios help in the comparison over time and between companies. Using the above abbreviations, two of the possible gearing ratios are $D/(SF + D)$, and D/SF.

It is important to ensure that the denominator and the numerator are kept consistent for all ratios being compared. For example, problems may arise with what to include in long-term capital. It can be sensibly argued that an overdraft is long-term capital, which differs very little from debentures for the purposes of gearing calculations. Also, such items as deferred taxation may not be consistent from company to company, thus necessitating adjustments.

Preference shares have seldom been issued since 1965 but remain as a past source of finance in many companies. These are similar to debentures because they have a fixed dividend, but they are similar to ordinary shares because the dividend does not have to be paid. It may be sensible to include them in fixed interest capital for the purposes of capital gearing in order to see how well the ordinary shareholders will fare when profit rises. However, when measuring the risks involved due to compulsory yearly payments, preference dividend could be excluded from fixed payments for the calculation on income gearing (see Section 10.6).

14.3 Profitability ratios

The various profit figures that are calculated and published have been mentioned in Chapters 10 and 11; the items added and subtracted include interest, taxation, extraordinary items and dividends. Therefore, when one profit figure is being compared with another, care is needed to ensure that like is being compared with like. The same applies to the choice of profit figures as parts of ratios.

It is necessary to be consistent not only from year to year and from company to company but also from numerator to denominator. For example, if a profit-to-capital-employed ratio were being calculated, profit should include debenture interest if capital includes debentures. The choice of the profit and capital figures will be determined by the availability of information and the purpose to which the ratio is being put.

Such return-on-capital ratios can be illustrated using the capital and profit figures of Bee Ltd in Table 14.3. Possible profit-to-capital ratios for Bee Ltd include:

		1998		1999
(1) $\dfrac{\text{Net profit before interest and tax}}{TK}$		$\dfrac{1{,}000}{10{,}000} = 10.0\%$		$\dfrac{1{,}250}{13{,}000} = 9.6\%$
(2) $\dfrac{\text{Net profit before interest and tax}}{SF + D}$		$\dfrac{1{,}000}{8{,}000} = 12.5\%$		$\dfrac{1{,}250}{10{,}000} = 12.5\%$
(3) $\dfrac{\text{Net profit after interest and tax}}{SF}$		$\dfrac{340}{5{,}000} = 6.8\%$		$\dfrac{390}{5{,}500} = 7.1\%$

The third ratio uses profit after preference dividend, and capital that does not include preference shares. The profit figure in this case could be called 'earnings'. This ratio is a good way of measuring the return on shareholders'

Table 14.3 Return on capital for Bee Ltd (£000)

		1998		1999
CAPITAL				
Ordinary shares of £1 nominal value		4,000		4,000
Reserves (partly distributable)		1,000		1,500
Ordinary shareholders' funds		5,000		5,500
Preference shares (£1, 6%)		1,000		1,000
Debentures (10%)		2,000		3,500
Long-term capital		8,000		10,000
Current liabilities		2,000		3,000
Total capital		10,000		13,000
PROFIT				
Net profit before interest and tax		1,000		1,250
less Interest		200		350
Net profit before tax		800		900
less Tax		400		450
Net profit after tax		400		450
Balance of profit brought forward		460		600
Profit available for distribution		860		1,050
less Dividends:				
Preference	60		60	
Ordinary	200	260	300	360
Balance of profit carried forward		600		690

funds from year to year or from company to company. Ordinary shareholders benefit from the profit after interest, tax and preference dividend.
However, if a measure of the efficiency of management were needed, one of
the two other ratios would be better, because management has less control
over interest, tax and preference dividends under most circumstances. The
first two ratios measure profit from the wider point of view of the whole
company rather than just the shareholders. In the case of Bee Ltd, we can
see that the company's profitability on total capital is being approximately
maintained and that the return on shareholders' funds is slightly increasing.

If there are exceptional or extraordinary losses or gains in any year, the
analyst should consider whether or not to include them in the profit figure.
The argument for exclusion is that they may relate to several past years and
that they are not expected to recur. Thus, from the point of view of measuring the efficiency of a company for one year in a way that can be compared
with other years or other companies they should be excluded. However, it
may be argued that, since exceptional and extraordinary items affect the
earnings that are available for distribution to shareholders, they should be
included in earnings.

The official requirement (as in SSAP 3) for disclosure of earnings per share
(EPS) requires all such items to be included. However, many companies
provide supplementary EPS figures which *exclude* extraordinary items and
many types of exceptional items. The *Financial Times* also uses this basis.

Analysis here can be continued by looking at the earnings per share and the dividends per share. For further ratios let us assume that the market price of the £1 nominal value shares in Bee Ltd is now £1.50 for both years. Then:

		1998		1999
(4) Earnings per share	$\dfrac{340}{4{,}000}$ =	8.5p	$\dfrac{390}{4{,}000}$ =	9.75p
(5) Earnings yield	$\dfrac{0.085 \times 1 \times 100}{1.5}$ =	5.7%	$\dfrac{0.0975 \times 1 \times 100}{1.5}$ =	6.5%
(6) Price/earnings (P/E)	$\dfrac{1.5}{0.085}$ =	17.6	$\dfrac{1.5}{0.0975}$ =	15.4
(7) Dividend per share	$\dfrac{200}{4{,}000}$ =	5.0p	$\dfrac{300}{4{,}000}$ =	7.5p
(8) Dividend yield	$\dfrac{0.05 \times 1 \times 100}{1.5}$ =	3.3%	$\dfrac{0.075 \times 1 \times 100}{1.5}$ =	5.0%

Earnings are split into retained profits and dividends, both of which belong to the shareholders. Some shareholders prefer small dividends, with consequently higher capital gains, because the tax on dividends is higher than the tax on capital gains for some taxpayers. Others may prefer a high dividend yield, because they want a substantial regular income.

Companies that are expected to earn higher profits in the future often have high price/earnings ratios. This is because investors are willing to pay a higher price than the company's present earnings suggest in order to gain the benefits of future earnings.

These various ratios (4)–(8) are called *investors' ratios* and may be used, in conjunction with other information about the strength of a company's management, customer goodwill and so on, when deciding whether to buy or sell shares.

14.4 Profit and sales ratios

An interesting way to look further into differences in return-on-capital ratios is to use the sales figure for ratios, thus:

$$\frac{\text{profit}}{NA} = \frac{\text{profit}}{\text{sales}} \times \frac{\text{sales}}{NA}$$

A company will be able more easily to explain falls in profitability or to plan for increases in profitability by studying these secondary ratios. This can be illustrated using the figures for Sea Ltd in Table 14.4. The ratios may now be calculated:

	1997		1998
$\dfrac{\text{profit}}{\text{NA}}$	$\dfrac{1{,}300}{10{,}000} = 13.0\%$		$\dfrac{1{,}400}{12{,}000} = 11.7\%$
$\dfrac{\text{profit}}{\text{sales}}$	$\dfrac{1{,}300}{4{,}000} = 32.5\%$		$\dfrac{1{,}400}{5{,}000} = 28.0\%$
$\dfrac{\text{sales}}{\text{NA}}$	$\dfrac{4{,}000}{10{,}000} = 40.0\%$		$\dfrac{5{,}000}{12{,}000} = 41.7\%$

This shows that the sales-to-capital ratio has actually improved and that the problem of falling profitability is due to a falling profit-to-sales ratio. This does not mean that efforts should not be made to increase turnover for a given capital, but it does suggest that particular attention needs to be given to the profitability of each sale.

The profit-to-sales ratio can be split down further for Sea Ltd:

$$\frac{\text{profit}}{\text{sales}} = \frac{\text{sales}}{\text{sales}} - \frac{\text{labour}}{\text{sales}} - \frac{\text{administration}}{\text{sales}} - \frac{\text{marketing}}{\text{sales}}$$

	1997		1998
$\dfrac{\text{labour}}{\text{sales}}$	$\dfrac{1{,}000}{4{,}000} = 25.0\%$		$\dfrac{1{,}400}{5{,}000} = 28.0\%$

Table 14.4 Sales and profit of Sea Ltd (£000)

	1997		1998	
		4,000		5,000
Sales				
less Labour	1,000		1,400	
less Materials	800	1,800	1,100	2,500
Gross profit		2,200		2,500
less Administration	700		800	
less Marketing	200	900	300	1,100
Net profit		1,300		1,400
Net assets		10,000		12,000

$$\frac{\text{materials}}{\text{sales}} \quad \frac{800}{4,000} = 20.0\% \qquad \frac{1,100}{5,000} = 22.0\%$$

$$\frac{\text{administration}}{\text{sales}} \quad \frac{700}{4,000} = 17.5\% \qquad \frac{800}{5,000} = 16.0\%$$

$$\frac{\text{marketing}}{\text{sales}} \quad \frac{200}{4,000} = 5.0\% \qquad \frac{200}{5,000} = 4.0\%$$

The ratios show that it is increases in labour, materials and marketing costs per sale that are causing the fall in profit on sales and hence in the profitability of the company. In real situations the problem of inflation will make this analysis much more difficult. The measurement of profit will be more complex, and different rates of inflation may be working on sales, labour, materials and so on. This will make it hard to identify the costs that really need control and how to control them.

A simple way to present these last ratios is to make an extra column on the profit and loss account and to use it to express all figures as percentages of the sales figure. For Sea Ltd in 1997 this would appear as in Table 14.5.

When comparing this with Sea Ltd in 1998 or with other companies, it will be useful to know that the gross margin on sales is 55 per cent, and so on. Unfortunately, using *published* accounts it will not always be possible to analyse them in this detail.

Just as it is possible to break the profit-to-sales ratio down, so it is possible to analyse the sales-to-assets ratio further:

Table 14.5 Sales and profit of Sea Ltd (£000) and percentages of sales

		1997	%
Sales		4,000	100.0
less Labour	1,000		25.0
less Materials	800		20.0
		1,800	45.0
Gross profit		2,200	55.0
less Administration	700		17.5
less Marketing	200		5.0
		900	2.5
Net profit		1,300	32.5

This may reveal, for example, that the ratio is worsening mainly because an increasing amount of working capital is needed for each unit of sales. As before, this may not be controllable, but an area for investigation will have been identified.

14.5 Summary

Interpretation of financial information is a hazardous process. Figures by themselves are of little use for decision-making. The comparison of figures from different years or different companies involves problems of consistency. Comparisons using historical cost information after years of heavy inflation may be dangerously misleading. International differences add other problems.

Ratios and percentages are useful because they put figures into context. There are many ratios, which can be used for different purposes. Profitability ratios, investors' ratios, liquidity ratios and gearing ratios have been considered here and in other chapters. Profitability ratios can be split into profit-to-sales and sales-to-capital ratios. These in turn can be split further to identify areas that need attention.

Often, there will be insufficient information for the calculation of the most suitable ratio. This may not matter, because trends in a substitute ratio may provide similar information. In general it is important to achieve consistency from year to year, company to company and numerator to denominator. When this is done and when current information is used, the various analytical techniques mentioned in the chapter should prove very useful in helping to interpret financial information.

Self-assessment questions

Suggested answers to the self-assessment questions are given at the end of the book.

1. The net assets of a company equal:

    (a) Current assets *minus* current liabilities.
    (b) Total assets *minus* current liabilities.
    (c) Shareholders' funds *minus* liabilities.
    (d) Shareholders' funds.

2. High gearing:

    (a) Is always good.
    (b) Is always bad.
    (c) Can be either good or bad.

3. If a company's share price falls, what happens to its P/E ratio and dividend yield?

P/E ratio	Dividend yield
(a) Increase	Increase
(b) Increase	Decrease
(c) Decrease	Increase
(d) Decrease	Decrease

4. EPS x P/E ratio gives:

(a) Market captialization.
(b) Earnings yield.
(c) Market price.
(d) Return on equity.

Tutorial questions

1. When comparing different enterprises over the same period, careful consideration needs to be given to the accounting policies chosen by the enterprises. Why is such consideration important, and what effects can changes in accounting policies have on an organization's reported profitability?

2. The finance department for the XYZ company has recently developed a computer model to assist in the prediction of profits, balance sheets and cash flows. By entering the sales forecast and the values of various parameters the model will print data about profit and an outline balance sheet. The parameters are as follows:

Gross profit as % sales	60%
Selling expenses as % sales	15%
Fixed costs, excluding interest	£12,000
Tax rate on profits	40%
Pre-tax return on capital employed	20%
Debt : equity ratio	1 : 2
Interest rate % on debt	10%
Ratio of fixed to net current assets	1 : 1
Current ratio	3
Ordinary dividend as % profit	25%

Making any assumptions you feel appropriate you are required to:

(a) Prepare a profit statement based upon the above factors which show, using a forecast sales figure of £80,000:

(i) net profit before interest and tax;
(ii) earnings available for distribution;
(iii) ordinary dividends.

(b) Determine the book value of long-term debt and current liabilities.

3. 'Financial ratios are only as good as the accounting information upon which they are based'. Discuss.
4. Explain the importance to management and to the shareholders of the debt: equity ratio.

Further reading

Holmes, G. and Sugden, D. (1994) *Interpreting Company Reports and Accounts,* 5th edition, Hemel Hempstead: Woodhead-Faulkner.

Lumby, S. (1994) *Investment Appraisal and Financial Decisions*, 5th edition, London: International Thomson Business Press.

Pendlebury, M. and Groves, R. (1994) *Company Accounts: Interpretation, Analysis and Measurement,* 3rd edition, London: International Thomson Business Press.

LIQUIDITY 15

Liquidity is very important for a company. If lack of control leads to too little liquidity, the company may be forced out of business by its creditors, who may be demanding to be paid. If there is too much liquidity, this is very expensive, because liquid assets are usually unproductive.

In this chapter we look at the company as a cash flow system, and then at the relationship between profit and liquidity. After this, methods of measurement and control of liquidity will be discussed, including cash flow statements and liquidity ratios. The reasons for, and the costs of, holding stocks, debtors, cash and creditors will be examined, in order to learn how to control them. Then cash forecasts and budgets are introduced.

Liquidity has been used to mean the level of liquid resources in the context of the expected calls to be made on them. There are other useful expressions to which more precise meanings can be given. *Solvency* is a state in which a company is able to pay its debts as they fall due. A company may be technically insolvent yet still able to survive if creditors can be persuaded to postpone their claims or if a third party is prepared to rescue the company. *Working capital* is the difference between current assets and current liabilities.

15.1 The cash flow cycle

In order to understand liquidity it will be useful to look at a company in terms of the generation and use of cash. In a simple case where stock is bought for cash and then sold for cash, the company's cash flow system can be presented as in Figure 15.1.

Usually, of course, some stock will be bought on credit, and some sales will be made on credit. This will mean that at most points in time there are outstanding debtors and creditors as well as amounts of stock and cash. This flow is pictured in Figure 15.2.

In order to include all the elements of working capital in our diagram we must add short-term borrowing and lending. There will be occasions when a company has either an unnecessarily large amount of cash or insufficient cash to remain solvent. This will usually lead to an adjustment of short-term borrowing or lending. For completeness it should be noted that tax payments and dividends need to be added to expenses as uses of cash. This leads to Figure 15.3.

It is easy to see that many of the flows that affect cash have no effect on profit. For example, since accounting profit is measured by using the accruals concept, credit sales are recognized before cash is received, and credit purchases are also included in the trading account irrespective of whether cash has been paid. Also, payments may not affect profit if they

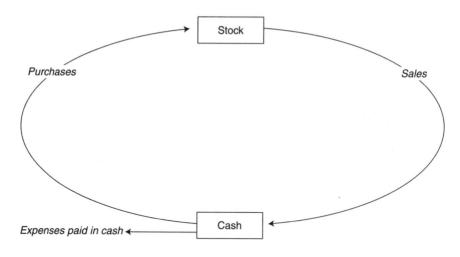

Figure 15.1 A simple cash cycle

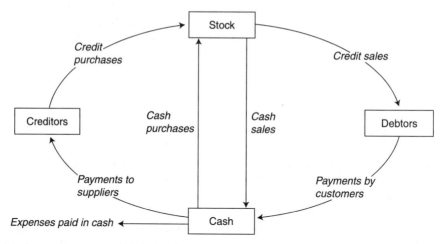

Figure 15.2 Cash cycle with debtors and creditors added

relate to a different year. Dividends are appropriations of profit, and so they affect cash but not profit. Neither does the adjustment of short-term monetary assets and liabilities affect profit. There are also long-term uses and sources of funds that do not affect profit. For all these reasons a *profitable* company may still have serious liquidity difficulties. Attention needs to be paid to the control of liquidity as a quite separate activity from seeking to maximize profit or pursuing any other of the company's objectives.

The long-term sources of funds mentioned above include inflows of cash resulting from share or debenture issues. The uses include the purchase of fixed assets or the redemption of debentures. This gives Figure 15.4.

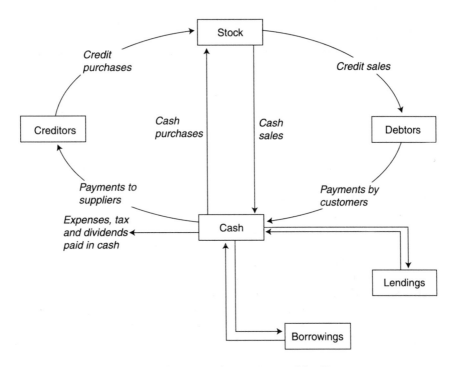

Figure 15.3 Cash cycle with short-term borrowing and lending

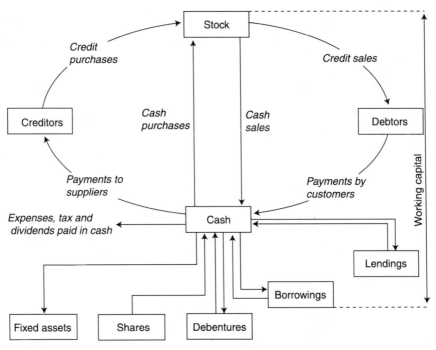

Figure 15.4 Cash cycle with long-term flows added

In many companies, current liabilities can be looked upon as financing much or all of the current assets. The balance, which has been called *working capital*, should be regarded as a long-term requirement of a company and should be financed by long-term capital.

15.2 Flow statements

One way of presenting information about the liquidity of a company is through a *flow statement*. There are many possible formats for such statements. In this section we shall look at one of the simplest. In the following section we shall look at particular rules and formats as proposed in the United Kingdom.

The simplest form of flow statement starts with the opening balance of cash at the beginning of the year and explains the various uses and sources that lead to the closing cash balance. Such statements record the changes in the various totals represented by boxes in the above diagrams. The statements should help their readers to understand the cause of any liquidity problems and the reasons for the difference between profit and liquidity.

Let us look at an example, starting with the simplified opening and closing balance sheets of Apollo Ltd (Table 15.1). In this simple case let us assume that there are no dividends or tax payments or sales of fixed assets.

A cash flow statement could use the differences between each item on the balance sheets to explain the difference in cash as in Table 15.2. The depreciation for the year can be seen to be £200, as the difference between the cost and net figures for plant has risen from £500 (i.e. £2,000 − £1,500) to £700 (i.e. £3,000 − £2,300). This depreciation is added back under profit in the cash flow statement, because depreciation has caused a reduction in profit but not in cash. For the same reason it can be seen that the amount spent on new plant is not the £800 difference between the net figures but £200 greater than this.

The stocks, debtors and creditors changes have been included because they correct for the fact that not all the profit is in the form of cash. For example, the fact that stocks have increased by £30 means that £30 of the

Table 15.1 Apollo Ltd balance sheets as at 31 December (£)

	1997	1998		1997	1998
Land	2,340	2,600	Share capital	4,000	4,000
Plant			Reserves	700	1,500
(cost 2,000)	1,500				
(cost 3,000)		2,300			
			Loan	500	1,100
Stocks	630	660	Creditors	840	1,000
Debtors	1,260	1,780			
Cash	310	260			
	6,040	7,600		6,040	7,600

Table 15.2 Apollo Ltd: changes affecting cash, 1998 (£)

Opening cash		310
Sources of cash:		
Profit	800	
Correction for depreciation	200	
Loans	600	
Creditors	160	1,760
		2,070
less Uses of cash:		
Land	260	
Plant	1,000	
Stocks	30	
Debtors	520	1,810
Closing cash		260

profit is not in the form of cash. Also, even that profit which has been received in cash may be spent in various ways (e.g. buying more fixed assets). Consequently, a substantial profit may be made while the cash resources actually fall, as in this example. Cash flow statements should help to explain such situations to businessmen, shareholders and creditors.

15.3 Cash flow statements

Cash flow statements are required by FRS 1 (as revised in 1996). The standard requires the statements to show cash flows under eight headings (as illustrated later) which then explain the change in the cash figure over the year.

Let us use a rather more complicated example than that in the previous section to illustrate a suggested format for cash flow statements. Jupiter Ltd has the balance sheets and profit and loss account extracts shown in Tables 15.3 and 15.4 respectively.

Assuming that no fixed assets were sold, the cash flow statement prepared according to FRS 1 would be like that shown in Table 15.5. Comparative figures have been omitted for simplicity.

The dividends and tax actually paid in cash during the year are the amounts that should be included as cash outflows. In this case they are the £7,000 and £42,000 relating to the previous year. The cash flow statement still works because the dividend and tax relating to the current year are added back into the profit figure. So, as with every other item, the figures for both years (or difference between them) are used in the cash flow statement.

Table 15.3 Jupiter Ltd balance sheets as at 31 December (£000)

		1997			1998	
ASSETS						
Fixed assets:						
Property and plant		900			1,000	
less Depreciation		45	855		140	860
Current assets:						
Stock	230			270		
Debtors	180			190		
Investments	40			30		
Cash	29	479		30	520	
Current liabilities:						
Overdraft	80			100		
Taxation	42			50		
Creditors	170			160		
Proposed dividend	7	299		8	318	
Net current assets			180			202
Total assets less						
current liabilities			1,035			1,062
Debentures			300			100
Net assets			735			962
Ordinary shares			200			300
Reserves			535			662
Shareholders' funds			735			962

Table 15.4 Jupiter Ltd extracts from the profit and loss account for the year ending 31 December 1998 (£000)

Profit before depreciation	320
less Depreciation	95
Operating profit	225
less Interest	40
Net profit before tax	185
less Taxation	50
Profit after tax	135
less Ordinary dividends	8
	127

15.4 The measurement of liquidity

Cash flow statements provide some help in measuring and understanding changes in liquidity. More precise measurements of changes and comparisons with other companies can be achieved by using liquidity ratios, some of which have been met in Chapter 14. In that chapter it was pointed out that ratios are useful because they put changes into context. For example, the change in the ratio of current assets to current liabilities is likely to be more informative than the change in the size of working capital.

Table 15.5 Jupiter Ltd statement of cash flows for the year ending 31 December 1998 (£000)

Operating profit	225
Depreciation	95
Increase in stocks	(40)
Increase in debtors	(10)
Decrease in creditors	(10)
Net cash inflow from operating activities	260
Returns on investments and servicing of finance[a]	(40)
Taxation	(42)
Capital expenditure	(100)
Equity dividends paid	(7)
Management of liquid resources	10
Financing[b]	(100)
Decrease in cash[c]	(19)

Notes: a The interest expense.
 b The shares issued (+100) and the loans redeemed (−200).
 c The cash difference (+1) and the overdraft difference (−20).

The liquidity ratios for Jupiter Ltd (the accounts of which are in the previous section) are as follows:

		1997	1998

$$\text{current ratio} = \frac{\text{current assets}}{\text{current liabilities}} \qquad \frac{479}{299} = 1.60 \qquad \frac{520}{318} = 1.64$$

$$\begin{array}{l}\text{quick ratio} \\ \text{(or acid test)}\end{array} = \frac{\text{quick assets}}{\text{quick liabilities}} \qquad \frac{249}{177} = 1.41 \qquad \frac{250}{168} = 1.49$$

The quick ratio excludes stock on the grounds that a going concern must usually replace stock immediately and that, at least in manufacturing companies, it may take months for stock to become cash (see below). To keep the current liabilities consistent with this it seems reasonable to exclude the overdraft, which may well last for more than one year, and the taxation in those cases when payments are not due for many months.

Using these definitions the current ratio remains much the same for the two years but the quick ratio shows a slight increase. There can be no overall guidelines as to what are safe levels for these ratios. Companies with a large proportion of sales on credit and the need for large stocks may have to keep current ratios well above 1.5 and quick ratios above 1.0. Such companies include manufacturers of heavy engineering equipment. On the other hand, such companies as supermarkets or chain stores may make all their sales for cash and have a very high rate of stock turnover. They may also dominate their suppliers to such an extent that they are never in danger of being sued for settlement of debts. In these cases current ratios may be safe even below 1.0, and quick ratios may fall to 0.2.

Because of the costs involved in holding large stocks or debtors balances and because of the unproductive nature of cash, it is important to guard against liquidity ratios that are too high as well as those that are too low.

Other ratios that are useful for understanding the changes in liquidity ratios include *debtors' turnover, stock turnover* and *creditors' turnover*. Let us assume that the following extra information about Jupiter Ltd is known, in addition to that shown above in the previous section:

(1)   At 31 December 1996 (£000):
   Stock 240
   Debtors 170
   Creditors 180
The changes in these totals have taken place smoothly over the two years.

(2)   Sales and purchases were (£000):

	1997	1998
Purchases (all on credit)	900	1,070
Cash sales	100	130
Credit sales	1,360	1,740

The ratios below can be calculated from this information. In each case average figures are used for the numerators. For example, the stock for 1997 is taken to be the average between the £240,000 at the beginning of the year and the £270,000 at the end of the year:

$$\text{Stock turnover} = \frac{\text{average stock}}{\text{purchases}} \times 365$$

	1997	1998
	$\dfrac{255 \times 365}{900}$	$\dfrac{285 \times 365}{1{,}070}$
	= 103 days	= 97 days

$$\text{Debtors' turnover} = \frac{\text{average debtors}}{\text{credit sales}} \times 365$$

	1997	1998
	$\dfrac{175 \times 365}{1{,}360}$	$\dfrac{185 \times 365}{1{,}740}$
	= 47 days	= 39 days

$$\text{Creditors' turnover} = \frac{\text{average creditors}}{\text{credit purchases}} \times 365$$

	1997	1998
	$\dfrac{175 \times 365}{900}$	$\dfrac{165 \times 365}{1{,}070}$
	= 71 days	= 56 days

Looking at the values of these ratios we can see that Jupiter has made useful moves in the direction of reducing stocks and debtors but that it has not been able to extract as much credit as previously. The average length of time that money is tied up as stock and then debtors for credit sales is still as high as 136 days in the second year. The importance of these changes will be discussed in the following sections.

There will be problems in finding the necessary information for these ratios from published accounts. For example, since both stock and creditors are in terms of cost prices, the purchases or cost-of-goods-sold figure should be used in ratios with them. These figures are not always disclosed in accounts. Therefore the sales figure may have to be used as a proxy. Also, the debtors' turnover ratio clearly needs the credit sales figure, whereas only the gross turnover figure is usually available.

A further problem relates to the use of average figures for the numerators of the above ratios. Averages between year-end figures (as above) will probably be more accurate than using just the closing figures. However, there may be seasonal movements of stocks, for example, which make stockholding levels at year ends atypical. Accountants will be able to solve these problems for the ratios of their own companies, but it will be more difficult using only the published accounts of other companies. In all cases it is important to be consistent from year to year, from company to company and from numerator to denominator. However, it is still worth calculating ratios when there is insufficient information to be consistent between numerator and denominator (e.g. when credit sales figures are not available). This is because one of the main values of ratios is to spot trends. These should show up despite such problems.

15.5 The Reasons for and costs of holding current items

15.5.1 Stock

Other things being equal, the more stock that a company holds and the longer the stock turnover period, the stronger the current ratio of a company will appear. However, because of the large and varied costs of holding stocks, most companies put great efforts into controlling their stocks and speeding up the turnover.

The reasons for holding stocks include the high costs associated with running out of stock. This gives rise to the need to hold buffer stocks as well as stocks for day-to-day transactions. Also, in order to take advantage of quantity discounts or special offers, order quantities may be very large, which implies a higher average stockholding level. High stock levels may also be incurred as a speculation against rising prices. The greater is the expected inflation or the possibility of disruption of supply or the planned increase in output, the greater the level of stock will be. Some companies may keep a high level of stock just in order to avoid the expensive process of having to monitor stock levels closely. This is unlikely to be a wise decision, however, in the context of the costs discussed below.

The costs of holding stocks include the cost of the money that is thereby tied up. This money could otherwise be used to reduce borrowings or increase real or monetary investments. This cost is clearly proportional to the size of stocks and is very significant when interest rates are high. Further costs are those associated with storing the stock. These include the use of warehouses, insurance and protection. In addition, the greater is the stock, the more difficult it is to control it and manoeuvre it. The losses due to theft, deterioration and obsolescence will increase, too, with larger stockholdings.

It is clear that it will be necessary to hold larger stocks as production volumes and diversity increase, particularly for production that involves several long processes. It is also clear that it may be worth holding larger stocks to hedge against scarcities or price increases. However, the above costs when added together are very great and should make the need for stock control systems obvious.

Stock control includes the analysis of the reasons for, and the costs of, holding stocks; making decisions about minimum re-order levels and quantities; and the installation of control systems to monitor the level of stocks, to identify slow-moving items, to initiate re-ordering and to identify stock losses. Such a stock control procedure will be expensive, but it may enable a company to hold much lower levels of stock and thus reduce all the other costs.

15.5.2 Debtors

It would be possible to run some companies successfully with a very small number and size of debtors. Indeed, many retail organizations manage this by making all their sales for cash. However, a majority of companies do have substantial sums due from debtors at any time. This is because the offering of credit to customers may be an aid to marketing, particularly if competitors also offer credit. In addition, the maintenance of credit accounts may avoid large numbers of cash transactions, which are inconvenient to both buyers and sellers. However, the costs of granting credit comprise a number of factors that may sum to a substantial proportion of the gross profit margin on sales. Consequently, it may well be more profitable in some fields of business to try to sell by offering lower prices rather than better credit facilities. At least a company should be aware of the nature and size of the costs of granting credit.

These costs include the interest (lost or paid) on the money tied up in debtors. Although the standard terms quoted are thirty days, the average length of credit taken is much longer. With today's interest rates this amounts to a very significant cost. For example, let us say that the interest rate is 10 per cent per annum and that the average length of a debt is ten weeks. In this case a £100 credit sale will cost about £2 (i.e. £100 × 0.10 × 10/52) in interest alone. Another cost will be the administration involved in recording the sale and information about the debtor, and sending an invoice and a monthly statement. Further administration is involved in processing the later receipt of money or in sending reminders and engaging in debt collection activity. As an example, this may amount to £1 on average in postage, staff time, computer time, paper and so on.

Further costs are the inevitable bad debts, which in some companies may amount to 2 per cent of debtors outstanding. On average 2 per cent bad debts means £2 on every £100 sale. In some areas of business, notably hire purchase, the figure may be much larger. Cumulating these three types of cost gives £5 on a £100 sale. Many purchasers might prefer an extra 5 per cent discount to the availability of credit.

If it is thought that, despite the above costs, debtors are an inevitable part of one's business, a system of control in order to minimize the average length of debt and the amount of bad debts will be necessary. Such a system may include the careful scrutiny of first-time credit buyers, maximum credit limits, quick invoicing, prompt-payment discounts, timely month-end statements, reminder letters after a fairly short period and the willingness to threaten and take legal action over debts in order to establish a reputation for taking debts seriously. All this implies efficient recording and data processing, which may be either manual or computerized. Such systems will be expensive, but they will usually pay their way by reducing the other costs of debts.

15.5.3 Cash

Cash is clearly an unproductive resource, except inasmuch as it is necessary in order to lubricate the operations of a company. Consequently, efforts should be made to reduce holdings of cash to a minimum. The reasons for holding cash are often divided into three types. First, there is the transactions motive, which means that a certain amount of cash is necessary to keep floats in tills and petty-cash boxes, to pay wages and so on. The larger are the number and size of regular cash transactions, the larger the transactions balance will have to be in order to avoid embarrassing shortages. Second, cash is held to satisfy the precautionary motive that arises from the necessity to be able to meet unexpected bills when they fall due or expected bills when they fall due unexpectedly early. Third, the speculative motive suggests that cash (or current assets that can easily be turned into cash) should be held in order to be able to take advantage of unforeseen bargains or investment opportunities. Some part of the total balance thought necessary to satisfy these motives can be kept on short-term interest-bearing bank deposits. However, this usually means that resources are still being used less productively than they might otherwise be.

This leads into the consideration of the costs of holding cash (and bank) balances. The most obvious cost is the interest forgone or the interest paid. Alternatively, some companies may look upon the necessity to hold cash as being the tying up of money that might otherwise have been invested in profit-earning machinery within the company. The money could then be said to be forfeiting the internal rate of return. Another view is that the cost of holding money is its decline in real value due to inflation. Anyway, it is clear that idle cash should be kept to a minimum.

15.5.4 Creditors and accrued expenses

The reasons for taking credit include the fact that by being in debt a company avoids having to use its money, thus avoiding an interest cost. In addition it may be convenient to settle several small invoices with one cheque. A company may therefore feel inclined to try to take as much credit as possible from its suppliers, particularly if they are in a dependent position. However, such a company should consider whether there is a point beyond which ethical issues become important and whether it runs the risk of pushing its suppliers into liquidity crises, which would damage all parties. Also, prompt-payment discounts may be more valuable than extra credit taken. Detailed attention should be paid to these matters.

15.6 Cash forecasts and budgets

Elements in the control of liquidity, even in those companies which do not operate extensive budgetary control systems, are accurate cash budgeting and detailed monitoring of cash budgets. A cash budget is a detailed numerical statement of intentions for several future time periods. It is drawn up using information about intended flows of cash resulting from sales, purchases, loans, investment, administration expenses, and so on. The cash budget is preceded by a cash forecast. If this predicts deficiencies or unnecessary surpluses at various times in the future, ways of avoiding these will be built into the budget. Such adjustments may include new issues of debentures or shares, additional overdraft arrangements and reductions in capital expenditure programmes or planned dividends. An example of a cash budget is shown in Figure 15.5.

When the budget has been set, it can be regularly compared with actual flows and balances of cash. A monthly budget period may represent a

CASH BUDGET 2001
Responsible Officer: J. Haydn, Financial Accountant

	January	February	March	April
Opening balance	5,000	8,350	13,950	4,550
Cash sales	10,800	9,000	10,600	etc.
Payment by debtors	20,500	21,600	19,500	
Loan raised	-	-	10,000	
Payment to suppliers	(15,000)	(16,000)	(1,550)	
Cash expenses	(8,950)	(9,000)	(9,000)	
Dividends	-	-	(5,000)	
Capital purchase	(4,000)	-	(20,000)	
Closing balance	8,350	13,950	4,550	

Figure 15.5 Example of a cash budget

reasonable frequency. Any discrepancies from the budget will be quickly discovered and can lead to changes of plans in order to avert a cash shortage or productively to use an unexpected surplus. In addition, in order to allow a margin for the unexpected without having to hold large cash and near-cash balances, a company may wish to make standby credit arrangements with commercial banks. This will provide a safety net, which will be particularly useful for a company whose future is especially uncertain.

15.7 Summary

Liquidity crises have forced many profitable companies out of business. This chapter has examined the nature of cash flow in a company, pointing out the ways in which profit may not equal cash. Formalized statements called cash flow statements are now a required part of published accounts. They should help in the attempt to understand changes in liquidity.

Methods of measuring and controlling liquidity include a variety of liquidity ratios, control systems and cash budgets. The steps that a company may take to control liquidity can be summarized as follows:

(1) Finance the working capital balance by long-term sources.
(2) Study the liquidity movements in the company with aid of cash flow statements.
(3) Make cash forecasts; rearrange plans in order to adjust for expected shortages or surpluses; monitor the resulting monthly cash budgets in order to be able to correct rapidly for the unexpected.
(4) Calculate quarterly liquidity ratios of various kinds to spot trends and to detect liquidity problems quickly.
(5) Study the reasons for, and costs of, holding the various current items; establish control systems to reduce the costs.
(6) Arrange standby credit in case of liquidity emergencies.

It seems sensible to carry out all these steps, for they are designed to achieve complementary purposes. For example, it is not clear how good liquidity ratios are at predicting liquidity crises, even when the ratios are used in the context of other years and other companies. However, when they are backed up by other explanatory ratios and cash flow statements, a picture of the company's liquidity position should begin to emerge. Fortunately, many companies have realized the usefulness of powerful control systems for stocks and debtors and of detailed cash forecasting and cash budgetary control.

Self-assessment questions

Suggested answers to the self-assessment questions are given at the end of the book.

1. Which of the following would be most likely to be classified as a current liability?

   (a) Mortgage payable.
   (b) Deferred tax.
   (c) Taxes payable.
   (d) Five-year bills payable.

2. Which of the following is a measure of liquidity?

   (a) Working capital.
   (b) Profit margin.
   (c) Return on assets.
   (d) Return on equity.

3. Current assets divided by current liabilities is known as the:

   (a) Working capital.
   (b) Current ratio.
   (c) Profit margin.
   (d) Capital structure.

4. One measure of capital structure or gearing is:

   (a) Current assets *minus* current liabilities.
   (b) Current assets divided by current liabilities.
   (c) Net income divided by total assets.
   (d) Total liabilities divided by total owners' equity.

5. The cash flow statement provides a useful complement to the other annual financial statements because:

   (a) It provides new information, not available elsewhere in the accounts.
   (b) It shows how much cash will be needed to run the business during the forthcoming year.
   (c) It summarizes the contents of the other accounts into a clearer form.
   (d) It presents the information contained in the other statements in a different way.

6. Which one of the following results in a cash flow?

   (a) An issue of bonus shares.
   (b) A rights issue of shares.
   (c) A depreciation charge.
   (d) Revaluing a fixed asset.

7. At the start of the year the written down value (WDV) of the fixed asset 'motor vehicles' was £26,000. During the year depreciation of £7,000 was charged on motor vehicles and one vehicle, which had a WDV of

£2,000, was sold for £1,000. At the year end, the WDV of the motor vehicles was £24,000. What was the cost of the vehicles acquired during the year?

(a) £4,000.
(b) £7,000.
(c) £6,000.
(d) £8,000.

8. In a cash flow statement, which one of the items below would appear as a cash inflow?

(a) Revaluation of fixed assets.
(b) Profit on disposal of fixed assets.
(c) Purchase of fixed assets.
(d) Proceeds on disposal of fixed assets.

Data for questions 9–13

The trading account of Bruno Ltd for the year ending 30 June 19x6 is set out below:

	£	£
Sales		860,000
Opening stock	100,000	
Purchases	625,000	
	725,000	
Closing stock	76,000	
Cost of sales		649,000
Gross profit		211,000

The following amounts have been extracted from the company's balance sheet at 30 June 19x6.

	£
Trade debtors	120,000
Prepayments	8,000
Cash in hand	12,000
Bank overdraft	16,000
Trade creditors	80,000
Accruals	6,000
Proposed dividends	10,000

In the questions that follow you should assume a year of 365 days.

9. Calculate the average stock turnover period in days:

(a) 33 days.
(b) 37 days.
(c) 49 days.
(d) 51 days.

10. Calculate the debtors' collection period in days:

(a) 51 days.
(b) 54 days.
(c) 67 days.
(d) 72 days.

11. Calculate the creditors' payment period in days:

(a) 45 days.
(b) 47 days.
(c) 50 days.
(d) 78 days.

12. Calculate the current ratio at 30 June 19x6.

(a) 1.25:1
(b) 1.93:1
(c) 2.04:1
(d) 2.12:1

13. Calculate the quick ratio (or acid test ratio) at 30 June 19x6:

(a) 1.25:1
(b) 1.28:1
(c) 1.37:1
(d) 1.50:1

Tutorial questions

1. Mosca and Vespa are two sole traders with the following financial statements (in euros) for the year ending 31 December 19x8. Using the information contained in the financial statements, calculate the following ratios and comment on the results of your analysis:

   (i) return on capital employed,
   (ii) gross profit margin,
   (iii) current ratio,
   (iv) inventory turnover period,
   (v) debtors' turnover period,
   (vi) creditors' turnover period.

   (Assume opening and closing stocks are the same.)

Income Statement

	Mosca		Vespa	
Sales		144,000		140,000
Cost of sales		120,000		120,000
		24,000		20,000
Selling expenses	7,000		10,000	
Administration expenses	3,000		6,000	
		10,000		16,000
		14,000		4,000
Net profit				

Balance Sheet

	Mosca		Vespa	
Fixed assets		54,000		30,000
Current assets				
Inventory	20,000		10,000	
Debtors	30,000		50,000	
Cash	10,000		5,000	
		60,000		65,000
Less Creditors		24,000		5,000
		90,000		90,000
Capital		90,000		90,000

2. Cross-sectional analysis (comparison between different businesses over the same period) and trend analysis (comparisons between the same business over different periods) both suffer from significant limitations.

What are the limitations of each form of analysis?
How can they be overcome, and to what extent?

3. The following information has been extracted from the recently published accounts of DG plc:

Balance sheets as at 30 April

	19x5 £000	19x4 £000
Fixed assets (NBV)	1,850	1,430
Current assets		
Stock	640	490
Debtors	1,230	1,080
Cash	80	120
	1,950	1,690
Creditors due in less than 1 year		
Bank overdraft	110	80
Creditors	750	690
Taxation	30	20
Dividends	65	55
	955	845

Continued

Net current assets	995	845
Total assets *less* current liabilities	2,845	2,275
Less creditors due in more than 1 year		
10% Debentures	800	600
	2,045	1,675
Share captial and reserves		
Ordinary share capital	800	800
Reserves	1,245	875
	2,045	1,675

Extracts from the profit and loss accounts

Sales	11,200	9,750
Cost of sales	8,460	6,825
Net profit before tax	465	320
This is after charging:		
Depreciation	360	280
Debenture interest	80	60
Interest on bank overdraft	15	9
Audit fees	12	10

The following ratios are those calculated for DG plc, based on its published accounts for the previous year, and also the latest industry average ratios:

	DG plc 30 April 19x4	Industry average
ROCE		
(Capital employed = equity and debentures)	16.70%	18.50%
Profit/sales	3.90%	4.73%
Asset turnover	4.29	3.91
Current ratio	2.00	1.90
Quick ratio	1.42	1.27
Gross profit margin	30.00%	35.23%
Days debtors	40 days	52 days
Days creditors	37 days	49 days
Stock turnover	13.90	18.30
Gearing	26.37%	32.71%

Required

(a) Calculate comparable ratios (to 2 decimal places where appropriate) for DG plc for the year ending 30 April 19x5. All calculations must be clearly shown.

(b) Analyse the performance of DG plc, comparing the results against the previous year and against the industry average.

VALUATION OF THE BUSINESS

16

In Chapter 2 we introduced the alternative approaches to the valuation of the business: valuation by assets and valuation by expected net cash flows. Using the knowledge and expertise gained during the subsequent chapters we can develop these ideas. First, the asset approach will be examined, starting with a summary of the problems involved in valuing assets included in balance sheets and going on to introduce ways of valuing those normally excluded. Then, a variety of approaches to the valuation of the business as an entity will be discussed, including economic values and market values.

The suitability of these alternative approaches will depend upon the uses to which a valuation is to be put. This will be mentioned from time to time in this chapter, and the threads will be drawn together in the summary.

16.1 Balance sheet assets

Accounting conventions are used to decide which assets should be included in balance sheets and how the assets should be valued. The conventions that we have met include prudence, money measurement and objectivity. These will ensure that any asset recorded in the balance sheet still exists in a form that is useful to the business and that at some point in time (either past or present) a monetary value that is verifiable in some way has been assigned to it. There is a strong tendency to prefer undervaluation to the risk of overvaluation. Losses are accounted for when they are foreseen; gains usually wait until they are realized.

These conventions lead to the exclusion of a variety of assets that a business may clearly own (e.g. customer goodwill, expert management, monopoly power, loyal staff). In order to arrive at a satisfactory total of assets for valuation of the business these must be included. They will be considered in the next section. Powerful doubts have been expressed about the usefulness of adding together all the assets as a means of valuation. These also will be considered later.

The assets that *are* included in the balance sheet have traditionally been valued at their historical costs. Market values of assets have been considered of doubtful relevance to external users of accounts because the business does not intend to sell them; and replacement costs or economic values have been rejected because of their lack of both objectivity and simplicity.

There are, of course, modifications to pure historical cost for valuations of various assets and liabilities:

(1) Land and buildings are often shown at current or recent revaluations.
(2) Precious metals are shown at selling prices.
(3) Fixed assets generally are shown after depreciation, where appropriate.
(4) Stocks are shown at the lower of cost or net realizable value.
(5) Debtors are shown net of bad and doubtful debts.

Further, market value information will be provided in notes for investments and property (in cases where the balance sheet does not show it). Monetary assets and liabilities will be shown at historical values, but these will also be their current values.

In general, and particularly for fixed assets, 'historical cost' balance sheets use an inconsistent mixture of different valuation techniques, including pure historical cost. This can cause similar items to be added together at widely differing values just because they were bought at different dates. Although such accounts may still be able to fulfil some of their original stewardship role, they would be very misleading if used to measure the value of the business for any decision-making purpose.

If a system of current cost accounting is being used, asset values will generally be based on depreciated replacement costs rather than historical costs, market values or economic values. This has been shown to be the normal outcome of using the concept that the value of an individual asset should be recorded at its value to the business. One may be rather happier about adding these current values together in order to use the total for calculating the net assets of the business.

Suppose that Paradigm Ltd has the balance sheet shown in Table 16.1. The value of the company to its owners on a balance sheet basis is £3m, and the underlying asset value of a share is £3m/1m = £3. The next section will deal with other assets that should be added in to make this method of valuation a little more realistic.

16.2 Other assets

Some of the assets traditionally excluded from balance sheets could be included in the existing scheme of accounting without much difficulty, because expenditure is involved in creating them. This means that the tests of money measurement and objectivity could be made to apply, and pru-

Table 16.1 Paradigm Ltd balance sheet (£m)

Net assets	4.5	£1 ordinary shares	1.0
		Reserves	2.0
		Debentures	1.5
	4.5		4.5

dence might be satisfied by strict attention to whether they really were valuable assets.

One example of this class of assets is research and development (R and D) expenditure. The best guide to practice is SSAP 13, *Research and Development Expenditure*. This suggests that some development expenditure may be capitalized and recorded as an asset after fairly strict tests about the certainty of the future benefits flowing from it have been satisfied. Earlier thinking was contained in ED 14, which proposed that no R and D should be treated as an asset. Clearly, then, R and D is on the borderline of the assets that can be included in balance sheets. The argument for including it is that the expenditure in successful cases relates to future periods when the benefits will accrue. Therefore, accruals accounting principles suggest that the R and D expenditure should be capitalized and not treated as an expense until it can be matched against future revenues. The arguments against inclusion are that future revenues are not sufficiently objective and that capitalization will generally be unconservative.

Similar arguments are used about expenditure on advertising and training. If a company spends large sums during one year to train its staff, its balance sheet at the end of the year will show a smaller total of net assets than it would otherwise have done. However, the company may be more valuable because of the greater future profits that will flow from better-trained staff. Similarly, sums spent on advertising are intended to create future sales and profit.

However, it is even more difficult than for R and D to be sure that expenditure *will* bring benefits and to tell which training expenditure or which advertising expenditure will lead to future profit. Consequently, the prudent and objective system of historical cost accounting has traditionally refused to capitalize these expenditures. Nevertheless, if it were wished to stress realism rather than prudence and objectivity, the value of past and present unexpired expenditures of this sort could be estimated as part of the calculation of net assets.

Training expenditure in particular is included in schemes of 'human asset accounting', which attempt to put a value on efficient management and skilled staff rather than leaving them as unspecified components of a nebulous goodwill. Items that could be capitalized include recruitment costs, induction and initial internal training and external courses. Capitalized amounts would be depreciated over time and removed when an employee left the company.

This system would not be a particularly accurate or complete recognition of the value of a company's human assets, but it could fit within the existing accounting framework, and it would be better than nothing when trying to put a value on a company's net assets. There is a considerable body of writing on this subject, which there is not space to review in this introductory textbook.

There are other elements of goodwill that do not obviously follow from specific expenditure and cannot therefore be capitalized and included in anything like a traditional balance sheet. Examples of such items are internally generated brand names, a reputation for good products and service, and a monopoly position. It would be necessary to throw objectivity and prudence to the four winds in order to include valuations for these as individual assets, based on their contributions to future profits. However, for some purposes it might be done.

So, it is possible to identify the assets traditionally included in a balance sheet and to value them at a current value, then to include such depreciated capitalized expenditures as advertising and the enhancement of human assets, and then to estimate values for even vaguer elements of goodwill. This would be done in order to arrive at a total of the net assets of a company.

However, we should ask what this total would represent. It would not be the break-up value of the company, which might be interesting as a minimum value. The goodwill elements will be worth nothing if the company ceases to trade, and the tangible assets have been valued not at net realizable value but at markedly different values (e.g. net replacement cost), because the company is viewed as a going concern.

If the nebulous goodwill elements cannot be estimated and included, a net asset valuation will not represent what it would be worth paying for the company, because a company is worth more than the sum of all its individual parts valued separately. The value of the net cash inflows from the buildings, machines, working capital and human assets combined together should exceed such a net asset valuation. However, a cash flow valuation (examined in the next section) is notoriously subjective, and the net asset valuation might be used as a comparison or check on it when calculating what it would be worth paying for the company.

Table 16.2 shows the situation when other assets are valued and added to the balance sheet for Paradigm Ltd. The value of the net assets of the business to the owners is now seen as £7.1m and the asset backing for the shares as £7.10 per share.

16.3 Valuation by expectations

The alternative approach to valuing a business by adding up its assets is to value it as an entity – a going concern. This recognizes that the worth of the business rests on its earning power, which comes from using the assets in mutual conjunction. The excess of this sort of valuation over a conventional net assets valuation may be called *goodwill*.

Table 16.2 Paradigm Ltd balance sheet with 'unconventional' assets added (£m)

Conventional net assets	4.5	£1 ordinary shares	1.0
Capitalized expenditures	1.8	Conventional reserves	2.0
Estimated goodwill items	2.3	Additional reserves	4.1
		Debentures	1.5
	8.6		8.6

The theoretically most satisfactory method of valuation by expectations is to discount the expected net cash inflows to the present. This is because cash flows *now* are worth more than those in the future. The cause of this time preference may be looked at from several points of view. Owning money *now* means either that one needs to borrow less (thereby reducing interest payments) or that one can lend more (thereby increasing interest receipts). Alternatively, if certain projects cannot be carried out without these present cash flows, the return on the projects will be sacrificed unless there is money now.

The degree of time preference is represented by a discount rate. If a company is thinking of using spare cash resources for either a project or an interest-bearing investment, the relevant discount rate can be the rate of interest in financial markets, which is a collective assessment of time preference. Alternatively, if investment in a project is seen as drawing upon the general long-term resources of the company, it may be more suitable to use an internally calculated average cost of capital. This will be the weighted average cost of interest on debentures, dividends on ordinary shares and so on. If new capital must be raised, the cost of that new capital may be more relevant.

Another factor to be considered is the level of risk (which is statistically quantifiable) and uncertainty (which is not quantifiable). A high level of risk or uncertainty may be taken into account by raising the discount rate. This places a greater emphasis on early cash flows, which are likely to be the least uncertain.

As an example, suppose that Exemplar Ltd is a company set up to sell the benefits arising from a wasting asset. For two years there will be a net cash inflow of £2,000 at the end of each year, then £1,000 for each of the next two years. After that there will be no more income and no assets worth selling. In this case let the discount rate be 10 per cent per annum. Without discounting it may be said that the value of the company is £6,000. With discounting:

$$\text{Value of Exemplar} = \frac{£2,000}{1.1} + \frac{£2,000}{(1.1)^2} + \frac{£1,000}{(1.1)^3} + \frac{£1,000}{(1.1)^4}$$

$$= £1,818.2 + £1,652.9 + £751.1 + £682.8$$

$$= £4,905.0$$

More generally, the *net present value* (NPV) of future income streams is given by:

$$\text{NPV} = \frac{C_o}{(1+r)^0} + \frac{C_1}{(1+r)^1} + \frac{C_2}{(1+r)^2} + \dots + \frac{C_n}{(1+r)^n}$$

where C_0 is net current cash inflow, C_1 is the net cash inflow at the end of year 1, and so on, and r is the appropriate discount rate.

In addition to the problem of determining the appropriate discount rate, this economic value approach encounters severe practical problems when it becomes necessary to predict flows of net benefit. Clearly, forecasting the future is so far from being objective, and including incomes for many years ahead is so unconservative (as though counting the chickens before their parents had set eyes on each other) that such a method is quite unusable for normal accounting purposes. Even for making an estimate of the value of a business it may usually be regarded as too uncertain.

For practical purposes a method of valuing a business using *superprofits* may be used. The superprofits are what an established company would earn in excess of the earnings of a new business with similar balance sheet assets. This can be formulated as follows:

$$V = A + \frac{\pi - rA}{k}$$

where V is the value of the business, A is net assets, π is yearly profit of the established business, r is the rate of return on assets in a new business and k is the capitalization rate of superprofits.

If there are established values for r and k for the particular type of industry in which the company operates, a measure of the value of the business may be obtained by capitalizing superprofits using the formula.

16.4 Market valuations

Alternative ways of valuation rely upon using the market for providing values of individual shares or of the whole company (i.e. all the shares). However, since the market value of a share depends on the marginal supply and demand at a particular time, it is clear that selling all the shares will not be possible at the same price as selling one share. Also, for a prospective purchaser, to use a market valuation is to beg the question. He wishes to know how much it is worth paying for a company rather than what its price is. However, for the purpose of takeover or for establishing a price for unquoted shares in order to make a first quotation or a tax valuation it will be useful.

The simplest form of using the market is just to look at the market price of a share and to multiply this by the number of shares that there are. This will give a market capitalization. If a company is not quoted on a stock exchange, it may be possible to establish an approximate share price by working out a suitable price/earnings ratio (P/E ratio) for the type, size and business of the company. Using the earnings per share figure for the past few years, this will produce a price per share.

The same technique can be applied to dividends rather than earnings. If it can be established what a suitable dividend yield for the company may be, a price can be worked out from this. These valuations can be illustrated by using Pattern Ltd – an unquoted public company to which the following data relate:

Facts:
Ordinary shares 100,000
Average earnings £40,000
Dividends per share 27p

Estimates
P/E ratio 16
Dividend yield 4%

Using earnings,

$$\text{earnings per share} = \frac{£40,000}{100,000} = 40p$$

$$\text{P/E ratio} = \frac{\text{price}}{\text{earnings}}$$

$$\therefore 16 = \frac{\text{price}}{£0.40}$$

$$\therefore \text{price} = £6.40 \text{ per share}$$

Using dividends,

$$\text{dividend yield} = \frac{\text{dividend \% } \times \text{ nominal value}}{\text{market value}} = \frac{\text{dividend}}{\text{price}}$$

$$\therefore 4\% = \frac{£0.27}{\text{price}}$$

$$\therefore \text{price} = \frac{£0.27}{£0.04} = £6.75 \text{ per share}$$

These two valuations are different because the estimated price/earnings ratio and dividend yield are based on averages, and Pattern Ltd is not exactly average.

16.5 Summary

There are many approaches to valuing a business. The one chosen should depend upon the use to which the valuation is to be put. For many purposes several simultaneous valuations may enhance decision-making. The approaches introduced in this chapter are summarized in Figure 16.1.

If a rock-bottom conservative valuation is wanted quickly and needs to be simple and objective, using the historical cost total of net assets may be

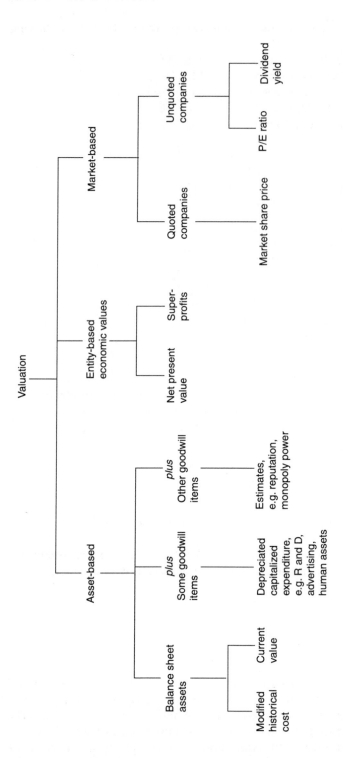

Figure 16.1 Valuation methods

appropriate. Even this may sometimes exceed the break-up value of the company, which would require a net realizable valuation of the net assets. However, if a more realistic, yet still asset-based, valuation is required, the assets should be valued at their value to the business, which normally means net current replacement cost. To this current value total of balance sheet assets could be added the depreciated capitalized expenditure on such items as advertising and training. This would require the suspension of complete objectivity and prudence. One could go further by adding estimates of other goodwill items.

However, for estimating what it would be worth paying for a business, a measure based on future net cash flows is needed. Practical approximations to theoretically sounder methods may be necessary. Also, market valuations will be useful for unquoted companies. These can be based on earnings or dividends.

This is a very complex area, to which it has only been possible to provide a brief introduction. More advanced courses take these matters further.

Self-assessment questions

Suggested answers to the self-assessment questions are given at the end of the book.

1. Accountants leave assets off of balance sheets if:

   (a) They are owned by someone else.
   (b) They are controlled by someone else.
   (c) They are expected to be sold soon.
   (d) Their replacement cost exceeds their book value.
   (e) They have no market value.
   (f) All of the above.

2. Advertising expenditure is not capitalized because:

   (a) It is usually paid for in the following year.
   (b) It is not clear how much it costs.
   (c) It is intangible.
   (d) It is not clear how much future benefit will flow.
   (e) It relates to future sales.

3. Ignoring difficulties of measurement, the worth of a business to an owner is best assessed by:

   (a) Cumulating future profits.
   (b) Measuring the value of net assets.
   (c) Cumulating future net discounted cash flows
   (d) Calculating the cost of replacing the net assets.

4. The market value of a listed company is not put into its balance sheet because:

(a) Market value goes up and down over time.
(b) Buyers of shares generally only buy a few shares.
(c) Readers of financial statements are trying to assess future value not present value.
(d) Market value is not known until the balance sheet date.

Tutorial questions

1. Why do accountants conventionally leave some assets off of a balance sheet?
2. For what various reasons might the market capitalization of a company exceed its balance sheet net assets? Could the reverse be the case?
3. Is it possible to buy a company at a bargain price? How is it possible to buy a company for less than it is worth to the buyer?
4. What difficulties are met when trying to value a company whose shares are not traded on a market?

SUGGESTED ANSWERS

Chapter 1
1. b
2. a

Chapter 2
1. d
2. a

Chapter 3
1. b
2. c
3. b
4. b
5. c
6. c
7. d
8. c
9. a
10. b
11. b
12. a

Chapter 4
1. b
2. b
3. c
4. d
5. c
6. b
7. d
8. d
9. b
10. c

Chapter 5
1. a
2. b
3. b
4. b
5. d
6. a
7. d
8. b

9. b
10. c
11. a
12. d

Chapter 6
1. b
2. c
3. c
4. c
5. b
6. d
7. c
8. b
9. a
10. b
11. a
12. b
13. a
14. c
15. a
16. b
17. b
18. c
19. a

Chapter 7
1. a
2. a
3. b
4. b
5. b

Chapter 8
1. a
2. c
3. c
4. a
5. a
6. d
7. c
8. b
9. d
10. c

Chapter 9
1. d
2. a
3. e

Chapter 10
1. a,b
2. c
3. b
4. a

Chapter 11
1. d
2. a
3. b
4. b
5. c
6. c
7. c

Chapter 12
1. a
2. b
3. c
4. b

Chapter 13
1. c
2. c
3. d
4. d
5. d
6. e
7. d

Chapter 14
1. d
2. c
3. c
4. c

Chapter 15
1. c
2. a

3.	b	9.	d	*Chapter 16*	
4.	d	10.	a	1.	b
5.	d	11.	b	2.	d
6.	b	12.	b	3.	c
7.	b	13.	a	4.	c
8.	d				

INDEX